8-26-74

ENCOUNTERING DARKNESS

ENCOUNTERING DARKNESS

Gonville ffrench-Beytagh

A CROSSROAD BOOK
The Seabury Press · New York

The Seabury Press
815 Second Avenue
New York, N.Y. 10017

This book has been edited by Alison Norman
from material which I dictated.

G. A. ff.-B.

The quotation from *Parson's Daughter* is reproduced
by kind permission of Esylt Newbery.

Printed in the United States of America

© G. A. ffrench-Beytagh, 1973

Library of Congress Cataloging in Publication Data

ffrench-Beytagh, Gonville Aubie.
    Encountering darkness.

    "A Crossroad book."
    Autobiogràphical.
    1. ffrench-Beytagh, Gonville Aubie.
    2. Church and race problems—Africa, South.
    I. Title.

BX5700.6.Z8F473   283'.092'4 [B]   73-17895
ISBN 0-8164-1149-2

Contents

ENCOUNTERING DARKNESS

'Theme'

'You don't preach Christianity, you preach shit!'

For eight days, I had this kind of abusive violence screamed at me, alternating with endless questions and long hours alone in my cell. Some of it I found very hard to stand. But through all my arrest, interrogation and trial, nothing gave me such an appalling shock as a casual remark during a 'soft-sell' period when my three interrogators were chatting to me over a cup of tea – a remark which had nothing to do with me personally at all.

They were asking me about the Church's attitude to the Immorality Act, which forbids sexual intercourse between Europeans and people of other races. Some time before, one of the bishops had condemned this Act and said that men and women should be able to marry each other if they wished, regardless of their colour. My interrogators were completely unable to understand this.

'Surely you know', they said, 'that sexual relationships between black and white are forbidden in the Bible?'

This I flatly denied.

They reiterated that I would find it in the Old Testament. I asked them what they meant.

'Well', they replied, 'don't you remember that it says in the Old Testament, "A man may not mix his seed with that of the animal"?'*

Suddenly I realized just what I had been fighting and why I hated it so much. Apartheid went far deeper than an economic and political denial of human rights and dignity. It was an attempt

* See Exodus 22:19; Leviticus 18:23 and 20:15.

7

to split off all the 'black', animal part of our nature, with the fears and hatred and sexual drives which we dare not acknowledge even to ourselves, and thrust it into a race whose skin happened to be dark. It was utterly irrational and utterly evil.

Until then, although I had been in the country for forty years, I had had no idea of the depths of this fear and envy of 'blackness'. I had heard the expression *'Hulle is nie mense nie'* – 'They are not men' – often enough, but I had taken it to be the same sort of half-joking contempt with which the English used to talk about 'wogs'. That men of the calibre of my interrogators (all of whom, incidentally, had told me that they were practising members of the Dutch Reformed Church) honestly thought of Africans as animals came as a revelation. (I must emphasize that they were not using the Bible to justify the law; they were claiming that the law had been enacted as a Christian duty because of the biblical injunction.) I suddenly saw what apartheid was in fact all about, even though the Afrikaner theologians would not teach it as doctrine and even their politicians would not say it openly. How can a white man have dealings, as an equal, with a mere creature, an advanced animal which is trying to reach out of its natural habitat into the place which God has reserved for real, pure, human beings? Anyone who thinks about apartheid or has dealings with it, or is aware of his own racial prejudices (which most of us have), must constantly remind himself that this is where it starts. *'A man may not mix his seed with that of the animal.'*

When I had a chance to think about what my interrogators had said, I realized that my own response to apartheid was equally a 'gut' reaction which was triggered off by my need to hold fast to my integrity as a whole human being against a force which was trying to control me and diminish me. God knows, I have enough 'blackness' in myself of irrational fears and insecurity and sexual drives. But I can only survive if it is acknowledged and healed and redeemed, not banished to some mental Bantustan. To try and explain this, I must go back to my own beginning.

CHAPTER ONE

Mixed-up boyhood

I was born in Shanghai on 26 January 1912 into what I suppose was a fairly typical expatriate family mess. My father was an Irishman who prided himself on his descent from the 'real' Irish as opposed to the descendants of sailors from the Spanish Armada and Cromwellian settlers. He himself had opted out of a Roman Catholic seminary, fought in the Boer War, and ended up at the time of my birth as the managing director of a cotton company in Shanghai. My mother was a widow, short and ugly but, from her ability to attract husbands, evidently oozing sex-appeal. She must have been in her middle thirties when she married my father and I was the first child by the marriage, though she had a son by her first husband. From my memory of her, she had no maternal feelings of any kind and we always called her 'Pegs'. In due course I was followed by a sister Pat and a brother Mike, in neither of whom our parents showed any more interest than they showed in me. We lived in solitary state on the nursery floor of our house in the French quarter of Shanghai and were cared for by Japanese *amahsans* with whom I can also remember no real relationship.

There is no doubt that my parents landed me with a collection of quite impossible names. Gonville was a family name, originally from some obscure connection with Gonville and Caius College in Cambridge. There was also a Captain Gonville Bromhead, who fought in the Boer War and got a VC at Rorke's Drift, who was related in some way. Goodness knows where 'Aubie' came from, but it caused me a lot of embarrassment when I was a young man in New Zealand and the usual response was, 'Well,

Aubie buggered'. As for ffrench-Beytagh, it is not really my surname at all. It was just plain Beytagh until my father, who from time to time had sudden attacks of snobbery, came round to my prep school and insisted that my brother and myself should from then on be called ffrench-Beytagh (ffrench being one of his own Christian names). Perhaps because I rather like being different, I have never managed to get rid of it again.

The memories of my early childhood are extremely fragmentary. There was the smell of cigar smoke, which meant that my father was back from the office; his infrequent fits of paternal attention when he allowed me to pretend to drive his smart new Buick, or took me to the races; being taken down and 'shown off' occasionally at the cocktail and dinner parties which my parents were constantly giving; and being given gin to drink on these occasions – ostensibly because it was a preventative for malaria – but actually I suppose because it was thought an amusing thing to do. I had my 'own' rickshaw boy, who took me daily to the French convent school, but remember absolutely nothing of the school itself. I must have had some friends, because my father scolded me severely when I was six for the size of my telephone bills, but apart from one Russian refugee family, I cannot remember them. Summer holidays were generally spent in Japan, where my mother had herself been born and brought up (her father, who was a chemist, must have been one of the very earliest settlers there). But again we were in the care of the *amahsans* and holidays did not mean that we saw any more of our parents. Christmas parties and present-giving, or any other kind of family festivity, never happened at all to my knowledge.

There are two incidents which stand out most vividly in my memory and which I have always thought of as representing the struggle with sex and alcohol which has plagued me all my life. One must have happened when I was very young indeed and was sitting on the verandah outside my nursery with my mother and the two Japanese *amahsans*: the three of them were semi-naked and were comparing the size of their breasts and giggling a great deal. The other was being taken one morning into my parents' bedroom by one of these Japanese nurses and shown a heap of bottles piled up in the corner, some of them broken; presumably my parents had been enjoying some kind of lost weekend. Certainly a great deal was drunk in the house and alcohol has been a problem with most members of my family.

'Pegs' was, as I have said, a figure so remote as to be virtually non-existent. I do not even remember when she finally faded out of our life in Shanghai. My father at least had some kind of identity as far as I was concerned. He went off snipe-shooting with his friends very early on Saturday mornings, and was a member of a voluntary fire brigade, with his helmet hanging in the hall. Once he took me to his cotton factory and showed me the huge flywheel. He was an ardent Sinn Fein supporter and when Michael Collins was killed he made me have a military funeral with my toy soldiers. Also he could not abide missionaries, who he said made the Chinese 'cheeky', and would keep his hand on the hooter when we passed a Salvation Army band. Occasionally I would get a diatribe from him on one or another of these subjects – and the last that I remember was to the effect that I should never, never, trust a Scotsman.

This meant nothing at all to me. But since my mother at about this time went off with a young Highlander called George Buchanan, I suppose it makes some sense. George Buchanan was an officer in the merchant navy – and younger than my mother's oldest son. How my mother met up with him I do not know, but when I was seven or eight she went off with him to South Africa and ceased to be, even nominally, around. Soon afterwards my sister Pat, who was then about five, left too – apparently she was sent to join my mother in South Africa in the care of some relatives who were going out there. My brother Mike and myself were left in the care of a succession of people who were engaged to look after us. One of them was an Australian 'housekeeper' who I am certain was sleeping with my father, but it all made little difference to our normal way of life.

Then there was a sudden and utterly complete break. My

father somehow persuaded a Miss Esylt Newbery, a teacher in the cathedral school in Shanghai, to look after us.

Esylt Newbery is quite beyond my capacity to describe. She has done it far better than I could in two books which she has written, *Parson's Daughter* and *Parson's Daughter Again*.* In these books she describes her childhood under the dominance of a terrifying parson FATHER (whom she refers to in capitals throughout the first volume), her escape to become a governess abroad, and her childhood ambition to be a widow with three children and a nice home of her own, having killed off the necessary but inconvenient husband by putting poison in his tea. By some astonishing coincidence our father found her and persuaded her to take over our legal guardianship and look after us in England while we were being educated.

So towards the end of 1919, Mike, myself and Esylt Newbery (whom we were told to call 'Auntie', and always have done since) set off by sea. Our father joined us in Hong Kong and when we got to Bombay, where we broke our journey, the whole family came together for the last time. My mother apparently came up from South Africa to discuss arrangements for divorce with my father, and she brought Pat with her to join Mike and myself in Esylt's care. Evidently 'Pegs' had some rather ineffective guilt feelings about her inadequacy as a mother since she bought us extremely expensive but totally unimaginative presents. I got a Kodak developing set – a sort of miniature dark-room in a handsome wooden box, with a handle that you turned, and an interesting smell – but as I did not have a camera it was not a great deal of use, even if I had had the faintest idea what to do with it. She must have gone into a toyshop and bought the first expensive-looking thing that caught her eye. What went on between my parents at this meeting I do not, of course, know. Esylt in her book said that my father simply decamped one morning leaving all the outstanding problems concerning our future unsettled. In any case, my mother went back to George Buchanan, my father went back to Shanghai (where he soon

* Published by Robert Hale in 1958 and 1960.

married again), and the three of us went off with Esylt to an utterly new life in England. There were various changes of lodging and school when we arrived, but eventually we all settled in a flat in Weston-super-Mare and I started as a day-boy in a local preparatory school.

I often wonder how many of the compulsive obsessions, irrational fears, and other anxiety symptoms which have plagued me all my life, were caused by the utter contrast in the two halves of my childhood. In Shanghai we had lived in a completely pagan household, aware even as children of adultery and drunkenness going on all round us (the permissive society is not nearly as new as it thinks it is), and then we were suddenly plunged into the care of the spinster daughter of a Victorian clergyman. I am very grateful for the years which she devoted to us. If it had not been for her we would have ended up in an orphanage of some kind, since my father was quite incapable of looking after us. I have no doubt too that after my personal rickshaw, my telephone bill, and my precocious taste for gin, a degree of discipline was very salutary – but to go from Shanghai life to a régime symbolized for me by daily cold baths and never being allowed jam *and* butter on our bread, was, to say the least, a bit of a jump. Esylt Newbery certainly did her best, however, and there are many things which I look back on with pleasure, such as our first 'real' Christmases, and picnics and long bicycle rides in the country, which balanced the rigid nursery-type control.

Until I reached adolescence I was, I think, an exceptionally 'good', docile boy. Pat could show her feelings by going into depressions (called sulks in those days) for days at a time, and sometimes roused Esylt to such a fury that she chased her round the flat whacking her with a hairbrush. Mike was always in trouble, running away from school and so forth, and I well remember my horrified admiration when he stole the detention book from our prep school, in which he had accumulated enough bad marks for some dire penalty to be awarded, tore it up, and put it down the lavatory in our flat. I was a school prefect at the time and had a terrible struggle with myself over whether or not

I should report him but I am glad to say that I did not and he was never found out. (I had incidentally been made a supernumerary prefect after a fight with one of the regular prefects over some kind of injustice or bullying. He was a good deal bigger than me but I managed to give him a thorough pasting and awaited retribution from the headmaster with some trepidation. When it turned out to be promotion, it was a considerable shock. It seems that a militant concern for justice was an early trait in my character.)

Inevitably there are difficulties when a single woman tries to bring up boys. From time to time there was an agony over clothes. Soon after we got to England I was sent for a short time to boarding-school with garments which were the greatest possible embarrassment to me. One was an object called a 'cholera-belt', which was simply a piece of woollen knitted stuff that I had to wear round my stomach; the others were one-piece 'baby' pyjamas with a large split up the behind. Every other boy in the school had ordinary two-piece pyjamas and I suffered public shame each morning when we washed in basins down the middle of the dormitory. On another occasion my brother and I were sent off to our day preparatory school in Norfolk suits which Esylt Newbery had found in a sale. (Norfolk suits are a Victorian combination of coat, knee-breeches and stockings, and as far as I know they had not been seen for forty or fifty years.) Mercifully the headmaster must have said something to her, because we did not have to wear them again.

It was of course not Esylt's fault that she could not provide us with a father who could have seen that things like this did not occur. She did do her utmost to see that we kept in touch with both our parents and insisted that we wrote to them regularly. My mother turned up once when we were at prep school, an embarrassing occasion for everyone, I think. My father sent money regularly for our support. He had, as I have said, married again, and continued to run the factory in Shanghai, but he came to England on leave or business about three times during my childhood and always came to see us. These visits were not an unqualified success. The one I remember most clearly was when I was fifteen and had just acquired my first dinner-jacket. Esylt Newbery had arranged a dinner party for him and invited the church organist and one or two other respectable friends, and after dinner they intended to go on to a dance at the Winter Gardens which had just opened. My father was very late and when he did arrive he was as tight as fourteen coots. It was a most embarrassing occasion. His great hairy chest showed through his unstudded boiled shirt and finally, at the dance, he left the party and went off with one of the local butcher's three very attractive daughters. On a subsequent occasion Esylt Newbery arranged for us to meet him at a temperance hotel in Bristol; but it took more than a temperance hotel to keep my father sober.

Eventually my father's second marriage also broke up and he came back to England and set up with a third partner (I never knew whether he married her or not). This lady wrote and told my mother that he had died of DTs in a London hospital in the early part of the second world war. Although he could obviously have been more of a success as a husband and father, I have good reason to be grateful to him. He did pay for our support and education until he lost his income in the slump, and he did do his best, according to his lights, to see that we were brought up in a stable, 'proper' home. Also, when I was longing to leave school, he exerted his authority by telling me in no uncertain terms that I was to stay there until I got my matric 'even if it takes you till you're twenty', and for that I have always been grateful.

My early religious background had been, to say the least, nominal. My baptism certificate showed that I had been 'done' in the Anglican cathedral in Shanghai – I cannot think why, since my father was a very much lapsed Roman Catholic and antagonistic to the Church in any shape or form, while my mother was, so far as I am aware, unbaptized. I can only suppose that she took me to the nearest church in a fit of superstition. My only early religious education was a solitary visit to a Sunday school when I was on holiday in Japan, again for no apparent reason. Esylt Newbery took us to church and must have tried to teach us to pray, although I cannot remember much about it. She used to make us learn the collect every Sunday, and when I finally left her care, she made me promise to say the collect for the nineteenth Sunday after Trinity every night, 'O God, forasmuch as without thee we are not able to please thee: Mercifully grant, that thy Holy Spirit may in all things direct and rule our hearts; through Jesus Christ our Lord.' Since my anxiety state does not allow me to make a promise without keeping it, I have, in fact, said this collect every night of my life, drunk, sober, or semi-conscious. Mercifully I managed to resist also promising that I would wash my hands before every meal.

After prep school I was sent to Monkton Combe, which was a very low-church, evangelical, minor public school, obviously chosen by Esylt to give me what she thought was a good church background. The religious teaching there left me largely unaffected – except to swear when I left that I would never voluntarily go near a church again. But when, ten years or so later, I changed my mind, the memory of the Monkton Combe services did provide a sense of familiarity and homecoming which I think was important. I left Monkton Combe too early to have got to the 'confirmation year' and so was privately instructed by an assistant curate in Weston-super-Mare. I imagine that he was as much afraid of me as I was of him. At least I have no remembrance of him talking to me about either the reality of the Church or the love of God for me, and if you leave either of these things out of the Christian religion it ceases to be Christian. I have learned since then that if he had started talking to me about myself and who I was, and then had tried to show me that I mattered to God, even though I obviously did not matter to my parents, it might have been a different story. Perhaps it was better to discover this later from actual experience.

What had much more impact on my religious thinking than home, school, or confirmation, was a number of holidays which I spent at the Varsities and Public Schools Camps, which were, I think, an offshoot of the Children's Special Service Mission. I suppose that Esylt Newbery found it a bit much to compete with an adolescent boy during the long summer holidays, and rightly thought it was better that I should be mixing with people of my own age, so I was sent off to these camps for several years running, and I cannot say that I went at all unwillingly. They were curious experiences. I cannot remember how many of them I attended but the personnel always seemed to be more or less the same. They were officered mostly by young undergraduates who were members of Christian societies at Oxford or Cambridge, and they were intensely religious, in what I think was not really the best sense of that term. There was plenty of time during the day for relaxation and games, although these were thoroughly organized so there was very little opportunity for individual initiative, but quite the largest emphasis was on Bible-reading, prayers and services. We sang 'choruses' interminably and some of these stick in my mind to this day. I kept being 'converted' each year at these camps, but although I think I genuinely meant to be a Christian it became increasingly clear to me that I could not possibly live up to the standards, especially in sexual matters, which these conversions were supposed to achieve.

This tension between faith and morals has been a factor throughout my life. It was not until I discovered that the Church existed for the sinner and that I did not have to be perfect before I could start trying to follow 'the way' that I had the grace or the courage to make any real effort to tackle my own nature and what seemed to me to be its foundation, since my childhood, of drink and sex.

However, I do remember having some affection for many of the 'officers' at these camps, among whom was Joost de Blank, who subsequently became Archbishop of Cape Town. And when I finally found a spiritual home in a more catholic presentation of the faith, this earlier evangelical experience gave it a very valuable foundation.

One of the problems about not having an effective father was that there was no one whom I could ask about sex. Talking to Esylt Newbery about this was of course impossible. She had had, as I have said, a very Victorian upbringing herself, and it simply was not done for a male and a female to talk about such things – even if she had been able to tell me what I wanted to know. This problem is best illustrated by a quotation from page 124 of *Parson's Daughter*:

> In some ways, it is easier to bring up children when there is no one to dispute your authority, but at times the absence of a father makes things a bit difficult. A father ought to talk to his boys about some matters as man to man, but I had to do this sort of thing myself, so I watched my opportunity.
>
> One day we were at breakfast, and Mike was stuffing himself with porridge, when suddenly right out of the blue he said to me:
>
> 'Auntie, how do babies come?'
>
> The other two stopped eating and listened with all their ears to what I would answer.
>
> 'This', I thought to myself, 'is it!'
>
> 'Why, you little goose! Don't you know a simple thing like that?'
>
> 'No, really I don't. How do they come?'
>
> 'Well, I suppose you know how a hen lays an egg? A baby comes from his mother in the same way, only it isn't in a shell, that's all. And don't fill your mouth so full, your porridge won't run away.'
>
> He was perfectly satisfied. 'Oh, *that's* it. I never thought of that! Now I know what the hymn means, what says "Where-a-Mother-laid-a-Baby-in-a-manger-for-a-bed".'
>
> He never asked me any more about it.

I do not remember this particular occasion, though it certainly sounds as if Mike was deliberately playing her up. But this kind of response did make it quite impossible to ask further. The first talk I had about sex was from the headmaster of my prep school just before I left. He had all the boys who were leaving into his study one night and gave us a talk about puberty and the evils of masturbation and so on which I don't think many of us understood at all at that age, but perhaps I was a late developer.

Monkton Combe was no more informative. It must have been unique amongst public schools in that sex was never even discussed among the boys, or at least if it was I never heard it. On one occasion we were summoned to the school hall and told solemnly but obscurely that a boy was being publicly expelled, but it was never made clear exactly what he had done and we could only assume that it was for some sort of homosexual misdemeanour. Like most boys, I got what information I could by surreptitiously looking things up in the public library.

When I had been at Monkton Combe for nearly a year two things happened. One was that I had some kind of 'breakdown', which I cannot remember at all, and was sent home to recover. The other was that the slump really hit the cotton industry and my father could not send enough to keep us at boarding-school. In consequence, I was taken away from Monkton Combe and became one of the thousand or so day-boys at Bristol Grammar School. This was almost as dramatic a change as the switch from Shanghai to Weston-super-Mare. I was saved, I think, by my talent for sport. I had already done quite well in cricket, soccer, boxing and rugby, and it happened that when I got to Bristol the school was extremely hard-up for a scrum-half so I was taken straight into the first fifteen. As a result I was plunged from my cold fortress into something of a sexual maelstrom. The other members of the team were much older than myself and tough types both athletically and socially. They not only knew about sex but had a considerable experience of it. In the bus, to and from the rugby matches, we sang the songs which I suppose will always be sung on such occasions. It was not a large repertoire but it was an earthy one and I certainly had very little idea what it was all about. However, I coped much better than I might have done, and this was largely due to the protective attitude that one boy called Peregrine adopted towards me. He was an extremely handsome youth with a devil's peak on his forehead and, I should think, extremely sophisticated. Somehow he took a liking to me, realized something of my bewilderment and embarrassment, and constantly came to my aid when I was obviously out of my depth in the kind of sexual joking and conversation that went on. I shall always be grateful to him, and I shall always be grateful, too, to the other people at Bristol Grammar School, because if I had not had this experience to pave the way I should have been completely lost when I got out into the cold hard world.

I did quite well academically at Bristol and, perhaps spurred on by my father's threat, I got a good matric. The headmaster wanted me to stay on and try for a closed scholarship at St John's College, Oxford, but I flatly refused to do this. I made all sorts of excuses, the main one being that Esylt Newbery was always complaining that my father was no longer sending any money, and telling us that we had got to start earning our own livings as soon as possible. But my real reason was that I was desperate to get away from a household run by a woman, where I was still treated as a child and sent to bed at nine o'clock. I not only wanted to leave home, I wanted to get as far away as I possibly could. I haunted the public libraries, reading up about foreign countries and scanning the newspapers for ideas.

The first job I tried for was in answer to a newspaper advertisement. It was for somebody to help on a farm in Canada, and I had to go up to the Midlands by train for an interview with the man concerned, who was over on a holiday. I was growing a lot of fuzz around my face at the time. I knew I ought to shave but I never had shaved, I hadn't got a razor, and I didn't know how to go about it. I was much too shy to talk to Esylt about this sort of thing. So with the little money I was given for my journey I bought a razor and I shaved for the first time in the lavatory of the railway train going up. I made a filthy mess of my face, my clothes, and everything else, and when I got home I hid the shaving gear. It was quite a long time before I was gradually able to let Esylt know that I was shaving.

I failed to get the Canadian job and I searched around all over the place for some other means of getting away from home. Finally, with Esylt Newbery's help, it was decided I should go to New Zealand under a special scheme by which about a dozen so-called 'public schoolboys' went for a year to Waitaki Boys'

High School in Oamaru, New Zealand, to do a short agricultural course there, before starting on a farming career. I left for New Zealand with this party of boys on 4 January 1929. I was not quite seventeen and it was all a very considerable adventure.

Perhaps predictably, I didn't last long at Waitaki High School. I was resentful of being sent to a further school at all. Getting away from home meant for me getting away from discipline and everything connected with it, so I was extremely troublesome and unco-operative, a complete switch from the docile sort of boy I had been in England. My rebellion culminated in being caught coming into the school grounds soon after midnight on a Monday morning. I and a friend of mine had cut chapel on the Sunday night, and had taken two girls out in a boat in the bay of the harbour to visit one of the ships. It was in fact a perfectly innocent affair sexually, but obviously I was setting out to defy authority and the headmaster of the school could not allow it to continue. Both I and my companion were soundly beaten and the headmaster cabled Esylt Newbery suggesting that I, as the ringleader, should be removed from the school as soon as possible. She had some friends or acquaintances who were small farmers near Havelock in the North Island of New Zealand and so I was sent away from the school to work for them. This was my first job.

My employer, Mr Mason, was a 'Cocky', that is he had a small mixed farm. The work was fairly tough. I don't think that I have ever experienced any pain worse than I had in my forearm muscles when I milked cows for the first time. There were not very many to get through, but I almost cried with the agony of trying to go on. However, I did enjoy the horse-riding and the general work of a shepherd. Mr Mason and his wife did their very best for me: they welcomed me into their home and invited girls for supper and bridge, and nobody could have been kinder, but I was determined that I was going to get completely free.

One night I simply walked out and left them, and had that strange exhilarating feeling of being completely unknown and having no responsibilities whatsoever. I suppose as a Christian one should never feel like that, but all through my life, when I am on holiday, I have liked to get away to a city or a place where no one knows or cares who I am. Not that I want to do anything bad, it is simply the sense of freedom that I enjoy.

The first night I just walked, trying to avoid cars on the road in case the Masons were looking for me. I spent the second night on a haystack and got chased off by a farmer and some police. It seemed to me the safest thing to do was to go back to the haystack, which I duly did and was not disturbed again. This sort of thing went on until I got to Wellington, where it was very difficult to earn a living because unemployment was so bad. I attempted to sell programmes in a cinema and also tried to get a job selling cars, but failed. I was sleeping meanwhile in a disused hut in the railway goods-yard and eventually the police, who I had not realized were looking for me, found some of my clothes there and caught up with me. Apparently the headmaster of Waitaki High School was formally my guardian and as I was still well under twenty-one he had started a search for me. After a lot of argument it was decided that I had not got to go back to school (where they certainly did not want me) and I was sent to work for some dairy farmers, this time in Taranaki, under Mount Egmont. Again I left them as soon as I could and took another job not far away. This was particularly arduous work on a dairy-farm which supplied milk for a milk round, and it meant that we went to bed about 7 p.m. and got up soon after 2 a.m. to start milking. (This experience in early rising was useful later when I became a priest and found how valuable it was to say some prayers before the early Mass.) Like all these jobs, the dairy-farm didn't last long because of my own truculence and desire to be free, and I set out this time really 'on the bum'.

The great slump of the late 1920s and early 1930s had already had a considerable effect on my life. The cotton industry had been one of the first to be hit and this was one of the main reasons why the supply of money from my father had dried up and why I had been determined to get out and earn my own living. But by the time I got to New Zealand the slump had hit that country pretty badly too and there was serious unemployment. Hundreds of men were, like me, wandering the roads looking for work. There were labour camps for the men who chose to go to them and work for ten shillings a week, but I was not prepared to do that, and stayed 'on the bum', living as best I could. I often stole cream from the cream cans waiting to be picked up outside the gates of dairy-farms, and stole vegetables and so on. There was an unwritten law at that time which said that any man who was really hungry could kill and eat a sheep, provided that he hung the skin on a fence so that the owner could clean and sell it. But I never really felt that I could cope with a whole sheep. People were very good and I often got a meal for doing an hour or two's work cutting firewood and other odd jobs. I met a varied collection of people on my travels. One was a boy who had been at prep school with me. Another, with whom I joined forces for a time, shook me considerably by taking me, with great confidence, into an ironmonger's shop (I knew that he had no money) and using me, in my innocence, to distract the shopkeeper's attention while he stole a rather expensive knife.

I wandered all over the North Island of New Zealand and travelled for several hundred miles on a goods-train under the tarpaulins. I got pulled in by the police on one occasion, because a Chinese market-gardener had been murdered and I had been wandering in the vicinity, but of course I had nothing to do with it and was released.

At some time I went back to the South Island and worked with a shearing gang up the Waitaki river. Here I got into a fight in which I got one of the worst beatings of my life, although it didn't do me any harm. When I first joined this shearing gang I was dressed rather 'poshly' compared with the rest of the gang, who were in dungarees. On our first night in the bunk-house of the sheep ranch, where we were to shear, all the rest of the gang got into bed in their shirts and went to sleep. I had a pair of pyjamas in my case, but I was so aware of the gaffe I had committed by arriving comparatively well-dressed that I followed their example, and left my pyjamas in the case. A few days later, when I was picking up the fleeces on the shearing floor, I tripped over one of the shearer's feet and caused him to stumble. As the shearers were paid by piecework and were going flat out, he called me a bastard, to which I replied in a peculiarly British fashion by insisting that he should come out and fight me. This he duly did. He was a great deal bigger than I was, and gave me an awful pasting, but I never find it easy to give up and I fought as long as I could. This somewhat increased my reputation with the other members of the gang. At 'smoke-oh' the conversation centred on the fight and one of the men remarked that he couldn't understand why I, who dressed and talked like a toff, should not possess a pair of pyjamas to my name. I have always remembered this and from it learnt that you get much more respect if you stick to your own habits and customs, and do not try to adapt yourself to your company.

I suppose that all through this time I must have realized, if only subconsciously, that I was doing violence to myself. I enjoyed the freedom and irresponsibility tremendously, but from time to time other things caught up with me. The warden of my theological college later told my bishop, 'ffrench-Beytagh has a good brain, albeit one of the most muddled ones I have ever taught', and I was not using my brain at all at that time. When I had the chance of good conversation I enjoyed it very much and at one time, when I was sick, I set myself to read Emerson's *Essays*, though I can't say that I enjoyed them very much. I suppose one can hardly put *Alice in Wonderland* in the same category but I gave myself a copy of it when I had been discarded by one of my girl-friends and wrote an inscription on the flyleaf saying that I was presenting it to myself, in the hope that from then on I would 'eschew the company of all women, cows, bitches, she-cats, etc.' From time to time I wrote poetry, which I suppose most young people do at some time in their lives. It was not good poetry, but it did help to express that part of me that yearned to be something more than a casual farm-labourer.

The strain between these two parts of me must have been much greater than I realized. Probably this was not only the conscious strain of neglecting my education and my talents, but also the continuation of the basic strain between the almost complete freedom of my early years in Shanghai and my subsequent upbringing under Esylt Newbery's strict discipline. All this resulted in some sort of breakdown which I have never clearly remembered or understood. It occurred some time between jobs, and all I can remember is that I found my way down to an almost dried-up river-bed with a stony beach. There I made myself a tatterdemalion kind of tiny tent out of dead branches and a couple of sacks, and there I stayed. How long I lay there, I have no idea, but it must have been several days. I have vague memories of getting up from time to time and there were certainly several empty tins around when I finally moved out, so I must have fed myself. I do remember that the tent was wet with dew or rain – and that was all I knew, or know. When it was over, all I could remember was a great darkness and a great exhaustion. It may have been what some psychologists call a fugue, it certainly was not a period of conversion or enlightenment or anything like that and I did not feel that I came out of it a better person in any sort of way. Except for the clearcut memory that it happened, I do not think it had any conscious effect on me at all. (I had a similar experience in Johannesburg while I was on remand, when I went for a few hours into a semi-catatonic state.) I suppose that when I subconsciously find things too much for me I just contract out. I am neither proud of this, nor particularly ashamed. It may well be part of the mercy of God that He helps me and heals me in this way.

Eventually the police caught up with me yet again, because I was still under age, and this time I was sent to work for the largest peach-growing farm in New Zealand on a place called 'the Island', in the middle of a river near Motueka in the Nelson province. I must have spent the best part of a year around here and a very tough experience it was. But by this time I had toughened up considerably myself and had a rather unsavoury reputation as a fighter. (After one fight the other man was in hospital for several days.)

The peach-growing area was also suitable for tobacco, and after getting fed up with peaches I started to work for tobacco farmers as a casual labourer. This was almost as tough for my back-muscles as milking cows was for my forearms. It meant staying crouched down all day, taking the suckers out from between the leaves of the tobacco plants. The tobacco juice covered my arms and hardened like glue. Altogether it was an unpleasant and difficult business, but at least I felt independent. I had no particular boss, and I was allowed to live in a 'whare', a little tin hut, on one of the farms. There was an extremely nice schoolmistress in the village who was most hospitable to me and I went to most of the local 'do's'. For the first time I really came across girls as girls. Until then I had steered clear of them. For instance, on the boat coming over to New Zealand several of the boys in the party were clearly having sexual affairs of one sort or another (probably a good deal less than they claimed) but I had been much too shy and frightened. It was still worse when the ship got to Colon on the Panama Canal and a group of us went on shore and ended up in some sort of combined brothel and night-club. I was horrified and got out as fast as I could, back to the safety of the ship. (We thought that one of the boys who stayed on had missed the boat but he turned up next day, dead-drunk, in a potato locker.) The New Zealand girls got me over this panic and really taught me what sex was about. I had affairs of varying intensity with quite a few of them and still correspond with some – though now of course they are happily married and mostly grand-mothers. Whatever the morality of all this may have been, it was a great deal of use to me in my whole emotional development, besides being great fun, and I am deeply in their debt, as I am to other women who have helped and befriended me since then.

Life drifted on in this pleasant but very aimless way until one day, as I was hanging over a farm gate doing nothing whatsoever, a man came up and claimed, much to my astonishment, that he was my mother's brother-in-law. He had been looking for alluvial gold somewhere in New Zealand and had been asked to find me by my mother, with whom I had completely lost touch. How he had done so, I don't know. He said that my mother was willing to pay my fare over to South Africa if I was prepared to go there. I was prepared to go absolutely anywhere, for any purposes whatsoever, and I jumped at the idea.

It is, of course, trite to say that I left New Zealand with mixed feelings – but they were *very* mixed. I started my journey, at the end of 1932, by sailing from Nelson to Wellington, in order to pick up the boat for Australia and South Africa. I have a clear picture of myself as I leant over the ship's rail and saw the sun coming down behind the mountains and sounds (fjords). I felt in my bones that I would never see them again, and I was leaving one or two very good friends behind. I had not achieved anything in particular, but I had learnt a great deal in all sorts of ways and not least about mixing with people and making friends. I was physically fitter than I have ever been, before or since, and although I was not quite twenty-one, I felt that I could hold my own in any company – which only goes to show what an arrogant young man I was. I must in fact have been a pretty revolting sight – a friend referred to me recently as 'one of the early hippies' and I certainly used what were then outlandish clothes to express what I thought about my elders and 'the system'. I wore the baggiest of plus-fours with two-toned 'co-respondent' shoes and brightly coloured socks. And as soon as I could get away from farm work I grew my fingernails long so that I could paint them white underneath; at one point I even affected a monocle. But underneath all this I had a desire to belong and the subconscious knowledge that somewhere, some time, I would find a place where I could belong – as I believe the true hippie does today.

To some extent this longing had become conscious. A little while previously, I had had to have two operations for severe blood-poisoning which I had got when clearing some virgin land. As I lay in hospital each day, I watched the other men having visits from their families and friends, while I had no one. My few friends were miles away and although one or two of them meant quite a lot to me, it was not the sort of long-term relationship which one can rely on through thick and thin. I remember waking up to the fact that there was no one within thousands of miles who gave a damn whether I lived or died. At that time I became aware that if I wanted to matter to anyone or belong anywhere, I would have to stop this casual wandering around and get stuck into something with some plan or purpose to it. I had tended to despise office-workers and city folk, with their daily monotonous round, growing older in the same old place, with nothing new to look forward to, but in that hospital bed I began to feel a twinge of envy for them. I remember thinking about a sentence I had once read to the effect that those who get into a rut at least make an impression on the earth's surface – and realizing that I was making none at all.

Although this was, as far as I remember, my first conscious realization of my need to 'belong', I now know that it is one of the great driving forces within me. It goes back, I imagine, to my childhood, when I did not really belong to my parents, and although Esylt Newbery did her best to provide a good home, I did not feel I belonged there either. All through my priesthood I have needed people, or a group of people, to whom I felt I mattered and who mattered to me. To be honest, I think that I am so selfish, or so much in need, that my need to be needed by them is the greater force.

So, as I have said, although I was a pretty brash young man on the surface, as the boat left Nelson that night, I was also pretty mixed-up inside. I was sad to be going, but experiencing again that sense of liberation which I had had when I first left England. I was going to a new country and a new life, and I felt ready for anything. I don't think that the prospect of seeing my mother had anything to do with it. I had not seen her since I was about twelve and then only for an hour or two. I might just as well have been going to Canada or China, so long as it was a new start, and carried with it the possibility of really getting my teeth into some real sort of job.

CHAPTER TWO

Reluctant Christian

Any landfall after a long ocean voyage has its own beauty – even the dreadful mud-flats of the Yangtze-Kiang river have a certain attraction – and certainly I shall never forget my first sight of Durban, with its great bay and long line of white buildings, and behind them the rising hills of Zululand. Here I saw 'the African' for the first time, and I saw him, of course, as a servant and a labourer, bustling about the ship getting ready for us to disembark. Here also, oddly enough, I had my first taste of racial discrimination, in a very personal way. Because many Chinese had become naturalized as British citizens and then emigrated to the Union, the South African government had decided that anyone born in China must be classified as Chinese and therefore be refused admission. My passport showed that I had been born in Shanghai and so I came within this category. Eventually I was given a temporary permit as an Asiatic and for over a year I had to attend the Immigration Office in Johannesburg at regular intervals to have this permit renewed. (In the end the law was changed and I was transformed from an Asiatic to being, as my indictment later described me, 'an European male'.)

It took quite a long time to get this sorted out and I had to get help from a friend of my mother, whose address was the only one that I had in Durban. I only had one Australian pound left, so this friend not only had to get through the red tape about my passport but also pay for a hotel room for the night and advance me the money for my journey up to the Eastern Transvaal where my mother lived. (It seems incredible now, but I searched that hotel room on the beach front in Durban to make sure that there

29

were no snakes, of which I have always had a neurotic fear. Just how I thought snakes could exist in the middle of a big city like Durban I do not know, but I record it as a fact.) Next day I set off on the train up through Zululand and Piet Retief to Graskop in the Eastern Transvaal. On the train I came across an Afrikaner for the first time. He was an old man who could not speak much English and he was only mollified at my incapacity to speak Afrikaans when I told him that I had only arrived from overseas the day before. He began to question me, and amongst other things asked whether London was all flat low veld, which did not indicate that his knowledge of the wider world was very great.

It was over ten years since I had seen my mother and getting to know her again was a quite extraordinary experience. I was so little conscious that she was, in fact, my mother that when I was handing round drinks at a sundowner party soon after I arrived I called her 'Mrs Buchanan', and I am not sure that she ever forgave me for this. She was then in her early sixties but still had her hair dyed red, as she had done when she visited us at prep school in England, and she still seemed very giggly and irresponsible. When, in the evenings, we played three-handed bridge, she used to cheat quite blatantly and got extremely angry when this was pointed out to her. I cannot say that we got on badly, but there was never any real relationship between us. Fortunately I liked her current husband, George Buchanan, very much indeed. As I have mentioned, he was a lot younger than 'Pegs' and was indeed a year younger than her eldest son. He had been an officer in the merchant navy but had developed tuberculosis and had emigrated to South Africa in the hope of a cure. At that time he was managing a forest called Driekop on the edge of the great berg which runs right across the Transvaal, and I spent a lot of time riding with him about the forest as he directed the work of the men who were felling and carting timber, most of which was used for props in the gold mines. There was no room for me to sleep in the house so I slept in a small but comfortable hut outside with a stable door whose top I left open through the night. I used to be woken, morning after morning, by the most glorious sunrises I have ever seen in my life shining through the open section of the door.

This was the high veld ('*Jock of the Bushveld* country') and a most beautiful part of the world. On days when I had nothing to do I would take my lunch with me and ride to the edge of the berg, where the cliff fell away almost sheer for thousands of feet, down into a sea of smoky blue haze. I used to sit here for hours and hours in a sort of conscious 'fugue', staring into that limitless blueness with the smoke of the kraal fires twisting up from the invisible low veld, far, far, below. It was like being on the edge of the world.

But in spite of the attractions of the forest and the berg, I very soon became unsettled, and felt it was time I got down to work. My half-brother Jack McIlraith, my mother's only son by her first marriage, was employed in the Colonial Service in the Bechuanaland Protectorate. He thought I might be able to get a job in that service, so after a couple of months I set out from Graskop to Gaberones where my brother lived. It was a long journey. I had to change trains at Johannesburg, which seemed simply a conglomeration of buildings and a long row of mine dumps and headgear, and then the train ran through the great flat dullness of the Western Transvaal to the edge of the Kalahari desert and at last reached Gaberones. At that time Gaberones was affectionately known as 'the Camp', which sufficiently describes it, though I understand it is now quite a town, has dropped the 's' from its name, and is the capital of Botswana.

I had never consciously met my half-brother Jack McIlraith before, although I believe he had seen me as a baby. Marriages don't seem to go well in my family. My mother tried three times and my father at least twice, and by this time Jack had divorced his first wife by whom he had five children. When I arrived to stay with him he had a 'housekeeper' who also had five children. (He eventually married her and they had a child together as well.) It says something for them that with a family of ten they were prepared to put me up. In fact they were quite extraordinarily kind to me. I did my best to repay it by teaching some of the younger children but I also had a rather traumatic affair with the housekeeper's eldest daughter.

Jack was an engineer in the Public Works Department and he spent a lot of time going out into the desert and attending to the pumps which supplied essential water to the semi-desert villages. I went on many of these trips with him and spent some weeks in Serowe, the largest native village south of the equator, where there was something radically wrong with the pumps. Although we camped here for some time our only contact with the Africans there was with those who came to sell us eggs or chickens. Occasionally we would see the paramount chief, Tshekedi Khama, out riding with his entourage, but we never met him. While we were there an Englishman was flogged by his orders, and later, as I went south by train, I passed a force from the Royal Navy coming up from the Cape to remind the chief where the power really lay. It was a typical 'gunboat' exercise.

As in my mother's house, I had nothing at all to do with Africans at this time. They were servants and neither I, nor anyone else, was interested in them as people. They were called by their nicknames and I never knew what their real names were. Jack had as his assistant a Coloured man called Martin who travelled everywhere with him and not only helped him throughout the day, but cooked his evening meal, while we sat outside the tent and had our sundowners. Occasionally Martin would be given half a mug of brandy, which he drank standing. In no sense did he mix with us. There was a typical South African relationship of affectionate banter which went on between him and Jack, but if he stepped out of line Jack was on to him like a flash and very often physically punched and kicked him, which, to be honest, he did not seem to mind very much. I accepted this state of affairs, as everyone else did, though there were a couple of incidents which made an impression on me. One was hearing a cultured English voice, and on turning round to see who this classy newcomer was, finding he was a coal-black African in Tshekedi Khama's entourage; another was seeing, for the first time, Africans chained together in a chain-gang, like animals (and this was not in South Africa but in the Bechuanaland Protectorate under British colonial rule). Also I do remember pointing out to my brother that in New Zealand the Minister of Railways had been a Maori and that you could not class people by their race, but that was as far as my concern went.

Again I became bored and it also became very clear that there was no prospect of a job in the Colonial Service as I had hoped. Finally one of my mother's influential friends got me an interview for a job as a junior clerk in Johannesburg with a mining machinery company, Holman Brothers. It was rather a sticky interview since the headmaster of Waitaki High School, who was the only reference I could give, was obviously not able to be very glowing about my character, and my work record was hardly encouraging. However, I explained what had happened as honestly as I could to the managing director and he took me on, though I doubt whether I would have got the job if it had not been for the influence of my mother's friend.

The firm sold mining machinery and equipment all over southern Africa and I had to take orders, quote prices to buyers, and see that stocks were reordered from our head office at Camborne in Cornwall when an item was running short – of course all in a very junior capacity. I could cope with the work all right, though I got into trouble for swearing in front of the office girls, but what impressed me most about the whole business was the amount of bribery that went on. This was quite blatant. There was intense competition between the various firms which sold new equipment, and the buyers could get almost anything they asked for as a sweetener. They would ring up the office and demand tickets for a big boxing-match or something of the kind and somehow the tickets had to be obtained – or else. Important customers would get an expensive radiogram or even a car as a Christmas present and all the salesmen kept what was openly known in the office as a 'bribery and corruption account'. I remember a doll costing £8 which had been given to some mine manager's daughter figuring in one of these. Since my own salary was £10 a month I resented this particular item a good deal. However, I managed to get a room over an undertaker's business in the centre of Johannesburg for a rent of £2 10s. per month and somehow lived off the rest. It was possible to get quite a good meal in those days for 1s. 6d., so I didn't do too badly and could occasionally manage a cinema if I ate a bag of chips or something on that night instead of having a full meal.

It was one of the loneliest periods of my existence. I hadn't got the clothes or the money to mix with my mother's friends, nobody at my work ever invited me to their homes, and with the amount of money I had to spare there was very little that I could do. Almost in desperation I decided to go to evening classes at the Witwatersrand Technical College and I started on a course to qualify for the Chartered Institute of Secretaries. I never did qualify, but it opened the way up for me into something which was eventually to change my life.

I noticed that one of my fellow students, a year or two older than myself, wore a Toc H badge. Toc H had been started during the first world war. The name came from the initials of Talbot House which had been run as a pastoral centre just behind the front line (Toc being telegraph code for 'T'). Many men had found a meaning to their lives there and after the war they helped its founder Tubby Clayton to start centres, which gradually spread all over the world, where service and Christian fellowship were combined. I had come across the movement casually in New Zealand and although I knew hardly anything about it, I made seeing this badge an excuse to go and talk to the man who was wearing it. His name was Herbert Shaw and he became one of my lifelong friends. He introduced me into Toc H in Johannesburg, and because I had a lot of time on my hands and nothing much which interested me, I soon became active in the movement. At this time I was a fairly convinced agnostic. I had thought about religion very considerably, and found it quite impossible to be an atheist, but I also rejected Christianity as I had known it. Since Toc H has a strong Christian foundation this caused some difficulty but I tried to be honest with the officials of the movement about my own position and they accepted me as a member.

Johannesburg was an extraordinary place to be living in at that time. When I arrived the slump was still casting a blight over everything and there was almost nothing going on, which was why I had found it so difficult to get a job. But very soon things began to wake up and I found myself in the middle of a hectic boom. The city was pulled down round my ears and rebuilt with flats and office-blocks (these turned out to have a useful life of about thirty years – they were almost all replaced yet again by the end of the sixties – so I have in effect seen three Johannesburgs). New mines were opened up and stock exchange business rocketed. I remember how envious I was of my friends who worked there as clerks and who made a packet on overtime (and no doubt a little quiet gambling on the side). I remember one of them urging me, 'For God's sake, if you've got twenty-five quid, buy Freddies' (shares in the new Free State reef which was just being opened up). The price of Freddies duly shot up to an incredible height, but alas, I did not have £25.   1821878

In spite of not having much money, as I made friends and the atmosphere livened up, I did have a lot of fun. There were several cheap dance-halls and night-clubs, like the Astoria Palais de Danse and Sunningdale (which then was right out in the veld along dirt roads, whereas now it is in the middle of a rich suburb). Often on Saturday nights, I and my friends made up a party to go to the five-shilling hop at the Wanderers Club, which was where the main railway station stands now. Here an incident occurred which made a deep impression on me. Another man in the party and I were standing at the bar around midnight and I offered him a drink. He glanced at his watch and refused. I said, 'Look, don't be an ass, it's my shout – I've had two drinks off you. What will you have?' And still he said, 'Thanks, but I don't want one.' By this time I was a bit hurt and angry and I went on pressing him for a reason why he would not accept a drink from me. Finally he said, 'Well you see, I am going to receive Holy Communion in the morning.' I was shattered. I had

had no idea that this man did anything about religion at all and I had never heard of fasting communion. That an ordinary person like him should care so much about a church service and have the guts to stick to his principles about it, made a very deep impression on me, although it had no immediate, practical result.

By this time I was doing quite a lot of work for Toc H, and when Tubby Clayton, the founder of Toc H, made a visit to Johannesburg in about 1935 I helped to organize his programme. One of the things which impressed me about Tubby Clayton was a remark which he made about friendship. He was, I suppose, one of the most outgoing and friendly of people, who travelled the whole wide world and made friends wherever he was. But he pointed out that no man could afford to have more than a very few real friends – meaning people with whom he would be willing to share his last crust, and for whom he would even be willing to die. I believe this to be true and, although I have been extremely fortunate throughout my whole later life as a priest in the friendships which I have made, there are probably comparatively few people who really know me as I am, with all my faults, and with whom there is no holding back of any kind. Tubby Clayton was accompanied by a young man, Jonathan Graham, who acted as his ADC and who later became a monk and finally superior of the Community of the Resurrection. I had a good deal to do with Jonathan in arranging the details of Tubby's talks and travels and during the week or ten days that he was in Johannesburg we had some long and pretty vociferous discussions about the Christian religion, sometimes privately and sometimes at Toc H meetings. There was no question that he had the better brain and produced a better argument, but I had had some practice in debating at school and made some effective though rather cheap scores. These arguments were certainly one of the factors which gradually helped to weaken my 'agnosticism'.

Another person whom I met at this time was Alan Paton who later wrote *Cry, The Beloved Country* and the other books which have made him famous. He came to Johannesburg after I had joined Toc H but he had been a Toc H member for many years and I heard a good deal about him before he arrived. I rather resented what I was told; he was obviously more than capable, a very considerable leader and much loved by Toc H members throughout the country, and I was prepared to be considerably jealous of him. I was pretty truculent to him when he arrived, and came to the forefront of Toc H in Johannesburg. But he completely disarmed me by asking my advice, so that very soon I too succumbed. His job in Johannesburg was an important one. The reformatories of the country had just been taken over from the Department of Justice by the Department of Education and the Minister of Education had taken Alan from his school-teaching job in Pietermaritzburg and put him in charge of the great African reformatory in Diepkloof, a few miles south of Johannesburg. This, when I first saw it, was a horrific institution, completely enclosed by a tremendously high barbed-wire fence, inside which were rows of cell-blocks, dank, dark and dirty, and warders armed with guns. It was Alan's task to change this from a prison into some sort of a school, and a magnificent job he made of it. Inevitably, as soon as the barbed-wire was taken down and the warders became teachers, many of the boys took advantage of this unexpected freedom, and the number of escapees increased alarmingly. I often stayed for the weekend at Diepkloof with Alan and his wife and sometimes we spent most of the time chasing boys over half the Southern Transvaal. Almost all the staff were Afrikaners and Alan took the trouble to take a degree in Afrikaans in order to identify himself with his staff. At the time of the Voortrekker celebrations, he even grew a beard, as most of the Afrikaners did. Alan, of course, was a strong practising Christian, as was Ronald Anderson who was the leader of Toc H in Johannesburg, and these two were my greatest friends, although I was a few years younger than both of them.

In some ways I was living a double life at this time. On the one hand there were the good things that I was attempting to do, centred on Toc H. For example I took an active interest in a slum-clearance and rehousing scheme in the slums of Fordsburg and also ran a small boxing club there for Coloured boys. I put a good deal of time and effort into working with these youngsters and for the first time tried to speak a little Afrikaans, which was their main language. At one time I taught in a night-school for African servants who wanted to learn how to read and write, and I was also involved in visits to European lepers at Westfort Sanatorium. (My first visit to the sanatorium was fairly traumatic. I have always had irrational fears of many kinds and they were certainly very much to the forefront when I first went to Westfort. We were not in fact allowed to touch the lepers – we indicated a shaking of hands with them by shaking our own two hands together – but we came into very close contact with them and we sat and talked to them for many hours.)

Yet combined with doing these 'good works' I was also running around with a pretty hectic and doubtful bunch of characters. My sister Pat had emigrated to South Africa in about 1934 and she and I set up a flat together. In spite of our lack of money we had a good many parties there, and some of them were fairly wild ones. She very soon went off with one of the crowd, a young man from a fairly rich family, with whom on one occasion I had a fight in a night-club. (She later married this man and became, like him, a Roman Catholic, but he developed into a hopeless and very irresponsible alcoholic and she was given special permission from Rome to divorce him. She remained a devout Roman Catholic and tried to make a good job of bringing up her two children – I am sure that her faith saved her from a quite disastrous life, as I believe mine has saved me.)

By the time Pat got married, I was earning the princely sum of £25 a month and I went off to live in a rather sleazy hotel called Sans Souci out in one of the suburbs. Here again, I mixed with the kind of crowd that one finds in rather sleazy hotels, and I earned some extra money by signing-in people for drinks outside proper licensing hours and things of that kind.

Eventually this sort of life caught up with me – oddly enough on a really 'double' evening when I dropped in at a party on my way back from a first-aid course which I was taking. Everyone was pretty drunk, though I was rather less so, having arrived late, and there was an argument about a girl. I have no idea what it was all about, but on my way home I was 'mugged' in the Braamfontein subway, and my jaw was broken in three places. The doctor said later that they must have used an iron bar. Somehow I walked the three miles back to the hotel, presumably in a very concussed state, and spread blood all over the place trying to put myself to bed. Fortunately, some other people in the hotel heard me groaning and came into my room. I had passed out again by that time and they took me to hospital. I woke up the next morning to find a vast Afrikaner policeman sitting beside my bed and when I asked him why he had come to question me in the state I was in, he said it was because he thought I might die! This gave me a considerable shock, since although I felt lousy I had not thought things were as bad as that.

The hospital made rather a mess of setting my jaw and I was there for some time. My first visitor was Alan Paton who took the trouble to come the ten miles from Diepkloof as soon as he heard that I was in hospital. Of course I could not talk much, but his strong presence was a comfort and a strength and I was vividly reminded of the contrast between his immediate visit and my loneliness when I had been in hospital in New Zealand.

Enforced idleness evidently has a salutary effect on me. In the New Zealand hospital I had first realized how empty my 'freedom' really was, and while I was lying in Johannesburg General I made another important step in the same direction.

At that period I was seriously thinking it was time I got married, though I don't think I had any particular girl in mind, and as I lay there, with nothing to do but think, I began to consider the responsibility of having children and to wonder what those children would be like. This was difficult because of the double life I was leading and so I began to wonder what sort of person I really was and therefore what I wanted my children to be. I found myself thinking of the various people that I admired. Some of these were the heroes of my favourite reading, Bulldog Drummond, Peter Cheney, and so forth. I liked to think of myself as being like these characters, a tough reckless creature who didn't give a damn for anyone, popular, capable, unconcerned, free of all conventional shackles. On the other hand, I knew some real people whom I admired most tremendously, particularly Alan Paton and Ronald Anderson. As I lay there, in pain and dopy with drugs, it began to become very clear to me that it was these flesh-and-blood people whom I really admired and the others were an exciting but quite impossible illusion. It may not seem much of a step to make, but I believe that if there was a moment of conversion, this was it. I discovered that the people I wanted my children to be like were Christians – completely reckless, daring Christians. And it logically followed that that was the sort of person I wanted to be myself.

I had a month or so of convalescence in the houses of various friends, and through all this time this conviction developed. I began to read something other than thrillers. One book I remember was *Christ and Communism* by Stanley Jones, which, although extraordinarily bad theology, made a deep impression on me because it took me to the person of Jesus in a way I had never conceived before. Jesus became real and alive for me.

Soon after I came out of hospital I went to evensong at a little parish church near my hotel. This was the first time I had been near a church for years. As I have already said, when I left Monkton Combe I had promised myself that I would never go to church again of my own free will and, except on one occasion when a girl-friend in New Zealand had dragged me to evensong, I had stuck to this resolution. The service was a pretty dull affair with a few old people scattered round the church and the sermon was utterly uninspiring, but I did find that the familiar chants of the *Magnificat* and *Nunc Dimittis,* which I remembered from the chapel at Monkton Combe, struck a deep and emotional chord.

The decision to attend services regularly was brought to a head by an invitation to join the Toc H Mark, a residential group of Toc H members which had just been started by the Rev. Tom Savage, who was a recent addition to the whole-time staff from England. When I was asked to be one of its first inhabitants, it was pointed out to me that I could not with integrity be at the heart of Toc H unless I joined in the regular meetings for prayer that were the centre of the house's work. I remember that for some extraordinary reason I felt indignant that my willingness to take part in such prayer should be questioned, and I can only suppose that I must by that time have become convinced that prayer was an activity in which I could take part with reality. So I joined the house and I began to attend, but not to communicate, at the communion services which were regularly held in the chapel. I had not been in the Toc H Mark for very long before I found my way to Johannesburg Cathedral which was quite nearby, and there, on an occasion which I cannot remember at all, I again received the Holy Communion.

One of the very few spiritual experiences of my life happened that Christmas in the cathedral. In those days the dean was very much afraid of the Midnight Mass being attended by the drunken revellers who were about the streets late on Christmas Eve, so the doors were closed and admittance was by ticket only. Naturally, as a result, very few people came, and the service was in a side chapel. The experience I had was not at all dramatic, but I have remembered it all my life and return to it for reassurance on the many occasions when I have been despondent and doubted not only my own integrity but the whole Christian faith as well.

It was a hot night (December is of course midsummer in South Africa) and as the doors had been closed, the air was completely still. I knelt at the communion rail, and as I knelt there I felt a very strong cooling breeze – and that was all. I do not think that at that time I had any idea what the word 'breath' or the word 'wind' means to the Christian, or even that the Greek word for the Holy Spirit means breath. I did not even think of Jesus breathing the spirit on his disciples. All I know is that this breath, or wind, which I felt, had a meaning and a content for me which I have never been able to communicate to anyone else, and still cannot describe.

I have never mentioned this experience to anyone in any detail before and I certainly did not talk about it at the time. In fact I never discussed my very immature growings in religion with anybody at all, in spite of having people about like Ronald Anderson and Alan Paton and Tom Savage. But gradually I began to know without any doubt or uncertainty that I had got to be a priest. This scared me stiff – it seemed almost ludicrous to me and it certainly seemed so to my friends. When I was having some drinks one evening with a Jewish girl with whom I used to go out a lot at that time, I told her that I had got an awful feeling coming on that I had got to be a clergyman. She just rocked and rocked with laughter, and I joined in. But laughter would not drive the feeling away. Nobody talked to me about it or suggested that I should pursue the idea. It was purely internal, the hand of God. It was a sort of pressure, a growing knowledge which wouldn't let me alone. The books I read, the things I heard about, the people I met, everything seemed to push me in one direction.

Eventually the pressure became unbearable and I had to give way. About six months after I had left hospital I wrote a postcard to the Bishop of Johannesburg, Geoffrey Clayton, asking if I could become a priest. Many bishops might have thrown my postcard into the wastepaper-basket, but he did not. I had put my phone number on it, and his chaplain rang me up to make an appointment for me to see him, after evensong.

To all intents and purposes I had never spoken to a bishop before in my life. I didn't know how to address him. He met me at the door of the cathedral after the service, shook me by the hand and asked me to wait in the car. 'I've got to see a lunatic about something', he said, and I took it that he literally meant a madman. (I subsequently learned that he referred to most people as 'lunatics' at one time or another, including me.) Then he took me up to his house, sat me down, and said, 'Tell me why you want to be a clergyman.' 'I don't want to be a clergyman', I said. 'The whole thing appals and frightens me, I want nothing to do with it; but I feel I have got to be one.' So we got down to practicalities. For instance, I was hardly a churchman, I hadn't got a degree, I hadn't any money to go to college, I hadn't even a baptism certificate nearer than England.

There were subsequent interviews, and when the question was raised of my possibly not being accepted at the theological college, I said, 'I shall sit on the doorstep until they let me in.' In the end, I was accepted. (Mercifully they did not have selection conferences in those days.) The bishop arranged for the fees to be paid and for me to have £25 pocket-money a year, while I extracted a promise from him that I could leave the college after two years instead of the normal three, if I passed the examinations.

So it happened that in January 1936, at the age of twenty-four, I found myself in the train on the way to St Paul's Theological College, Grahamstown, in the Eastern Cape Province. I had not the faintest notion of what I was letting myself in for, but I started finding out only too quickly. Travelling in the train with me was the Senior Student, also from Johannesburg, called Norman Luyt, and he told me that every day at the college started with Mass, which the students were expected to attend. I almost got off the train there and then: the thought of doing without my cigarette and early morning cup of tea was so terrible. Then we discussed the list of things which I was supposed to have taken with me, one of which was a cassock. I had never heard of cassocks and did not even know what they were so I had not bothered to get one.

The college turned out to be a rather mausoleum-like, dull, brick structure which to me had the psychological impact of a prison. After all my years of 'freedom' I had got myself back into an institution and getting down to the slog of institutional routine was one of the hardest things I have ever done. To make matters worse, we had Lent in our first term (the academic year in South Africa begins in January) and a pretty severe Lent was kept in comparison with customs today. Food was cut down all the way through, but Fridays were the worst. We had pumpkin fritters – ugh! I have never been able to look a pumpkin in the face since, although it is one of the national foods of South Africa.

There were probably fewer than twenty students when I was

there, although the college could have taken more. They were all white and came from the English-speaking section of the population. Even then, the government would not allow black students to attend a white college. The warden when I arrived was the Rev. A. P. Hill. He was an old Etonian who had turned down at least two bishoprics. He left after a year to become a monk in the Society of St John the Evangelist (the Cowley Fathers), but I was extremely fortunate to have been there with him. He had been warned about me by the bishop and was sympathetic about my difficulties. Soon after I got there he extracted a promise from me that I would not walk out of the college without seeing him first. This stood me in good stead: there were several occasions when I would have bolted if the thought of having to tell Hill why I wanted to go had not held me back. But the most important thing about the warden was that he was always praying. If he was wanted on the telephone or something he was always in the chapel on his knees, and this was an example which I have never forgotten.

At that time the tension between high and low church ways of thinking was very strong in the college. I had experience only of the evangelical tradition, and I remember that at the first Mass most of the congregation genuflected at the *Incarnatus* in the Creed. I did not know what was happening when they all flopped down and felt an awful fool. But soon I began to discover this Catholic aspect of the Church and to find that I had unconsciously longed for it. I really owed this discovery, not to the college authorities, who were pretty middle-of-the-road in their teaching, but to one of the other students, Reg Petersen. He lent me books and talked to me about the Reality of the Blessed Sacrament and the Catholic concept of the Church as the living body of Christ. Naturally, I went from one extreme to the other and got very enthusiastic about all the accessories of Catholic religion. I thought the purple vestments for Lent were ghastly and said that they made me feel sick; Father Hill said that that was what they were meant to do.

Probably the most crucial step for me at college was making

my first confession and it took me well over a year to get down to this. I was driven more and more into a corner, knowing that I was accepting all the pleasant things in the Catholic faith – its colour and its joy – and refusing the part that was hard. I went through all the arguments for and against it – on and on and on, although I don't remember arguing it out with anyone else. I thought of finding someone to confess to in secret, but then a new warden, Cecil Alderson, arrived and I made my confession to him. It was a very traumatic experience with lots of tears. I did not have any very great sense of relief but there was a sense of having won this particular battle and I have practised confession ever since.

I have never in my life succeeded in living up to the true moral standards of the Christian faith, and it was because I knew that I could not do this that I had rejected the evangelical teaching that I had had as a boy. The Catholic wing of the Church demands no less a standard but somehow it does not seem to be so condemnatory of failure. If you are prepared to confess your failures aloud before a priest, a fellow Christian, and are really prepared to make yet another attempt, then you are in absolution freed to do so. It is not that you can be absolved and cheerfully intend to go and repeat the sin. There must be a resolution to try to do better. But it is the present and future that matters, not the past.

Throughout my time at college I had a sense of urgency and impatience. When I was in Toc H I was involved in all sorts of socially concerned activity and now I was stuck behind the four walls of a theological college in a quiet academic cathedral city which seemed to be utterly remote from real life. I wanted to be up and doing, and there I was stuck with theology and Greek. It was all very stupid, and I realized later that if I had spent the full three years there, instead of the two for which I had bargained with the bishop, I might well have been a better priest, both in praying and teaching. However, spurred on by my desire to get out, I worked hard and at the end of two years got an honours pass in the examinations for a Licentiate in Theology. Then to my horror, the bishop suggested that he should send me to his old college, Pembroke, at Cambridge University, to read for a degree. I just could not bear the thought of this, any more than I could when I was a boy and the headmaster at Bristol wanted me to try for a university scholarship. I simply had to get out into the world as a Christian priest and start some active work. (I have had this sense of urgency in getting things done all through my priesthood. Some of my friends call it an obsessive neurosis, which perhaps it is.) Anyway, I managed to persuade the bishop that I simply could not 'waste' a further three years in studying (I was almost twenty-seven by this time) and he made me deacon in St Mary's Cathedral, Johannesburg, at the Advent ordination in 1938. I was sent as assistant curate to Springs, which was a tough mining parish, about thirty-five miles from Johannesburg, to work under Tom Savage, my old friend from Toc H days, who later became Bishop of Zululand. A year later I was ordained a priest.

CHAPTER THREE

Ministry to White and Coloured

Putting on a dog-collar made me feel rather a fool. At once you become marked and people stop behaving naturally with you, especially in pubs and so on. I was very conscious of being cut off (which is one reason why I never wear clerical clothes when I am not being formal now). But Tom Savage was a good man to work under. Again he was a man who really prayed most faithfully and I learnt from him to value the privilege of the daily Mass as the core of my prayer and work. He also taught me the importance of really listening to people and giving them time to talk in a relaxed atmosphere, until they are able to get out what they really want to say. This meant constant visiting, and while the mornings were devoted to desk-work, sermons, hospital visits, and so forth, almost every afternoon and evening was taken up with seeing people in their homes. This required a good head for alcohol, which fortunately I have.

As Springs was a mining town most of our parishioners were miners. At 4 p.m. we would go and see the ordinary workers who had been on the early shift and have tea or a beer with them. Then at 5 p.m. the shift bosses came up and visiting them meant beer or a glass of brandy. Later still the mine captains came up – and that meant brandy or whisky – and last of all the managers, which again meant brandy or whisky, the alcohol content rising with the social scale. Of course it would have been possible to refuse these drinks, but if you accepted, it made for a much more relaxed atmosphere since they had been hard at work all day and naturally wanted to put their feet up a bit.

Although I realized the importance of this pastoral work, I came more and more to believe that one of the chief functions of an ordained Christian priest is to offer the sacrifice of the Mass, day by day. It seemed to me that as the covenant between God and man is broken every day by our rejection of it, so we daily need to renew our acceptance of Christ's offering to the Father and receive his healing power for our minds and bodies and souls, and not only for ourselves but for 'the whole state of Christ's Church', to which no man can set limits. This meant so much to me that, perhaps sometimes selfishly, I have insisted on saying Mass myself every day of my life, apart from holidays and sickness, since then. I still believe that doing something – regardless of 'feelings' – is important, but I would now put much more emphasis on prayer, love, and concern for the individual than I did then.

It was largely this increasingly 'Catholic' attitude that led me to my first change of parish. Soon after the second world war had broken out, I was suddenly sent for by my bishop, Geoffrey Clayton, and asked to go to Germiston. This is a large town, close to Johannesburg, where a man called Gerald Vernon was priest-in-charge. Vernon was a high-church Anglican of the deepest dye who had been appointed bishop in Madagascar. War broke out while he was on his way to his see, and Madagascar was blockaded so he could not get there. He agreed to remain as priest-in-charge at Germiston for the time being, but because he was so high-church, his curates had gone on strike. Clayton thought that I was sufficiently spiky to cope and I agreed to go, on condition that I could say Mass myself every day.

Gerald Vernon and I got on fairly well, though I did not always agree with his very rigoristic attitude. He introduced me to various 'high' services and practices – Benediction, High Mass, quantities of minor saints' days and six candles on the altar – and he also taught me to be very meticulous about the way I said Mass and conducted services. He may have been over-finicking about this, but he certainly conveyed the order of God, the rightness of reverence, and of doing things properly, and for this I have always been grateful.

After a few months, however, a boat became available which was running the blockade to Madagascar. So Gerald went off on it, and I was left by myself holding the Germiston baby as priest-in-charge.

I was on my own at Germiston for most of the war. When I was a non-Christian I was very much a pacifist (in spite of my talent for getting into fights) and I used to support the 'martyr nation' theory – that if everyone laid down their arms and said, 'Come and take us over', war would become impossible. It was a stupid theory, but I believed it. The Thirty-nine Articles of the Church of England, which you have to sign before you can be ordained, say, 'It is lawful for Christian men, at the commandment of the magistrate, to wear weapons, and serve in the wars', and I told Geoffrey Clayton before I was ordained that I could not believe this in any circumstances. When war broke out, I was one of four priests who even voted for a pacifist motion in synod.

But it was not just a question of pacifism. The whole of white South Africa was split on the question of whether or not we ought to be involved in this particular war, and many of the present Nationalist party leaders were thought to be so sympathetic to the German cause that they were interned (this may account for some of the current bitterness of the Afrikaners towards the English). Men in the police and the army were allowed to enlist for home service only, and if they had volunteered to go overseas they wore red tabs on their lapels. Sometimes open fights broke out between the two groups within the services and a great deal of bitterness was felt over the whole issue.

By and large, the Afrikaners felt that the war was none of their business (though there were, of course, very many exceptions), while the English-speaking people felt that they ought to do their share. But I had so taken on a South African attitude myself that in 1939 I felt that a European war wasn't really much concern of mine – quite apart from the broader issue of pacifism. Then I saw the film, *Mrs Miniver*, with shots of English towns being bombed and planes crashing in English fields, and I suddenly realized what was really happening and wanted to go and do something about it. I was offered a job as chaplain in a unit of the South African Medical Corps which was going overseas, and wanted very badly to accept. But Clayton discouraged me from making such an irrational volte-face after my public defence of pacifism, and so I stayed in Germiston in rather a schizoid state, wishing that I was doing something rather more useful than running a parish.

The war hardly made any practical difference to our lives in Germiston. Some non-essentials were in short supply, but there was no rationing and it gave me quite a shock when I went down to Cape Town on holiday and encountered my first 'dim-out'. What did make staying at home as a civilian priest fairly costly, however, was that at the beginning of the war the clergy were given the job of telling families when their sons and husbands had been killed, wounded or captured. The government thought it would be easier for these people if bad news was broken by a clergyman rather than by getting a bald telegram – so the telegrams came to us. This was, as may be imagined, a terrible duty, especially when, as happened to me once, I had to go to the same family twice in one week, bringing bad news. (Mercifully, the second son was only missing and later turned up.) After a time, this policy was discontinued at the clergy's request, because it became impossible to pay an ordinary pastoral call on a family without everyone fainting at the sight of you coming up the garden path. Nevertheless, it was very hard to be on the sidelines when other people, some of whom had far less reason to be involved than I had myself, were fighting in defence of the country of which I was still a citizen and where I had been brought up. I have no doubt that it was very good for me that this time I could not escape from the situation, as I had from school and theological college, and I just had to stay and get on with the job I was doing.

However, life as a priest-in-charge of Germiston was no sinecure – particularly for a brand-new priest like me. Germiston is a large railway junction and 'the railways' featured largely in its life. It was also a mining centre (although the mines have now for the most part been worked out) and a growing industrial centre. The parish covered a wide area and has now been divided into four. Even then its normal staff was three priests, but I had to run it by myself for most of the war years. This meant miles and miles of very rushed travelling, especially on Sundays, when I had to get round the five main churches as best I could. The strain was bound to catch up with me and on one occasion I found myself crying at the altar at High Mass on Sunday and had to be taken off to hospital for sedation. It was at this time that I started having stomach ulcers and also some trouble with my heart which the specialist diagnosed as 'coronary insufficiency'.

Bishop Clayton made every effort to get a rector for the parish. He hawked the position around all the senior clergymen in the Union of South Africa and a whole series of priests came for a day or so to look around, but none of them would touch it, so in the end Clayton offered it to me. Like a silly fool I got on my high horse and said, in effect, 'You try everyone else, and when no one will take it, you try me; you can stick it up your jersey!' He hauled me into his house and told me exactly what he thought of me and that I had to do it or else . . .

One of the most traumatic things that happened to me in Germiston concerned a young married man who had been one of our parishioners at Springs. This man had joined up at the beginning of the war and become a commissioned officer and I had lost touch with him. One Sunday night after evensong he presented himself at the front door, drunk, dirty and unshaven. He told me that he was totally broke, had deserted from the army, and had been living in a hotel at Randfontein, about thirty miles west of Johannesburg, with a young girl he had picked up somewhere. While he was telling me this he suddenly pulled out his army revolver and threatened to shoot himself. I was scared stiff but I finally managed to take the revolver off him and put it into the church safe. We went on talking until all hours and finally it was agreed that I should go to Randfontein and talk to the proprietor of the hotel about the complete unlikelihood of his ever being paid, and that I should then try to get the girl back to her parents in Durban. He himself would return to the army headquarters at Robert Heights and give himself up. We went to bed and in the morning he seemed to me to be almost entirely rational. He washed and shaved and we cleaned up his clothes as well as we could. Before I left for Randfontein he pointed out that if he took his revolver with him when he reported back to the army, he might get away on a charge of being AWOL rather than of desertion. This seemed reasonable enough to me and I gave it back to him.

I went off to Randfontein, found the hotel, and talked to the girl with whom he had been living. She was one of the most beautiful women that I have ever seen in my life. I told her what we had arranged about her boy-friend's future and her own and she seemed perfectly willing to fall in with it. While I was talking to the proprietor of the hotel he called me to the telephone. At the other end was the young man, who by that time should have been back at military headquarters but who was still in the rectory at Germiston. He told me over the telephone that he was going to shoot himself and said, 'Would you like to hear the shot?' I did my best to reason with him but he rang off. One of our church councillors worked in a bank near the rectory so I telephoned and asked him to hurry round and see what he could do, then we had to sit and wait. An agonizing ten minutes later he rang back to say he had found a body in my study with a bullet wound through its head. I bundled the girl into my car and we tore the thirty or forty-odd miles back to Germiston faster than I have ever done it in my life. When I got back the police were, of course, in the house and I had to go at once to the mortuary and identify the body. Then I had to fix up somewhere for the girl to stay until arrangements were made for her to go home.

To add to the nightmare quality of that day, the stop press of the evening papers reported that a short fair-haired man had been found dead from a bullet wound in Germiston rectory, and of course all my friends, including Bishop Clayton, thought that it was me. The telephone rang constantly that evening to ask if I was still alive, and, being the kind of person that I am, I suddenly developed an irrational fear that someone was going to shoot me.

That night was hell, but one of the church-wardens took me in and looked after me, and the acute panic faded fairly quickly. The memory of the experience stayed however, and indeed until I left Germiston there was a bullet-hole in the ceiling of my study to remind me of it whenever I looked up.

In spite of traumas like this, it was what I suppose one has to call a 'successful' parish in that the congregation grew, vocations to the religious life and the priesthood were produced, and I worked hard with all sorts and conditions of folk, although they were always white ones. I think I grew myself also in my understanding of what a priest's job is in other ways as well as the sacramental ones.

There is a very old definition of a priest as being a man who represents God to man and man to God. I think that this is true, but by 'represent' I really mean 'introduce'. Men need someone to show God to them and a priest should be able to do so from the authority of his own personal experience – not by standing behind the authority of the Church and thinking that wearing a dog-collar makes him an expert. A priest should himself have found Jesus as saviour – to put it in the most Protestant terms. And then he should present God to people by listening to them and accepting them as God listens and accepts. He should be unflappable and unshockable, and when he is trying to help people to find their way spiritually, he should encourage them to find the way which means most to them personally, which they always know deep down in their own hearts, and then to follow it. When I try to help people in the Christian religion, I generally say to them, 'For the love of Mike, read this book, try things this way and then do come back and see me again because what I am saying may be entirely unsuitable for you. If what I have said doesn't help, then obviously I have been wrong; and there are dozens and dozens of other ways of praying, dozens and dozens of other ways of beginning to love God.'

This way of looking at things has, of course, been built up and modified over the years, but its foundations were laid in Germiston, especially when, at the end of the war, I was lucky enough to get some senior and experienced men, who had been chaplains in the forces, and had taken an awful hammering, to come and work with me as curates. It was a most humbling experience having men of this calibre technically working under me, but with their help the life of the parish really grew instead of being kept just on the boil.

During my time at Germiston, for at least the third time in my life, I thought seriously of getting married. On this occasion I asked Geoffrey Clayton's opinion and he advised me against it. Rightly or wrongly, I accepted what he said. I suppose the truth is that I had very mixed feelings about tying myself down in a lifelong commitment to one person, just as I have never felt I could tie myself down in one place indefinitely. Also the series of disastrous marriages which my parents and all the other members of my immediate family had made were hardly encouraging. On the other hand, I had been quite certain at college that I was morally quite incapable of coping with being an unmarried clergyman, and sure that I had either got to get married or join a religious order. I did make various rather tentative efforts at different times to join the Community of the Resurrection and the Cowley Fathers, but always had a rather discouraging response and again was too uncertain of my vocation really to push it. So in the end, as so often happens, I found that I was being called to do what I had dreaded most and to cope as best I could with being an unmarried priest. I have no doubt, looking back, that not having to worry about a wife and family has freed me to give time and love to my parishioners and to God – and also to take political risks – in a way which would just not have been possible if I had been married.

In Germiston, however, none of this was clear, and I did have various girl-friends. One of them was a Sunday-school teacher who had also won a beauty competition, and who was, in my opinion, a very beautiful girl indeed. I took her out to dinner in Johannesburg one evening on my day off, she all dressed in her best and wearing a huge-brimmed black hat on her blonde head. She looked like an anarchist's mistress. There was a heck of a row coming from a group of fairly drunk men at one of the other tables and suddenly I saw that one of them was my half-brother, Jack McIlraith, who was evidently up in Jo'burg from Bechuanaland. I had not seen him for the best part of ten years, so of course I went over to speak to him and introduced my friend to him as one of my Sunday-school teachers. He said, 'Like Hell!' and I said, 'Well she is!' which was perfectly true. I think his concept of a clergyman's life changed a bit after that. Certainly, he never forgot how beautiful this girl was, and talked to me about her years later when he was very seriously ill in Salisbury General Hospital, not long before he died.

Inevitably one of the parishioners took umbrage at this shocking manifestation of secular human interests and wrote to Geoffrey Clayton complaining that the rector 'had women in the house'. Clayton, as he always did in such circumstances, sent the complaint on to me and asked, 'What do I say?' I wrote back and said, 'Tell her (or him) I always send them away before breakfast.' And I heard no more about it.

Another time Clayton asked me what was happening at Germiston, with a view to approving, or not, of the various high-church services we held and feasts that we celebrated. This information was provided and he approved of everything except the feasts of the Sacred Heart and the Precious Blood, which are not in the English Prayer Book. With some high-church parishioners I wrote nearly six pages of argument about why these two feasts ought to be observed. His reply ran:

> Dear ffrench-Beytagh,
> No.
> Yours sincerely,
> ✠Geoffrey Johannesburg

An absolutely brilliant letter.

It must be obvious how much my relationship with Geoffrey Clayton meant to me and how much I owed him. As time went on we became great friends and often went on holiday together, although he was so much older, more senior and more intellectual than I was. He was a hugely fat man, a constant chain-smoker (I think he only used one match in the day, for the first cigarette of the morning). He always laughed at his own jokes (often obscure Greek puns which meant absolutely nothing to me) until his great belly shook. He never suffered fools gladly and could be extremely rude. 'The trouble with you is that it's only what *you* think that matters', he said one day on holiday when I had disagreed with him on a trivial issue. But his bark was far worse than his bite, and he would generally apologize in some indirect way if he had been snappish. Luckily I was able to stand up to him and was never afraid of him, which I suppose was why he liked having me about.

We must have been an unlikely pair and sometimes got into some absurd situations. There was one occasion, on holiday in Lourenço Marques, when I, dressed in my usual holiday corduroy trousers and khaki shirt, was sent for by the hotel manager. (It was a very grand hotel, but since Geoffrey wanted me with him, and he had a very classy taste in hotels, he paid my bills) In the manager's office I found a young man whom I immediately thought of as 'the Archangel Gabriel'. Never have I seen such an exquisite dove-grey uniform or such a vast pink sash as he had across his chest. He turned out to be the Governor's ADC and evidently saw me as his 'opposite number'. He had come to invite Geoffrey on a trip in a special train through the game reserve with the Governor of Southern Rhodesia, who was also there on holiday. Geoffrey was delighted – so was I, since it gave me two days on my own in the bars of Lourenço Marques, which was much more my line than wild animals.

On the appointed morning I duly drove to the station in my tiny Ford Prefect, which we were using on the trip, accompanied by this vast archbishop in purple stock, pectoral cross, and so forth, only to find that the road was lined with ceremonial guards who would not let us pass. Eventually we got through on foot and I staggered a good half-mile to the station with two heavy suitcases and Geoffrey striding regally in front of me past the guards and the crowds. Over the last hundred yards, there was, literally, a red carpet. The station staff were all in frock-coats (though one man had evidently forgotten his braces and had a large leather belt across his paunch). I was deeply relieved to hand over Geoffrey and the suitcases and retire to my normal social level.

Although he had his idiosyncrasies, Geoffrey was a great bishop, a scholar, and a very sincere Christian. I think it is true to say that I really loved him and I trusted him implicitly, even to the point of giving my confessor permission to talk to him openly about me when I was wondering whether to join a religious order. This friendship made me feel that I must be worth something as a person and a priest, in spite of my inner anxieties and my ignorance of the whole ecclesiastical set-up. Perhaps I also felt that I got an affection and support from him which I had never had from my own father.

Looking back, I think I grew considerably during my time in Germiston in personal maturity and priestly competence, but I remained extraordinarily unaware of the whole racial situation. The colour bar was a fact of life (as it had been during my childhood in Shanghai) and I never thought about its implications. I would, for instance, cheerfully sit down and write passes for my African servants to go out at night without any awareness of the absurdity of having to give adult men and women permission to do what they liked in their free time. The same unawareness pervaded my relationship, or rather lack of relationship, with the African Christians in Germiston. Even today there is still extraordinarily little contact between black and white priests in the diocese. Only recently an African priest told me of how, when he went to call upon his European counterpart, he was made to go to the back door like any African servant or delivery 'boy'. But it was even worse then.

When I got to Germiston I did make a conventional effort to get to know the African priest in charge of the African township, which was then called the Location. I invited him to come and have morning tea with me, and I went out and bought a special cake from a local shop with which to entertain him. The conversation however was entirely stilted and formal, and we never got away from the South African relationship of master and servant, although I was in no way his ecclesiastical superior. He did eat heartily however and finished the whole cake, which I had expected to last for several days, so presumably at least he enjoyed that. Our acquaintance never really became any closer during all the ten years that I was in Germiston. I was simply not aware of what was happening in the African part of the Church. We had no services in the parish church for African servants on Sunday afternoons when they were free, and neither the African priest nor I ever invited each other to preach in the other's church. It wasn't a question of any deliberate ill-will but simply the awful effect of living in the South African atmosphere where, even in those days, black and white simply did not mix together.

I did manage to break through this 'perception barrier' to some extent with the first servant that I ever employed, but it had a sad ending. Being a bachelor, I had to have someone to cook, housekeep and so on for me, and after I had been at Germiston for a few weeks one of the priests from the Community of the Resurrection rang up to ask if I would take on their cook, Andrew Seabi, as general cook and bottle-washer.

Andrew was a bachelor of about thirty, a very religious and intensely sensitive man, who had been in the service of the CR for many years. In a moment of genuine Christian love and affection he had put his arm around one of the women lay missionaries who worked with the CR. This had so frightened the silly woman that they felt they were bound to get him another job. This whole incident preyed most tremendously on his mind, and he kept talking about it and about the rejection of his gesture of affection. Soon it became clear that the whole incident was more than just preying on his mind. He used to listen to the wireless, and in the evening when I returned from work and we had supper together, he would ask me why the people on the wireless were threatening his life. Finally the CR and I between us decided he must go to a psychiatrist who eventually certified him as insane and sent him away. I did my best to prevent this and said that I was willing to keep him in my care, but the psychiatrist thought he was homicidal and might well turn on me, so reluctantly I let him go. For many years I kept in touch with the superintendent of the mental hospital at Fort Beaufort where he was and I have prayed for him every Friday since then.

Another African whom I had some relationship with was a young man called Martin Kaunda. He was a university student from either Nyasaland or Northern Rhodesia who needed a home and job during his vacations. I took him on and paid him a very small sum to act as church cleaner and general factotum. He did not do this work really well and I suppose may well have felt that with his brains and education he ought to have had a better job. I lost touch with him completely until, years later, when I was Dean of Salisbury, I met him at the airport, wafting off to some international conference as a representative of his country.

However, these few personal contacts did not make me any more aware of the wider implications of racialism. Only one incident jerked me briefly into some concern. This happened within fifty yards of the rectory in Germiston, in broad daylight. As I was passing, I saw a European policeman reach out and grab an African and give him a terrific kick. I stopped him, took his number, and told him that I was going to report him. As far as I can remember, he let the African go. I went back to my house and wrote to the Minister of Justice setting out the details and saying that I thought something should be done. (The United Party, not the Nationalists, were in power at this time.) Later I was sent for by the authorities at Boksburg, the East Witwatersrand Command of the South African Police. I was met by the officer in charge and the constable was brought in and rebuked in front of me – and both of them were grinning. I had a feeling that they actually winked at each other. This made more emotional impact on me than the kicking, and it started my mistrust of the police.

From time to time, other things did awaken me a little, such as Michael Scott's reports on conditions on the potato farms, down in the Eastern Transvaal, and his own refusal to pay income-tax, and his subsequent imprisonment. I believe now that he was right about a good many things, but at the time I simply wrote him off, as most of us did, as being a good-hearted, but slightly hot-headed man. Even in later years, I thought of men like Trevor Huddleston and Bishop Reeves as sometimes going a bit far. I supported the liberal motions which they put before the diocesan synod, and I admired them in many ways, but they were dealing with things in which I did not feel a particular interest and which I thought did not concern me personally. I sometimes read reports in the newspapers of heavy sentences imposed on Africans for offences for which Europeans would receive either no sentence at all, or a very light one, and got angry and indignant – but that was as far as it went.

In 1948, just before I left Germiston, Jan Smuts's United Party was, by a very narrow margin, defeated at the elections, and the Afrikaner Nationalists came into power. Until then the colour bar had been a fairly negative form of control. There were certain things that Africans could not do and places where they could not go, but there was no attempt to push them back into tribalism or prevent them from getting as much education as they could. The emphasis, in fact, was on urbanizing and 'civilizing' them. No one seemed to give much thought to their future political role, but there was no real suggestion that they were essentially less human than anyone else.

All this changed in 1948. The Afrikaners believed that God had vindicated his people and had called them to establish a promised land where they could rule in cultural and racial purity. For the first time we heard the doctrine of *apartheid* and began to hear phrases like 'separate development' and 'separate freedoms'. The new prime minister, Dr Malan, broadcast an appeal to all church leaders that they should support his government in its task of apartheid development for all races, and the new government lost no time in entrenching itself by amending existing laws, such as the Citizenship Act, reorganizing constituencies to its advantage, and bringing in completely new legislation like the Group Areas Act. The Nationalists were determined to unscramble the racial omelette and it was from the first a totally impossible task. 'Homelands' for the various tribal groups were set up, where

Africans had some civil rights and a very limited degree of self-government, but these 'Bantustans' will always be ethnically, economically, and politically unviable. To talk of 'separate development' and 'separate freedoms' in the context of these pathetic scattered patches of parched land, is at the best Alice-in-Wonderlandish and at the worst blasphemous. But to the dedicated Afrikaner (as later became apparent at my trial) what matters is not what actually is real and practical, but what he thinks ought to be. His belief, as I said at the beginning of this book, comes from his guts and not from his brain, so the utter impossibility of his policies makes little difference to him. The will of God (and the Afrikaner) must be done. If people suffer in the process it is just too bad.

For the time being, however, I was very little concerned with these issues. In 1949, Ambrose Reeves, who had replaced Geoffrey Clayton as Bishop of Johannesburg, asked me to take on the full-time job of organizing a three-year mission to the entire diocese. So, after ten years in the parish, I said goodbye to Germiston and went to live with the Sisters of St Margaret in their orphanage in Johannesburg, where I was able to continue to say Mass every day. From there I either polished my behind at a desk in the diocesan office, writing letters, drumming up ideas and generally administering, or drove all over the diocese trying to get the parish priests and their parishioners enthused about the whole idea.

The first year was devoted to getting Christian families to see themselves as 'the Church' in each of their homes. The second year concentrated on revitalizing church congregations, and the third year was focused on 'mission' to the outside world. As with most missions, it really got off the ground in the parishes where the imagination and enthusiasm of the priest and the practising Christians had been caught (which was my job) and was rather a damp squib elsewhere. Also – again as with most missions – its effect was to revitalize existing congregations rather than bring in many outsiders. However, I do still come across people who tell me that their faith was strengthened and deepened by it.

It seems astonishing, looking back, that it never occurred to any of us that the African part of the Anglican Church should have been included in this evangelism. We called it a mission to the whole population of the diocese and yet we excluded three-quarters of the diocese from it. However, my next job shattered, for good and all, my ability to ignore the existence of the non-European South Africans and brought me my first personal experience of the meaning of apartheid.

I was appointed in 1952 to St Alban's Mission, which covered all the Coloured churches in the Johannesburg area. This meant work among a deprived community, which had very little identity, and was rejected by both black and white. Coloured people, in South African terminology, are, of course, those of mixed race – as opposed to Europeans and Africans. There was every conceivable ethnic strain amongst them – Indian, Chinese, and Malay, as well as European and African – and their colour varied from apparently white to as black as the ace of spades. The community also contained the whole range of the social scale, from some wonderful families to some of the most depraved and squalid individuals I have ever met. Most of the Coloured community lived in the Cape, but there was also a big population in Johannesburg and at that time six or seven churches in different areas of the city had been set apart for their use. I had two priests to help me to minister to these churches, and pretty busy it kept us.

The rectory, if that is what it could be called, was in Ferreirastown – in the heart of the Johannesburg slums – and it was a pretty traumatic place in which to live. The African bootleggers, who made an extremely potent and fierce kind of drink called 'skokiaan', used to brew this stuff in the neighbourhood and use the churchyard to hide it in. The police were perpetually round the place with spades, digging up the ground. My successor, who, unfortunately for him, was married, had the whole house barred and burglar-proofed, for which I can hardly blame him. However, I was lucky enough to have the companionship of two (white) friends, Cyril and Ann Maasch, who came over from

Germiston with their little daughter to live in the rectory and look after me, and they were tough enough to cope perfectly happily, in spite of the shouting and brawls which went on. During the two years that I was there, there was a succession of dramatic incidents. My car was stolen from outside the house and smashed against a telephone-pole on the way to one of the African areas; a Coloured man who had been in considerable trouble with the police and whom we had employed as a house-servant walked off with one of the church collections, and so on.

But I came to love the Coloured people almost more than I can say. They were deeply affectionate and responded tremendously to love. Of course it is impossible to lump together a whole community but I can't help generalizing about them. They tended to be a rather feckless lot, living very much for the moment (and who can blame them?), and they had a great deal of religion. As their parish priest I probably spent more time than I ought to have done at parties, because parties are a great thing amongst them and very well they do them. Weddings, anniversaries, christenings, almost anything is an excuse for a party, with all sorts of exotic foods – Indian, Chinese, African or whatever else occurs to them – and there is always plenty to drink, in fact too much. I have seen the best man at a wedding party dive over the top table, pulling out a knife from his hip, but fortunately failing to stab the man he was after, and this sort of incident was not uncommon. I have also seen a white woman, bared to the waist, in one of the slum courtyards just below the church, punching herself out of a drunken attack by the Coloured inhabitants of the courtyard. (This particular woman wanted to get herself classified as Coloured, did so, and is now married to a senior server in one of the Coloured churches.) They were a very quarrelsome people – but always made up their quarrels before making their Christmas confessions. Religion and the supernatural meant a great deal to them, but Dagga('pot')-smoking was very common and many of them had no sexual morals at all – I repeat again that the permissive society is nothing new. But for the Coloured community I think this kind of behaviour was an escape from their often appalling living conditions and their sense of hopelessness. In any case, not having much in the way of morals myself, we got on very well together and I cannot imagine a more rewarding ministry, though physically it was very hard work indeed.

The people whom we cared for lived over a very scattered area – not just in Johannesburg but in places like Kliptown, Protea, and Noordgesig, which were as much as twelve miles from St Alban's church itself. We were often called out at night to these areas and we regularly administered communion to many sick and bed-ridden folk in their own homes. Always when we went to a household, we were received, not only with joy, but with a real, deep, reverence and devotion – not for ourselves but for the Church and on behalf of the person who needed our help. We also did the best we could with the agonized longing of the adolescent young as they struggled to find some sort of job – any sort of a job, with or without a future – when we all knew in our hearts that the Coloured people were not really wanted and had no future at all. We preached and taught that God loved them – even though they were disinherited, and rejected by both blacks and whites. But it sometimes had a very hollow ring.

At St Alban's, for the first time, the utter nonsensicality of racial discrimination really hit me. Some of the Coloured people whom I knew 'played white'. That is they lived and acted as though they were white people – and if they were lucky they got away with it. There were a lot of rather bitter jokes about these amongst the other Coloured people, who had no hope of doing this, and there was a good deal of jealousy, although the 'play whites' were also much admired for getting away with it. Sometimes 'playing white' became a necessity within a family. For example, I knew one family well where the colour range was fairly large. When the mother went to hospital, which was often, she went to the European Hospital in Johannesburg, while the father, who was darker and was also sickly, went to the Coronationville Hospital in the Coloured township. The lighter children visited the mother and the darker children visited their father – and all this was quite cheerfully accepted as one of the facts of life.

But it could also become a major tragedy. I knew personally one young man who was extremely light-skinned and who committed suicide when he failed to 'pass' as white.

At about the time I was appointed to St Alban's there was an attempt by the Nationalist government to tighten up racial classification and so prevent people from crossing the colour-line successfully. Of course, this was just not possible on any scientific basis and the government kept changing their criteria for classification as a result – but at this time they had decided to define racial grouping on the basis of the community with which the person concerned normally mixed. Inspectors of various kinds went round the houses in the Coloured areas to inspect birth certificates and assess the racial background so that identity cards could be issued according to the 'correct' racial classification. The immediate effect, as far as I was concerned, was that every family photograph was whipped off the walls of the houses which I used to visit, leaving light patches on the wallpaper where they had been. Photographs of weddings, baptisms and parties were particularly dangerous to have around if people in the group were dark – and especially if they were African. The whole thing became a fantastic lottery. Some were lucky, and I still have personal friends whom I know to be Coloured but who now carry a white identity card. A slight difference in pigmentation and a lot of luck at the right time has made them one of the privileged 3·7 million while their slightly darker or unluckier friends and relatives are stuck for life in the Coloured ghetto.

It was also during my time at St Alban's that I first came across any technical points in connection with 'separate development'. One particular Coloured man, who worked in the Post Office, came to me with the most tremendous joy because, now that there was this thing called 'separate development', he was being appointed to a higher position in the Post Office than he had ever been able to occupy before. This was, of course, because the Coloured post offices were to be staffed purely by Coloured men, and in his own particular area he could advance further than he could if he had to compete with Europeans. One could see the logic of his argument, but it first brought home to me how vicious that argument in fact is. It means that the man is being bribed to accept himself as being separate from the really free human beings who are the Europeans. He could become a large fish in a very much enclosed and small pool, but never could he swim where there was any freedom.

Unfortunately the immediate advantages of 'separate development' made a considerable impact on many of the Coloured people and the different political parties that have arisen amongst the Coloured people since then show that some of them still think along these lines. Others have accepted that there is no real future for them in South Africa and many of the Coloured families whom I knew have emigrated to England, Canada, and even Australia. They are not perhaps the most belligerent part of the population but some of them are the cream of the Coloured people and their going is South Africa's loss. One cannot blame them, and indeed I encouraged some of them to leave, because the future for them and their children is utterly and wholly intolerable in the Republic of South Africa.

In some ways I think of my time with the Coloured community as being the most worthwhile period of my priesthood. It was certainly not the most successful by any of the usual standards, in fact I had very little impact on them. It was rather the other way about – they made a very deep impact on me. We had a real affection for each other and their spontaneousness, their capacity for laughter and grief, their dignity in the face of constant humiliation, and their real reverence for God made a deep impression on me. With this experience it was utterly and wholly impossible for me to go on ignoring a racial policy which treats such people as subhuman and I did begin to think in terms of trying to do something about it. My first real gesture of protest was resigning my South African passport when the Bantu Education Act was brought in (a gesture which I was later deeply thankful I had made). But for the time being I ceased to be much concerned with South Africa at all.

CHAPTER FOUR

The failure of 'partnership'

My sudden loss of interest in South African affairs occurred because in September 1954 I received what seemed to me a very astonishing letter. It came from Bishop Paget in Southern Rhodesia and it suggested to me that I should come up and see him, at his expense, about the possibility of my becoming the Dean of Salisbury. I had never thought of Rhodesia and I certainly had never thought of becoming a dean of anything.

Fortunately for me, Geoffrey Clayton, who by that time had become Archbishop of Cape Town, was staying at the Carlton Hotel in Johannesburg. I rang him up and asked if I could see him urgently. He agreed and I tore round there at once. I showed him Bishop Paget's letter and asked him what on earth I should do about it. I was brought down to earth considerably by Clayton's response which was simply, 'Oh, he has chosen you, has he?' Apparently Paget had asked Clayton's advice as to a possible dean for Salisbury and Clayton had given him four names, of which mine was one. I can only presume that Paget had tried the other three without success and now he was scraping the bottom of the barrel – at least that was the impression that I got. Clayton told me not to go up to be inspected, but to write to Bishop Paget and say that if I was offered the job I would accept, and go up to see him later, but if he wasn't prepared to offer it to me on Archbishop Clayton's recommendation without inspecting me, I wouldn't touch it. I took this advice and was offered the job.

After we had finished our discussion Clayton took me down to dinner in the Carlton dining-room. I had rushed round on my day off and was wearing an open-necked shirt and corduroy trousers. The head-waiter would not let me in. I am not sure that I have ever seen Clayton in such a rage as he was at this slight to his archiepiscopal authority. Finally, he won and we were hidden away in an obscure corner of the vast dining-room of this very posh hotel.

Salisbury was a little horrifying at first. The staff of the cathedral where I was to be dean were all older than I was; some of them had been there for a good many years and it was quite obvious that I wasn't really a very acceptable person to them. Perhaps the letter I wrote on Geoffrey Clayton's advice, refusing to be 'inspected', made them feel I was 'uppish', though I had of course gone up to Salisbury after I had been definitely offered the job. In any case, when I finally arrived there as dean on 29 December 1954, I was met at the airport by the bishop and one of the church-wardens, put in a room in the best hotel and severely left alone. I had no idea at all as to what the Sunday services were, or indeed what time the Mass would be next morning. I went to the cathedral and found a parish magazine from which I got the name of the other church-warden, who hadn't met me, and phoned to ask him if I could come out to his house. He agreed and so I was able to find out when I was to be installed and something of what was expected of me on the coming Sunday. It wasn't at all an auspicious beginning, but the problems worked themselves out and in fact my ten years in Salisbury were a very happy time indeed.

It is hard to imagine a greater contrast than that between Salisbury and Ferreirastown. In 1954 Salisbury was still essentially the urban centre of a middle-class farming community, with wide arcaded streets and colonial-style buildings where now there are great blocks of flats, offices and supermarkets. The white suburbs, with their spacious gardens and swimming-pools, and endless avenues of jacaranda trees, were most pleasant places to live. When the jacaranda petals were falling I used to drive down to the cathedral in the early morning over an almost unbroken purple carpet. The white population of Salisbury was well under ninety thousand, so it felt as if everyone knew everyone else and it was all very suburban, cosy and comfortable.

The cathedral was rather a magnificent building in its own way – designed by Sir Herbert Baker in a heavy Romanesque style and built from hewn granite – but the nave ended ingloriously in corrugated iron, since no one had got around to finishing it. As soon as I saw that, I made up my mind that somehow I would see it completed in a way which would be worthy of its purpose and of its setting, next to Cecil Square in the heart of the city, and in this at least I succeeded.

When I arrived in Salisbury, the Federation of Central Africa, that is the political union of Southern Rhodesia, Northern Rhodesia and Nyasaland, had just come into being. In fact my first big job as dean was the inauguration of a new Church of the Province of Central Africa, since it was thought that the ecclesiastical boundaries should follow the political ones. There was a tremendous ceremony for which the Archbishop of Canterbury came to Salisbury to hand over the dioceses of Nyasaland and Northern Rhodesia to the new province, and Archbishop Clayton came up from Cape Town to hand over the diocese of Southern Rhodesia (which was soon to be subdivided into Mashonaland and Matabeleland). It is very sad that although the new province still survives, the Federation which was its *raison d'être* has ceased to exist.

I ought to be able to comment a good deal more profoundly than I actually can on the reason for the failure of the Federation. I had access to all the leading political figures of the time and there was often conversation at sundowner parties at the British high commissioner's or elsewhere about what was really going on. But, as will already be clear to anyone reading this book, not only was I a late developer in political awareness, I was also not at all an acute observer of political trends. I realize now that I should have been aware of the tremendous importance of the Federation as a unique experiment in racial partnership and should have done far more to try and make it a success. Whether it ever could have worked, I do not know. Certainly a lot of cards were stacked against it.

My general impression was that the Federation was a beautiful scheme which had been dreamed up in Whitehall and then rather pushed at the countries concerned. The Southern Rhodesians, who were the richest of the three partners, felt that they were being bled financially to finance development in Northern Rhodesia and Nyasaland and also that they had to contribute much more than their share of technical skill and know-how, while politically they were only on equal terms with the other two. Many of the officers in the Colonial Service in Northern Rhodesia and Nyasaland were equally unenthusiastic. They felt that the Africans in these territories would have less chance of acquiring real responsibility if they had to compete with white Southern Rhodesians than if they remained under colonial rule, and that the real wealth and power would flow to the federal capital in Salisbury – and also of course they knew that they would lose their own jobs if federation really got off the ground. The result was that although officially they were supposed to 'sell' the idea of federation, in fact they tended to suggest that it really meant absorption by Southern Rhodesia and to emphasize the strength of the South African element in the white Southern Rhodesian population. Their general message was that the northern territories would be much better off as they were, under beneficent colonial rule (remember this was twenty years ago when very few African states had achieved independence). Presumably the African Nationalists in the north were also working against the whole concept of federation.

But the Churches must also take their share of the blame, and particularly the Anglican Church. We simply were not sufficiently aware – as we should have been – how desperately important it was that the Federation should work and that its expressed policy of partnership between black and white should become a reality. The Church has a very considerable influence in central Africa, not only in terms of actual Christian adherents, but also through its involvement in education at all levels and the extremely varied work of its missions. Almost all the leading African politicians have been educated under church auspices of one sort or another. We could have done far more than we did to emphasize the importance of 'partnership' and to make people feel that federation was a tremendously exciting experiment. Instead, in the Anglican Church at least, we spent hours and hours working on the canons of the new province and things of this kind while the Federation for which the province was created fell apart around us.

In my own ministry I kept coming across evidence that partnership was a myth and that white Rhodesians, like English-speaking South Africans, regarded the African as an undeveloped creature, happy in his ignorance. They knew only their servants and felt, as my father had in China, that all the fuss about liberation was the fault of the missionaries who were giving Africans ideas above their station. I sometimes saw the tragic results of not making 'partnership' a reality. For instance, there was the gradual change in Herbert Chitepo. As a boy he had gone barefoot to school at the Penhalonga mission and had struggled through every obstacle to qualify, finally, as a barrister in England. Then he had come back to Rhodesia only to find that, in spite of there being, in theory, no colour bar, he could not for a long time get an office in central Salisbury and he could not get a house in the 'white' suburbs. I used to meet him for lunch from time to time – picnicking in the cloisters because Africans were not allowed in the cheaper European cafés, only in the most expensive hotels – and I saw him gradually change from being a person of good-will, who wanted to make partnership work, to a bitter, anti-white extremist. I don't blame him. It was no use his being accepted by the more liberal European individuals if he was rejected by the whole social system.

The European Southern Rhodesians often justified their attitude by pointing out how incompetent many Africans were at the jobs into which they were thrust by the federal system. Of course, this was perfectly true. They simply had not been allowed to have the sort of technical experience and training which would have enabled them to run all the complex administrative and political machinery of a modern state. But if 'partnership' had been taken seriously on both sides, this could have been openly and honestly recognized, and the Europeans who were fortunate enough to have the technical experience and skill required could have trained the Africans to their own standards – not with a *de haut en bas* attitude, but with the feeling that they were working together to build the Federation and the sooner Africans could cope competently with full responsibility in running the Post Office or the nursing service or the electricity supply, or whatever, the stronger the Federation would be. As it was, there was far too much suspicion and resentment on both sides for this to happen. So the Europeans felt justified in believing that Africans could never take administrative responsibility, while simultaneously the Africans became convinced that they would never be allowed real responsibility and power in a federation dominated by the South. It is never hard to find evidence for one's own prejudices.

In Salisbury one of the most immediately noticeable effects of federation was that it was almost impossible to move without falling over a politician or a governor. It was reminiscent of the Gilbert and Sullivan song about the kind-hearted king 'who to the top of every tree, promoted everybody'. There was a governor of Rhodesia and a governor-general of the Federation, and both came formally to church. The Rhodesian governor, Sir Peveril William-Powlett, being the junior, had to make sure of arriving before the other one, Lord Llewellyn. Their staff rang each other up to plan the journeys and make sure that their chiefs arrived in the right order. There were also federal and Rhodesian prime ministers, with their respective cabinets and parliaments. But they seemed to function as office-boys as well. For example, when I was organizing the inauguration of the new province I rang up the government protocol department to suggest that a dinner should be given for the archbishops and was told that all arrangements must be made with the prime minister, Mr Garfield Todd, personally! I never came to know him very well, but I do know from personal contact that he is a Christian and a man of great integrity. Judith Todd, his daughter, is also a person whom I admire. I also met Sir Edgar Whitehead, Sir Roy Welensky and Lord Malvern at one time or another. Obviously, I did not agree with all their opinions, but it is, I think, true to say that none of them was a professional politician, out for his own ends. They were all struggling to find a future for the Rhodesia which they loved, though they saw that future in different ways, and each in his turn was forced to give way to pressure from the right wing, whose ideas were based largely on South African concepts of race relations.

Tragically, the rationalization for this steady move to the right came largely from the failure of the Federation. As I have said, 'partnership' in any real sense, and therefore the whole federal concept, was probably doomed from the start, but the Southern Rhodesians were able to blame Dr Banda in Nyasaland for the actual act which broke up the Federation (though they could hardly expect him to remain 'in partnership' with a country which had imprisoned him). The result was that they believed they had 'proved', after ten years of effort and sacrifice, that partnership did not work and that the South Africans were right – apartheid was the only answer. They still say to visiting 'liberal' VIPs, 'Look, look at the evidence that we have that multi-racialism does not work. We have not tried to stay isolated like the South Africans. We have lived in harness with the African for ten years; we have had him in parliament with us, and what is the result? The Africans have shown that they don't want to be in partnership, and they have shown that they are not capable of running things themselves. This is the only way left to us.' They feel *righteously* committed to the path that they are on, and it is very important to realize this.

It has proved, of course, to be a very steep and slippery path. Many people who were thankful when the Federation disintegrated were horrified by the Unilateral Declaration of Independence. This happened of course after I left Rhodesia and most of my information about it came from the white South African press, which, however 'liberal' it may be, is still South African. Still, I did talk to many of my Rhodesian friends when they came down to Johannesburg and I know how divided Rhodesia was at the time of UDI and what agony their divided loyalty caused them. There were men like the governor, Sir Humphrey Gibbs, who refused to vacate Government House, and the many people who came there to 'sign the book' on official occasions to show where their loyalty really lay. There were also men like a very senior police officer whom I knew, who wanted to retire and buy a farm in Natal because he could not face breaking his oath of loyalty to the Queen – and he was in line for even higher promotion if he stayed on. Many people still make a considerable effort to go down to Pretoria to renew their passports because they are determined to remain British citizens.

But there is also the other side of the coin. Many Rhodesians would sell their souls (almost literally) for Rhodesia to be absorbed into the South African Republic, and the Afrikaner element in Rhodesia grows stronger every day. At one time they were rather despised and resented, but this is not so now. Also, as Salisbury has grown and developed industrially, there is now a fairly large proportion of artisans and technicians amongst the European population who feel acutely threatened by any prospect of real African advancement because they would lose the privileged position which the colour of their skin gives them at present. Many of these people found Rhodesia a fairyland when they emigrated after the war from the decaying slums of industrial Britain. Now they have their own houses, cars, servants and swimming-pools, and are socially accepted in any but the snootiest 'Government House' circles. It is no wonder that they are willing to fight desperately to keep what they have got. The middle-class and upper-class English settlers who came out in the twenties and thirties are perhaps much more ambivalent about Smith and the whole UDI issue. All most of them really want is to preserve themselves, like flies in amber, in the proper life of the English gentry. They simply want nothing to change. They work hard on their farms, but they also have a lot of leisure for polo and racing and sport and sundowner parties – made possible of course by an unlimited number of servants. They treat their servants with kindness and liberality, they may even send a bright lad to university, but in the last resort they are too comfortable as they are to make any real stand against the Smith régime.

One factor in South Africa's growing influence on Rhodesia which has perhaps not been emphasized enough in other writings on the subject is the whole problem of educational standards. South African universities admit students who have got their matric (the equivalent of several good English 'O' levels) while the University College of Rhodesia and Nyasaland, and, of course, all the British universities, will only accept students with 'A' levels. The result is that until very recently Rhodesian boys educated at the famous South African schools could only get into South African universities, particularly Rhodes and Cape Town, where, of course, they do not come up against living experiences which might upset their concepts of racial superiority, and where they are not required to work or think so hard as they would be elsewhere. On the other hand, Rhodesian Africans who want to go to the University College in Salisbury have to meet stringent 'A'-level requirements and may finish up better educated than their European contemporaries, though socially of course they are increasingly ostracized.

It is all a complex and a tragic situation but the issues have become more and more polarized so that thoughtful and well-meaning people of both races, who once could have listened to each other and tried to reach a compromise, are now glaring at each other over the colour line. Even the tiny Centre party, which contains many of my personal friends, came down against the Pearce Report, which disappointed me a good deal. But I am in no position to talk. I was in Rhodesia, in a position of potential influence, when the seeds of the present situation were being sown and, apart from getting some Africans into the cathedral congregation and getting an African priest, Father Murindagomo, appointed to the cathedral staff, I did virtually nothing to make 'partnership' a reality or the Federation a going political concern.

Not that I managed to keep out of trouble – but it was ecclesiastical rather than political hot water. It is hard to realize how small the country is and how a chance remark can create a furore.

For instance, I said in the parish magazine one month that I could not see why I should bury people who never came to church, and argued that there should be civil burial officers for non-Christians, just as there were civil marriage officers. Some reporter came to see me and provoked me into an argument about this. I got a bit angry with him in the end and pushed him out. 'I suppose you would leave corpses in the street?' he said and I replied that that was all right by me. It made the headlines – DEAN WANTS CORPSES IN THE STREET, or something of the kind – and there was an awful row, with people writing letters saying that they were going to leave the Church. But in fact more came to see the fellow who could say such shocking things. When television came I was often asked to go and explain my views about marriage and baptism, and other similar matters, and always for controversial reasons. I did not mind this; an advertisement was still an advertisement, good or bad, and it was one way of bringing the Church to people.

Rightly or wrongly, what I felt mattered was building up in the cathedral a congregation of people who were really trying to lead a disciplined prayer life and to make their religion a reality in their lives. By the time I left, there were forty or fifty people coming to Holy Communion every morning and I spent a great deal of my time talking to people about their religion and trying to help them pray.

It was at this time that I discovered the uses of an 'office ministry'. I did very little visiting in the usual way, apart from accepting invitations to sundowners or dinner. But when I met someone who gave any indication that they would like to talk to me at greater depth, either from their confession, or a letter or a casual conversation at a party, I did my best to get them to make an appointment to come and see me. In an office you are on much stronger ground. You don't have to waste time on social preliminaries, coffee, drinks, and so on; you have your books on hand if you want to recommend one and a telephone at your elbow if a call to a doctor or someone seems indicated. And with a good secretary as watchdog you are free from interruption for a clearly defined length of time. In this sort of setting, I tried to listen and advise in the way I first learnt at Springs and Germiston and I made a lot of deep friendships which continued in less formal ways.

As some of these men and women began to find God they found their ordinary worldly friends and occupations less and less satisfying. Christ and love – love for men and women and for God – became more and more absorbing and quite a number found a religious vocation, as priests or as monks or nuns in a religious order. Many others found their way to a much more genuinely fulfilling life in the ordinary world and, if they needed it, healing from loneliness or frustration or mental sickness.

It is often said that the Church is full of neurotics and hypo-crites, and this is perfectly true. The Church should want them, when everyone else regards them as nuisances, and I wish the Church had more of them. There are too many people who treat the Church as just another interest in their lives – who are interested in religion just as they are interested in golf. The Church is the place for those, like myself, who know that they are in desperate need of the healing of love, both human and divine, and who can go from strength to strength because they are gradually enabled to give as well as to receive.

As a congregation, we tried to do a good deal about caring and giving, both individually and in various organizations. A number of things were started including an orphanage for African children and a multi-racial club, but I always felt that the most important was a branch of the 'Samaritans'. As most people know, this is an organization of voluntary counsellors who run a twenty-four-hour telephone service for those who are feeling suicidal and also try to give support and friendship to those who ask for help. About a hundred people were trained for this work and quite a few of those who started as agnostics found that they really could not do it unless they became Christians themselves.

In running the Samaritans, of course, I had to work very closely with doctors, psychiatrists, police, and the clergy of other denominations, and very co-operative I found them. I felt that my relationship with the psychiatrists and other doctors was particularly important, and as we got to know and trust each other we often sent people to each other for help which we could not give ourselves. (People with spiritual difficulties often need treatment for depression and vice versa.) I think that the clergy should make much more effort to build up this kind of co-operation and also that we do not do nearly enough to utilize the potential of professional skills and personal gifts which exist in our congregations. When I wanted to build a block of offices on the site of an old church hall in Salisbury I found businessmen and accountants in the congregation who really knew how to set about it in a professional way, and did so. Part of a priest's job, I think, is to look round and see where the real talents lie – for friendship, for hospitality, for organization, for care of the church, or whatever – and then get them used. In that way all the potential of the congregation is employed, whether it is the compassion and sensitivity of a shy, withdrawn person or the acumen of a business expert. I have often said jokingly that I let other people do all the work and then take all the credit, but in fact it is true, and I am proud of it.

One of my failings, both in Johannesburg and in Salisbury, was that I never took sufficient advantage of my position. I was an honorary member of the Salisbury Club and I ought to have gone there much more often and mixed with its members. My natural tendency is to work among the obviously deprived and it is easy to forget that the rich may also be deprived spiritually and emotionally. I should have ministered more to the 'establishment' and gone to the right clubs and the right parties, and perhaps I did not do so because I was afraid that I would not be very successful with this sort of person. If you are frightened of not doing a job well you tend to leave it undone and this is wrong.

I was very conscious of my lack of social know-how when I went to Rhodesia, and this sometimes got me into some funny situations. For instance, soon after I arrived I was summoned to dinner at Government House with Princess Marie Louise, who was staying there and would not dine without a clergyman present. It was a big formal dinner, and not understanding how many courses there would be, I overdid the first ones and got completely stuck half-way through. Later there was another grand dinner for the archbishops when the new province was inaugurated and remembering my previous experience I prudently missed the entrée, only to find that the next course was the dessert! Afterwards one of the staff told me that dinners were graded: a princess rated dinner number one and an archbishop only dinner number four.

It was in Salisbury that, for the first time, I saw the inside of a prison. On one occasion I had to visit a man who was under sentence of death. He had killed several people in what seemed to me had been a completely insane fit of rage over difficulties into which he and his family had got themselves, and to me it was a tragedy that he was hanged. I also used to go out to the prison regularly to see a friend of mine who had had a longish sentence for homosexual offences and to see a priest imprisoned for the same reason. I found then how much visits to prisoners mean, even though nothing effective seems to be achieved by them. I did not talk much to these men about religion. Perhaps I should have done more in this way, but I felt that my purpose in going to see them was to reassure them of love. Although one can assure people of the love of God, it is sometimes more important to show them the love of man, and that they are remembered by Christians outside the prison walls. This experience may well have been a factor in my later concern that African political prisoners on Robben Island should be visited by their families.

My own immediate family (if one can call such an unattached collection of people a family) ceased to exist even nominally while I was in Rhodesia. As I have said, my father had died early in the war, and my mother's husband, George Buchanan, died of TB while I was at college. My mother went into an old people's home in Vereeniging and she died there at the age of eighty-four, when I was in Salisbury. My sister Pat had an awful struggle to make ends meet and bring up her children after she divorced her husband, but she had become a very devout Roman Catholic and this pulled her through. There was much more suspicion between the Churches then and this affected our relationship, but we stayed in touch and saw each other occasionally on my leaves until she died of a heart attack soon after my mother's death.

I never saw Mike again after I waved goodbye to him on the station at Weston-super-Mare when I left for New Zealand. He joined the regular RAF, was a brilliant dare-devil pilot, and became a wing-commander and the liaison officer between the RAF and Winston Churchill. He also had the reputation for being one of the heaviest drinkers in the air force. After the war he was given a crash course in colonial administration and made ADC to Sir Andrew Cohen in Uganda, but I gather he irrevocably blotted his copybook by putting an extra nought into an order for red carpet when Princess Elizabeth was due for a visit, with the result that every colonial civil servant in Uganda was swamped with the stuff for years and years. We did write to each other at this time and tried to make arrangements to meet, but it never came off. After a period in northern Uganda, he ended as district commissioner in Pemba, an island off Zanzibar, where he died, apparently from falling down his verandah steps when drunk. Like the rest of us, he had difficulties over marriage and in fact divorced and remarried the same person. Obviously he had his faults, but he must also have had a lot of talents. He was much loved in Pemba and when he was buried the sultan ordered a day of public mourning.

Perhaps more important to me than these family deaths was the loss of Geoffrey Clayton. He died very suddenly of a heart attack one Ash Wednesday and I have always been convinced that it was because he, who was, as I have mentioned, a constant chain-smoker, invariably gave up smoking completely in Lent. Presumably his system just could not stand the strain. He had meant a great deal to me, and I felt very bereft.

However, I gained friends as well as lost them, and among the many whom I met in Salisbury was Alison Norman, who was later to figure as a 'co-conspirator' in my trial. Alison was then a woman of about twenty-seven who, after Oxford and a job on *The Economist*, had spent eighteen months working in south-east Asia and had decided to have a look at Africa before settling down. She got a job on a paper in Salisbury and stayed for eighteen months. During that time she came back to the Church, and she kept in close touch with me and her other Salisbury friends after she went back to England to train as a social worker. When she had a large financial windfall in England, she sent it to me to administer for her in financing anything I thought worth while. This turned out to be extraordinarily fortunate, because it showed that Alison had been sending me money years before I became involved with South African political prisoners.

My first contact with people in political trouble was with Europeans, refugees from the Belgian Congo who flooded down into Southern Rhodesia. They were in a terrible state. Some of them had been physically wounded and maltreated and some were in a state of shock from the loss of their relations or their livelihood, but they were all victims of unleashed African violence. That is why I have consistently said that I am as opposed to African nationalism as I am to white nationalism. Both of them need violence to maintain themselves and I abhor any régime which is based on force.

Very soon force was being used in Rhodesia too. Large imprisonment camps were set up at Wha-Wha and Gonudgazwinga for Africans who were being detained without trial as political malcontents. To my shame, I did not concern myself much with this, although I did give some of Alison's money to a fund which was started to help them and their dependants. Oddly enough, I felt more strongly about the imposition of the mandatory death-sentence for a number of crimes, including throwing stones at cars. The Chief Justice, Sir Robert Tredgold, resigned on this issue because he felt it was making a mockery of justice. I had always thought him the wisest man in the Federation and supported him wholeheartedly in making this stand. He hoped, as I hoped, that many people would follow him, but in the event very few people did and it is one of the tragedies of Rhodesia that Sir

Robert Tredgold has had to be on the sidelines in these past years, because a man of his integrity and wisdom could have been of the most tremendous value. (It is odd that I should have felt so strongly about this particular issue of a mandatory sentence, because it was clear from what the judge said when I was tried myself that he would have given me a suspended sentence if the law had not made five years' imprisonment the minimum he could impose.)

After I had been six or seven years in Salisbury, and everything was going pretty smoothly – at least as far as the parish was concerned – I began, as usual, to feel that I was in a rut and to get impatient for something new. The congregation was thriving; the cathedral, which, as I have said, had been left half-built for the last twenty or thirty years, was at last on the way to completion and the £120,000 needed to pay for it had been raised; a ten-storey block of shops and offices had been successfully built on the site of the old church hall; even my gaffes had become part of the accepted scene. But white Salisbury seemed a very suburban, cosy place. I wanted to be nearer the heart of things – either with people who were in desperate need, like the Coloured community in Johannesburg, or with men and women who were wholly dedicated to God in the religious life, since it is part of the paradox of the Christian faith that spiritual warfare is most acute either in a situation of extreme suffering and deprivation, or in a situation of total dedication to God. For this reason when I was offered the job of chaplain to a religious community in England, I wanted very much to accept it, but eventually turned it down on the advice of my bishop, and the then superior of the Community of the Resurrection, who was my old friend Jonathan Graham. They both thought that I should stay where I was, and this I did until 1965. Then out of the blue came a call from the Bishop of Johannesburg to go back there as dean. This was a job which I had always secretly longed for, though I had not expected to get it, and I had no doubt at all that it was also what I ought to do. Johannesburg was where my life as a practising Christian had begun and where I had been ordained. It seemed absolutely right that the wheel should turn full circle and there was no doubt too that it was a job in the middle of the political and spiritual arena. But I always break my heart when I leave a parish and the friends that I have made there, and when I left Salisbury the sadness and excitement were so mixed that I felt that I would burst.

CHAPTER FIVE

Dean of Johannesburg

The South Africa to which I came back in 1965 was a very different country from the one I had left ten years before. While I had been away there had been the Sharpeville massacre and the series of big 'treason' trials. The practical implications of the doctrine of apartheid had been clearly spelt out and rigidly enforced. Practically every vocal liberal, or person who dared speak out for freedom, had been imprisoned, exiled, banished, detained, or forced to flee the country. Even Alan Paton had had his passport confiscated. There was practically no one left who was in a position to speak out against the régime.

But if South Africa had changed, I had changed too. The failure of 'partnership' in the Federation of Central Africa, and my own sense of guilt at having done absolutely nothing to prevent it, had made me very aware of my own political responsibility, and although I had been out of South Africa I had followed what was going on there to some extent. While I was still in Rhodesia I had made a comment about South Africa being ruled 'by the whip and the gun', which shows that even then I had some awareness of what was really happening. (I was questioned about this remark by reporters as soon as I arrived at Jan Smuts airport in Johannesburg, so it did not take me long to get into political hot water.)

Looking back, I think that perhaps it was providential that I was out of the country for those ten years. If I had been there, I would, I hope, have been brave enough to identify myself with those who were fighting apartheid, and I have no doubt I would have been silenced like them. As it was, I came back without any reputation except as a churchman, and with an acute awareness that the Church had a responsible political function to perform.

The Anglican Church is the biggest of the English-speaking denominations in South Africa (though the Dutch Reformed Church is of course the biggest 'white' Church in the country), and I was to be dean of the cathedral in the biggest city of South Africa. I did think sometimes of Mordecai's remark to Queen Esther when she was afraid that she would be put to death if she went to the king to plead for the Jews: 'Who knows whether you have not come to the kingdom [or Republic] for such a time as this?'* From the beginning, therefore, I felt a conscious responsibility to take an active part in all that could be done by freedom-loving people to stem the torrent of an apartheid policy which I was convinced was contrary to the essence of the Christian religion. I was, honestly, neither just a 'political clergyman', nor a seeker for publicity for its own sake. But as my ministry in Johannesburg went on, I became more and more urgently concerned to bring the white people of the Church to a realization of what they were really doing. To most white South Africans apartheid had become simply part of the scheme of things, part of the 'South African way of life', which I used to refer to as the 'South African way of death'. I felt that I had to try and get them to see that it was the very antithesis of love, and utterly destructive both to those who practised it and to those who suffered under it.

On the surface, of course, things did not look too bad – as they still don't to the casual tourist. There were more Africans about on the streets than I had ever seen before, and they had become a significant part of the buying public. This was especially true around the cathedral whose main west door opens on to the street which leads directly to the African entrance of the Johannesburg railway station. Opposite the cathedral were shops catering especially for the African trade, with loud, jazzy music blaring day in and day out. Even at night a few Africans could be seen about. But each person had to have a special and particular

* Esther 4:14.

permission to be in Johannesburg at all and he had many miles to travel before he could get home on the crammed trains to the house or hostel where he was ungraciously allowed to live while he was part of the Johannesburg work force. And the police were absolutely everywhere in that apparently free crowd, checking passes, and watching and waiting for the smallest sign of trouble.

This was brought home to me very strongly soon after my return to Johannesburg when I was getting into my car just outside the cathedral. About half a dozen African youths suddenly crowded around me and one of them pulled out a knife which he held at my stomach while they demanded money from me. Fortunately my left hand happened to be on the hooter so I pressed it and the group of youths suddenly disbanded and disappeared. As they disappeared a white plain-clothes policeman in an open-necked shirt came tearing along with a revolver in his hand, accompanied by a plain-clothes African. He caught one of the young Africans as he was running away and brought him to me to be identified. I said to the policeman that I was much too interested in the knife which was at my stomach to notice the faces of the young men concerned so they let him go. This incident showed not only the ubiquity of the police, and indeed their competence, but also the very changed attitude of Africans towards the Church. Some years before, it would have been inconceivable that a priest dressed in a cassock could have been attacked in this kind of way.

The police are equally ubiquitous at night – especially in the raids which they make on the servants' quarters of European households to make sure that no illegal visitors are being entertained after 10 p.m.

One of our own subdeacons in the church (a subdeacon is a layman licensed by the bishop to administer the chalice at Holy Communion) recently committed the crime of going to bed with his wife. The man himself worked as a house-servant in one of the northern suburbs of Johannesburg while his wife worked in the same capacity in the southern suburbs. He was not allowed to stay with her without special permission, but he took a chance on his day off and spent the night with her. He was caught, and for that offence he was sentenced to a month's imprisonment.

African husbands and wives who are lucky enough to live together for most of the year are the exception rather than the rule. Men who are useful 'labour units' are forced to come to the big industrial cities like Johannesburg because there is no work in the Bantustans, and are housed in vast hostels, while their wives and children subsist in the 'homeland' on whatever their menfolk choose, or are able, to send back to them. The women often go as domestic servants in order to make ends meet or because, not surprisingly, they have been deserted by a husband they hardly saw. They have to leave their children in the care of some relative, often hundreds of miles away. It becomes impossible for a family to fulfil its responsibility of caring for its members. For instance, one of our priests who was serving in Johannesburg had at one time been the priest of the African congregation in Randfontein, a town about thirty miles west of Johannesburg, and there his son had been born. The son, aged now somewhere in his late teens or early twenties, was working in Johannesburg and living in one of the African men's hostels. There was no room for him to live permanently at home even if he had been allowed to do so. He became sick and went to hospital and as he got better his father tried to make arrangements to have his son to stay and convalesce with him in his own house in Soweto (a Johannesburg African township). Permission was refused; the boy was born in Randfontein, he belonged to Randfontein, and Randfontein was the only place in which he was allowed to live or stay unless he was working in Johannesburg and therefore allowed to stay in a municipal hostel. So here was a family prevented from having their own son in their own house even for a short period of recuperation.

One could go on for page after page giving examples of this kind. In a single month taken at random (July 1972) the Johannesburg advice bureau of the Black Sash interviewed 68 people who had been ordered to leave the area, 30 who were in trouble over the issue of reference books, 19 with housing problems, 26 in trouble over work permits, and 52 in trouble over residential permits. There were 53 with other varieties of similar difficulties with the authorities. Each one of these cases is a heart-breaking story of family separation or refusal of the right to work.

The Black Sash is an organization of white women throughout South Africa whose first object has always been to protest in an extremely passive and yet effective way at evil legislation. Their name comes from their technique of demonstrating against some act of the government by standing silently wearing black sashes of mourning. Their advice bureaux in Cape Town and Johannesburg are staffed by voluntary women workers who have made themselves acquainted with the law as it affects Africans and the regulations about where they can or cannot live. Day in and day out men and women, many of them in tears, come to try and find some possible means whereby they may be allowed to continue to live in the place where they have lived for many years or to have their children reunited with them. The Black Sash workers, with the help of friendly lawyers, try to help by persistently approaching the authority concerned, and by trying to find some way through the awful tangle of legislation which besets the African at every turn. Often it is because of clerical mistakes on the part of the authorities that papers are not in order, and although a claim is perfectly genuine it takes a very great deal of persistence to peg away until (occasionally) justice is done.

There are always long queues outside the various pass offices in the southern end of Johannesburg down around Polly Street. Sometimes our African priests from the cathedral staff went down to try to buy food for some of these people, who queue for the whole day long and sometimes longer, but there is very little that can be done to help them. They are just not people in the eyes of those who deal with them; they are simply numbered cases.

There is a pathetic belief amongst the Africans that if only they can persuade a European to go down to help them put their case there is a lot more chance of success. Certainly I know from my own experience that if I went down with an African I did not have to wait in a queue and this certainly gave the African with me an unfair advantage. But I never found that my advocacy really did anybody any good. The law was quite implacable.

There is a public holiday in South Africa every year called Family Day. The family is still a very important thing indeed to the Afrikaner in spite of the drift to the towns. The old Afrikaans family with its daily family prayers and its Bible-reading was an admirable institution, and the Afrikaners know how important the family is in building up a nation. (It is perhaps for this reason, subconsciously at least, if not consciously, that the Nationalist government is so completely determined to break up African family life.)

On Family Day I, in common with many other churchmen, took very particular care to publicize as widely as we could this important and very clear distinction between the building-up of the white family, which the government so strongly advocates, and the break-up of the black family, for which it also so clearly legislates. On more than one occasion the Council of Churches, of which I was a member, produced placards showing this contrast in policy as vividly and as emotively as possible. Once it was a photograph of an African man reading a letter in an urban African setting, with a piece of barbed wire separating him from another photograph of his wife and children at work in their fields at home. On another occasion John Vorster, the prime minister, played completely into our hands. He had said in a speech to a Nationalist party congress, referring to terrorist activities, 'I want to say to the world – you can push people around, you can fight them and you can insult them. They will take all this to a certain point, but you must not try to take a man's home away from him. You must not even think that you will go unpunished if you estrange a man's fatherland from him.' All we did was to publish a big photograph of the prime minister together with this statement and an excerpt from one of the apartheid laws. This poster was so effective that we tried to get some further copies printed. The printer told us that he had already had a government order of considerable value cancelled because he had produced the poster and there was no chance of getting him to do anything of this kind in future.

Thus the most passive kind of protest was blocked by blackmail – a use of force quite as effective as more overt methods, and one at which the Security Police are pastmasters.

When people like myself talk about the violence being inflicted on the African people it is usually supposed that we are talking about the physical violence with which they are often treated by the police and which I have several times seen with my own eyes, or that we are referring to the way they are sometimes flogged and maltreated by farmers, as is often reported in the South African newspapers. But this is not the only kind of violence. The break-up of family life is a violent attack on the family. Not being allowed to move around as you like, not being allowed to have your own son in your own home, not being able to sleep with your wife, not being able to make the most passive and legal sort of protest – all these things are violent attacks upon a man and his integrity as a human being, and I felt I had to say so as clearly as I could. I wrote in the parish magazine:

We have done violence to him. I do not speak of the physical assaults upon his person, which are made not infrequently by the more brutal among us, but of the deep and more traumatic violence which each man offers to the African simply by claiming his status as a white man and by walking free with the African always in his shadow. It is a violence of word and sneer and smile. It is a violence of constant and consistent arrogance.

I went on to say that almost every European is guilty of this kind of arrogance. The white liberals tend to think of the Afrikaner as being the source of all the evil in South Africa, but unconscious arrogance is part of the make-up of almost every white man in the country, unless he wakes up and consciously recognizes what he is doing, and alters his attitude. I often heard white people saying that Africans should 'be treated like human beings', which of course implies that they are not *really* human. I continued:

[This arrogance] is very much there in the Church and it is a wholly unchristian thing. It diminishes and degrades both the white man who despises and the black man who is despised. The black man is seen, not as a fellow human being, but as some lesser breed, and centuries of the white man's arrogance have convinced many of them in their bones that they are, in fact, inferior. A slave mentality has developed.

Again and again I tried to say this as forcefully as I could in the parish magazine, knowing that the national press would pick it up.

We have done and are doing violence to their status and their stature as human beings. We have done it by the attitude we adopt with them both individually and as a race. The kindnesses that we show are from *de haut en bas* and not among people. We smile at him as we smile at a child to give him confidence and to show him that we are not as terrible as we appear to be. We turn and rend him if he steps out of line. We say things to him that we would not dare to say to white people for fear of civil or violent action being taken in response. We do not have to be careful about what we say to an African. We treat him well as and when he serves us well. Any sign of independence we regard as cheek. Any sign that he may show of bettering himself is treated with sneers, if not to his face then behind his back. Sometimes that attempt to better himself is by seeking further education through a correspondence course, sometimes it is by dressing more smartly or buying a better bicycle or wireless set and sometimes even by saving to buy a motor-car. 'Who does he think he is?' we ask and that is the 64-dollar question. He may be beginning to think that he is meant to have some of the privileges of being fully human or he may be so conditioned and punch-drunk with the indignity poured upon him that he may not be able to think at all. Who does he think he is? But perhaps just as important is the question: who do you think he is?

As well as writing this kind of polemic, I was, of course, also doing my best to see that in the cathedral congregation, at least, we behaved as if we knew we were all redeemed and beloved children of God.

When I came to the cathedral, one of the tasks which the bishop had given me was the unifying of the black and white congregations who worshipped there. The black congregation had mainly come from St Cyprian's mission church. This church was founded in the days when black and white residential areas were not nearly so clearly defined and it served the Africans who were living in central Johannesburg. Later it mainly catered for domestic servants who lived with their employers and it was finally closed down because it was in the way of a road which the City Council wanted to build. The African priests who had served the mission continued to do so, using the cathedral as their centre, but the two congregations were almost completely separate. They worshipped at different times and had almost no contact with each other. Remedying this state of affairs took almost four years of persistent effort.

The first step was to get to know the African priests and find out what they were really doing – mainly in outposts at the huge hostels which had been built for African workers on the outskirts of the city. Then I had to get to know the leading members of the African congregation and to try to treat them exactly as I would Europeans – trying to make a real reciprocal relationship, with the same demands and the same friendship as I would expect in my relationship with a European churchman.

Gradually the mixed congregation became a reality. On average we had about 250 Europeans, and 150 Africans, Coloured people, and Indians at the 9.30 High Mass. Gradually, also, people stopped standing in separate corners during tea afterwards and really became one crowd. The Africans and Coloureds who came to the High Mass on Sunday mornings had to come a long way in from the townships, so they were people who had a particular concern for making a success of an inter-racial congregation. Most of them had some education and understood enough English to follow the services. There remained a part of the non-European congregation who were never really integrated with the rest and these were the servants who lived locally but who were working on Sunday morning and were not free to come to church until the afternoon. Many of them could only understand enough English to carry out orders and they included Zulu, Xhosa, Tswana and Sotho people. For these we had to have special services in the afternoons, using their own languages and always with two interpreters for the sermon – which made preaching a lengthy business.

We put a great deal of effort into social functions and social integration. There were barbecues in the deanery garden, parish dances, lectures and parties. Particularly valuable were the lunches which one of our parishioners, Barbara Waite, organized at her own house almost every Sunday, with children of all races bathing in her swimming-pool while their parents recovered from the quantities of excellent food.

As I have said, the cathedral was very close to the entrance of the station and thousands of Africans passed by every day, so I asked our African priests to stand at the cathedral door during the rush hours in the afternoon. They talked to the passing Africans and handed out pamphlets of various kinds, some setting out times of the services in the cathedral, and generally tried to make the Africans feel they were welcome. I also caused a big notice to be printed in several African languages saying that the cathedral was open to people of all races.

The most important step was to get Synod to agree that St Cyprian's Mission should be formally abolished and the priests who served it become full members of the ordinary cathedral staff. This was the crux. It meant that we had African priests administering the Holy Communion to Europeans, preaching to Europeans, and generally acting in exactly the same way as the European clergy. Some mornings you would come into church and find an African priest celebrating Mass and on other mornings it would be a European. It is difficult for an Englishman to imagine what this means to someone who is used to living under an apartheid régime.

Also of great importance was the Kiss of Peace. In the Liturgy as we used it in the cathedral 'The Peace' comes after the consecration prayer – God has come amongst us and we exchange his peace with each other. This we symbolized in the cathedral by each member of the congregation taking his neighbour's hands into his own and looking into his eyes. One person says, 'Peace be with you', and the other answers, 'Peace', and then turns to the next person and does the same thing so that it passes round the whole congregation, starting with the celebrant. I am quite certain that this physical touch between men and women of different races is one of the things which built the congregation together, and there is no doubt that it was one of the things that the authorities in South Africa could not abide. You cannot really *look* at someone and consciously reach out to touch him and yet continue to deny his humanity.

Of course, many people left the cathedral congregation when it became genuinely mixed and almost every white child had already been removed from the Sunday school when my predecessor brought in the St Cyprian's children. But then other parents began to bring their children deliberately so that they should have a chance to mix with children of other races and an ex-Methodist minister turned up to run the Sunday school because the cathedral congregation was the only inter-racial group of Christians he could find in the city. As the hard-liners left, the liberals came in, and overall the numbers increased. But what was more important was that the fellowship and prayer and service, which should be the heart of any congregation's life, began to become real.

None of these activities endeared me to the authorities, but one of the things which I think annoyed them most acutely was an article which I wrote on the proper meaning of the word 'Republic'. The occasion for this statement in the parish magazine was that I had been asked to take part in a service of thanksgiving on the tenth anniversary of the Republic and I had refused to do so. It seemed to me that the majority of the inhabitants of the so-called Republic had had very little to be thankful for since its inception. Things had been bad enough when South Africa was part of the British Commonwealth, but since it had become a republic they had got a lot worse, and so I wrote, in an article called 'No Republic This'.

If you look up the word 'republic' in the *Oxford English Dictionary* you will find it is defined as follows:

1) 'The State, the Common Weal.' I do not believe the common weal of all its people is the object of this republic. It is concerned with a separated weal of its European and African people.

2) 'A state in which the supreme power rests in the people and their elected representatives.' This country is fairly obviously not a republic in that sense either, because most of its inhabitants have no elected representatives in its government.

3) The third definition in the *Oxford English Dictionary* talks of a 'community of persons, animals, etc., in which there is a certain equality among the members'. The less said about that the better.

The object of this kind of protest was of course to try and make people aware of the facts so that they could be changed. 'Change' is a dirty word in South Africa and I discuss the Christian implications of this fact in more detail in the last chapter of this book. No one wants change or wants to think about it, so gradually I was forced into saying and writing, with all the strength at my command, that unless there was a change of heart amongst the white people and a change of circumstances for the black, there would be a violent confrontation between the two. I thought, rightly or wrongly, that if I could not persuade people to change their hearts and minds out of Christian love then I should try to persuade them to change out of fear. I hoped that if they really came to fear the violence that would follow their lack of love they might in some way begin to think of the African as a human being and therefore begin in a very seminal way to love him because they had at least recognized his existence.

It was this talk of violence which led me at my trial to be accused of inciting people to violence. This I never did, not because I thought the African had no moral right to rebel, but because I did not think a revolution was 'just' unless it had some hope of success, and this will not be the case in South Africa for many years to come. The South African state is as monolithic as it claims to be. What I warned people against, and tried to make them fear, was the spontaneous uprush of bitterness when suffering boils over into fury, and, in the long term, the utterly certain destruction of everything which 'white' stands for in South Africa.

It may sound from all this as if, in spite of my disclaimer at the beginning of this chapter, I was, in fact, just a political priest. But it is important to get the political aspect into proportion. Like most 'colonial' cathedrals, St Mary the Virgin, Johannesburg, is also a parish church, and many thousands of people lived within the parish, including the inhabitants of Hillbrow, the Soho of Johannesburg, with its bars and night-clubs and great tower-blocks of flats, and its highly mobile white population. (Hillbrow is said to be one of the most densely populated places in the Western world.) Apart from the people who lived in the parish, the cathedral drew an eclectic congregation from all over the city and we were also responsible for chaplaincy work in the many nursing homes and hospitals in the central area. Patients came to Johannesburg for treatment from anywhere between Zambia and the Cape, and when they went home they had to be commended to their own priests, which meant a lot of letter-writing. Equally, people came to work in Johannesburg with commendations to us, and this meant visiting and trying to draw them into the cathedral's life.

Most of this work, of course, I delegated. There were normally five priests and a social worker on the staff as well as an Anglican nun for some of the time. (The African priests could not, obviously, work in European hospitals.) My secretary, Laura Clayton, bore the brunt of all the secretarial work which we generated and was often working until ten or eleven o'clock at night. I myself was in a constant conflict between my wish to be available for people and my administrative responsibilities. There were absolutely endless meetings of one kind and another: the Council of Churches, the council of St John's College, the Christian Institute, the Diocesan Board of Finance, etc. etc., not to mention weekly meetings with the bishop and my fellow archdeacons, our own staff meetings and the parochial church council and its committees.

One of the tasks which demanded a great deal of time was set me by the bishop when I was appointed as dean. This was the rebuilding of a six-storey building next door to the cathedral, called Darragh House. It had been built by the Church in the early 1930s, and consisted of two halls, shops, offices and flats. It was in a bad state of disrepair and was only bringing in just over one per cent return on the nominal capital involved in the ownership of the land and the building. Obviously something had to be done but the question was what. Some people felt that the site should be sold to a developer and the proceeds invested. Others wanted the whole block, including the cathedral itself, to be sold, and the cathedral and its ancillary buildings moved to a site near the university where the setting would be much more attractive and dignified. (We were offered millions of Rand to do this and had a lot of commercial pressure put on us to accept.)

I was determined to do neither. I did not see why a developer should make a profit instead of the Church and I did not believe in leaving the city centre empty of any significant witness to the Christian faith, even if it would be quieter and more pleasant in a suburb – I had seen too much of the results of doing that in the United States. I was determined that we should develop the Darragh House site ourselves, as I had successfully done with Pax House in Salisbury, and eventually the cathedral council and the trustees agreed, though it was an uphill struggle. I got together a small but influential and expert committee of laymen who knew about loans, mortgages, building costs, and so forth, and they hammered out a viable scheme on a strictly commercial basis. After seven years of steady slog a twenty-two-storey block of shops, offices and flats is going up on the old site, while the cathedral stays firmly where it always has been, in the heart of the city.

I do try to listen to advice, but I am not much good at compromising when I am certain that I am right, and inevitably members of the congregation often disagreed with me – as many did over the Darragh House issue. When I first arrived as dean, for example, I insisted that the cathedral's great west doors should be kept open right through the day, so that the crowd passing on the pavement outside could see the high altar and the cross. In winter this was sometimes pretty draughty and an anonymous comment in the visitors' book begged God to 'preserve us from this dean who is freezing us all to death'. It was also noisy because of jazz blaring out from shops catering for the African trade, traffic hooting, and so forth, so that many sincere people felt with some reason that the quietness and reverence of the place was being disturbed (though you could in fact pray without much difficulty). I realized the disadvantages, but the fact remained that as soon as the doors were left open, people started to come – to pray, to take the weight off their feet, to cry, to light a candle, or just to sit and 'be' for a little while. Among them were Indians in saris who often left flowers and packs of unlighted candles before the statue of our Lady, perhaps in veneration of a universal symbol of motherhood. Often, too, people would just stand outside on the pavement for a few minutes, looking in, before they went about their business. The church was hardly ever empty, and although the background noise of the street could be a nuisance, it did remind us of our involvement with the secular city, and our responsibility in it. All in all, I was certain that the cold and inconvenience were well worth while.

Another running fight was about using the cathedral for secular purposes. I used to allow African choirs to give concerts there because there was no other suitable place which they were allowed to use. Some of the most faithful members of the congregation felt that this was a misuse of a consecrated place, and admittedly we did have to clear up a few cigarette-ends and quantities of sweet-papers afterwards, but I felt that this particular bit of hospitality was worth giving, and it did introduce people to a building (and, hopefully, to an atmosphere) which otherwise they might never have come anywhere near.

In spite of these tensions, the congregation did stay extraordinarily united and faithful. Although some people left because they could not bear a multi-racial congregation, many others, who did not like my political line in the least, were nevertheless loyal to the church so that we had the whole range of political opinions in the congregation. Occasionally personal dislike of me reached embarrassing levels, however. There was one old lady with whom I remonstrated about her very ostentatious devotions, which were disturbing other people during Mass. She biffed me on the head with her handbag and afterwards turned away and hissed whenever I passed her pew in a procession, though she still kept coming to Mass, bless her. The bishop had pages and pages of illegible letters from her about my misdeeds. Another large though elderly man kept threatening to murder me, though I was never clear what it was that I had done to annoy him. As he claimed to have been sentenced to life-imprisonment for some violent crime in Australia and used to come in early in the morning when few people were about, I was understandably nervous about this. He had two false legs but the toughest hands I have ever seen. The police later confirmed that he was a dangerous character and warned him off.

It was always difficult to know what to do about the drunks who wandered in. As Christians, we are supposed to be welcoming to all sorts and conditions of men, but they could be disturbing and frightening to other people, as on one occasion when a man started inveighing against the failings of the Anglican clergy at the top of his voice, and in very colourful language, from the high-altar steps.

It was also difficult to know what to do about people who were in obvious distress. Should one speak to someone who is crying, or leave them alone? I often wished that we had some retired priest who would make it his ministry to spend most of the day in the building and be available when he felt some need. I sometimes talked to people when I went in to say evensong or pray for the parish, which I did each day for half an hour from twelve-thirty to one o'clock. I felt that it was important to do this publicly and I tried to keep the time for it sacrosanct since I believe that interceding for one's parish, its organizations, its servers and servants, its life and worship, its involvement in the city of which it is a part, the suffering, the faithful, the lapsed, the pagan, and the seekers after God, is a very important part of a priest's work. I did this according to a worked-out scheme, but I tried to make it as immediate and relevant as I possibly could.

I was, of course, also in church in the early morning, from about 5 a.m., and even then there were some 'regulars' who came on their way to work to light candles and offer the day to God. My own early rising had been a gradual process. Having worked on a dairy-farm, I was not as frightened of the early morning as many people are. Also I had belonged since the early years of my priesthood to a very loosely knit group of priests called the Society of the Holy Ghost, which has a rule demanding certain times of prayer, study, and so on each day. Although I have been a very bad member of this group, I have always taken its rule as a guide to the kind of routine that I myself should keep. My day had not always started at 4.30 a.m., but I gradually worked back to this time because I found that when I was tempted to get slack the only way to cope was to make my rule harder than before, on the grounds that if the Devil found his tempting had a reverse effect, he would give up in disgust. Whatever the theology of this, it worked well in practice, though I think 4.30 is about my limit in this direction. The result was that I had time for personal prayer and matins before saying Mass at 6.30, and afterwards a period of quiet and thanksgiving before going home for breakfast at about 7.30. I could then fit in the hour's spiritual reading which my rule required before going to my office at 9 o'clock. (Often I did not manage this and had to catch up on my reading later in the day.)

This routine, it seemed to me, was a sheet-anchor. However useless and frustrating the rest of the day might seem, at least I had done *something* for myself, the world and God (whatever doing something for God might mean). And I kept it up on my day off, though I spent the rest of the day (apart from a shortened period of intercession) at home asleep or reading thrillers. This insistence on keeping my rule on my day off stemmed from my early days as a priest when it seemed to me quite unreasonable that we should ask the laity to give up their one free morning (people worked six days a week in those days) in order to come to church, if the clergy reckoned to have a lie-in on *their* day off. If I had kept to my usual rule I felt that even my day off was not wasted.

Of course, one never knows what is wasted and what is not. There was preaching and the preparation of sermons (I gave at least one each week), and generally some kind of talk to an outside organization once a week as well. There were the social gatherings which helped to cement the congregation and the Friday night open evenings at the deanery which later figured so prominently in my trial as hotbeds of subversion. There were the adult confirmation classes, which I always took myself and which were attended by people who wanted a 'refresher course' in their faith, as well as by those seeking confirmation. These took place weekly from Easter to November each year and I think that they were a valuable ministry. There were frequent invitations to sundowners or supper from parishioners. As far as possible I tried to avoid formal dinner parties but I liked to go to supper with a family so that I could get to know them personally, as a friend.

In general, I don't think that I did the job of being dean of Johannesburg justice in terms of making contact with the leaders of business and industry. As in Salisbury, I should have gone to the right clubs and accepted more invitations to talk to welfare societies, and such like. In fact I did very little to minister to those in places of power. I dare say that if I had felt really confident in this kind of work, I should have found the time and energy to do it, but I had so many other problems which I did not feel that I was beginning to tackle – leaving aside the whole apartheid issue. One of these was Hillbrow.

Because Hillbrow is such a pagan part of the city I had a particular concern with evangelistic work there and took an active part in the Mission Committee of the cathedral which was particularly concerned with that area. We did not achieve much, but I was determined to establish some sort of presence there, and, until the time of my arrest, on almost every Saturday night I walked around Hillbrow in my cassock for an hour or so. This walk often had its difficult moments due to encounters with drunks of various kinds, and on one occasion one of the younger priests who came with me was extremely shaken when three very drunken Coloured ladies followed us around for a whole hour singing, in a rather dirge-like manner, the 'Our Father' to a tune which is familiar to the Coloured people. Although several members of the cathedral staff came with me at first, they gradually came to feel that it was useless, and finally I found that I was doing it by myself Saturday night after Saturday night. Sometimes people did come and talk to me, but for the most part they were Spanish, Italian, or German immigrants who mistook me for a Roman Catholic. Once or twice there were quite helpful encounters which were followed up by visits. But I really cannot claim that I did anything more than just establish the fact that I was interested in Hillbrow and that I wanted to show that the Church had a concern with it. (I was also involved in a coffee bar which the Council of Churches started there and which did quite a good job of work for a year or so, but eventually collapsed for lack of funds.)

Another chronic headache was the Dean's Shelter. This had been started by the famous Dean Palmer during the slump of the 1930s and it was meant to provide temporary accommodation for European men while they searched for the few jobs that were going. When South Africa entered a period of great prosperity, its original function became unnecessary, and by the time I came back to Johannesburg it had become a sort of 'hoboes' home' which only encouraged European tramps to hang around Johannesburg and not attempt to seek for work. Over the years we gradually changed it into a longer-term hostel for men with a wide variety of problems. We accepted men with 'inadequate personalities' who were in sheltered employment, men who had just come out of prison, alcoholics (on condition that they were undergoing treatment), and others. It was a very difficult place to run because there was a constant change of staff and we never had the money to get the fully trained workers whom we needed.

Next door to the Dean's Shelter was a home for sixty old-age pensioners called God's Providence House and this too was a constant headache. There were a lot of bars in the neighbourhood and the old men were often very heavy drinkers, so on pension day there was always trouble.

We had a reputation for taking people into the Shelter whom no one else would touch, and so the welfare agencies and the government's social welfare department consistently sent us men who were notoriously difficult. Just as consistently these men, if they were working, stayed for a month and left without notice when they got paid and their bill for board and lodging was due. But in spite of many failures, the Shelter did produce some good results and it also cared for some mentally retarded and socially inadequate people who would otherwise have been in an institution or in prison. Here again, I did not personally do nearly as much as I ought to have done. A very old friend of mine, Vivienne Mason-Jones, and her husband took the brunt of running the place, and neither the Shelter nor God's Providence House could have continued without them.

Of course none of the cathedral's activities could have gone on for a day without the devoted work of the full-time staff (both clerical and lay) and the immense amount of time and energy which many members of the congregation were willing to give. As in Salisbury, others did the work and I took the credit. And at the basis of all this there was of course the daily Mass (we had, on average, over forty daily communicants) and the disciplined prayer life of very many people. Again, quite a few of these found a vocation for the priesthood or 'the religious life' in a more formal sense. But I hope that I have demonstrated that I did have a concern for my job as a whole and, although I thought political witness to be very important, I did not pursue it at the expense of other responsibilities.

It is, of course, not really possible to draw any hard-and-fast distinction between my activities as dean and unofficial work, but there were areas where I tried to make a personal contribution rather than as a spokesman of the Church, and people with whom I got involved as a result. These personal activities figured very largely in my trial and I must try to explain what it was all about.

CHAPTER SIX

Aiding and defending

When I first came back to Johannesburg, I expected, as dean of its cathedral, to be someone of some importance, as I had been in Salisbury. I was quickly disillusioned. The cathedral in Johannesburg was no longer even the city's principal Anglican church, in terms of the worldly importance of its congregation, since the influential people had moved out to the suburbs and rightly went to church where they were living. More importantly, I was no longer 'someone' as far as personal counselling and direction were concerned. In Salisbury I had built up this ministry, in Johannesburg I had to start all over again in a set-up where I did not know the doctors and the social workers and where the members of the congregation did not know me well enough to come to talk to me about the things that mattered to them. The result was that, although I was physically busy, I was in something of a personal vacuum. I felt that I was going through the motions of being a priest without really doing anything. I felt like a damp squib – which was very good for my pride.

Perhaps it was because of this that I reacted so quickly when D. & A. was banned. For some years the International Defence and Aid Fund had been very active in South Africa. Its work, as its name implies, is to provide defence for those charged with political crimes and to give help to them and their dependants. One of its officials in Johannesburg was a priest, John Davies, who was chaplain to the Anglican university students, and it employed Winnie Mandela as a social worker to investigate need and distribute funds. Winnie is the wife of Nelson Mandela, who was one of the leading lights of the African National Congress and who is now serving a life-sentence on Robben Island. She is herself constantly in political hot water.

Obviously this situation was asking for trouble. It was natural for the government to assume that Winnie Mandela was using the money to advance the interests of the African National Congress, and the government has never needed encouragement to jump to conclusions. The prime minister, by virtue of the powers invested in him under the Suppression of Communism Act, declared the Defence and Aid Fund to be an unlawful organization. It became illegal to receive money from it and the money which was still in its account was impounded.

I read of this in my paper one morning towards the end of March 1966 and it made me extremely angry. I did not know much about Defence and Aid's work but I was quite clear in my mind that the wives and children of convicted people should not be penalized deliberately because of the acts of their husbands or fathers and I was also convinced that anyone, no matter what he was alleged to have done, should have the chance of adequate defence in a court of justice. These seemed to me to be minimum criteria in any nation which called itself civilized. So when Defence and Aid was banned, and I was simultaneously at something of a vocational loose end, I felt I should do something about it. So, I subsequently found, did Alison Norman.

Alison, as I have mentioned before, was a friend whom I had known in Salisbury some years previously and who had helped me financially with various projects there, including starting the Samaritans and building a small orphanage for African children. She had offered to do anything she could to help in Johannesburg and so I wrote and asked if she could raise any money to help me carry on the work which Defence and Aid had been doing. Almost simultaneously, as it happened, Alison wrote to me expressing her concern about this particular issue and offering to raise and send money to carry on the work if I was willing to administer it.

The government banning order had made it pretty clear that

it was only money from D. & A. itself which was banned and not the action of helping political prisoners. They just wanted to stop what they felt was the use of D. & A. money as a tool of the African National Congress. I was in no sense the tool of the ANC and so there was no reason for the government to object. I was rather uncertain whether or not I would be contravening a law which forbids the use of foreign money for 'political purposes'. However, I took legal advice and was assured that paying for legal defence, school fees, and so forth, was not political activity within the meaning of this Act and I was in the clear. (This advice turned out to be sound, since I was never accused of this particular misdemeanour.)

I was so convinced that there was nothing illegal about what I proposed that I asked John Davies to ask the Security Police for his records and give them to me. He had often been interrogated at 'The Greys' (at that time the Johannesburg headquarters of the Security Police before they moved to John Vorster Square) and it must have needed a lot of nerve to go back voluntarily and ask for his files, but he did it and was given them. He also let it be known through his connections that I would be carrying on the work, though of course not using Defence and Aid money with which to do it. It is worth emphasizing that we were quite open about this and the Security Police knew about it from the start. They let me do the work without interruption for about six years, and I presumed, when I thought about it all, that they preferred to let me carry on, rather than let it fall into the hands of some *sub rosa* organization which it was harder to keep an eye on. Whatever their reasons, they did let me go on, and I still feel some sense of injustice that they did not give me some official warning if they wanted me to stop. At least I would then have had some clear idea about what they were objecting to and why they disliked it.

When I sat down to think about what I had taken on, it was immediately clear that I could not possibly cope by myself and I enlisted the help of John Turnbull, who was then working in the parish office. John had been a young executive in a Johannesburg company but had become dissatisfied with the rat race of Johannesburg commercial life and I had persuaded him to come and work as parish secretary at a very much reduced salary. Soon administering the 'Alison Norman fund' got too much for John to cope with in addition to his other work so I managed to persuade a Mrs Jean Webb, who was working in an office in the city, to come for three mornings a week at a nominal salary and do the basic interviewing and paper work. These two bore the brunt of the whole thing and I was only involved in borderline cases when it was doubtful whether a person should be helped or not.

In fact, John did not use the list which we had got from the Security Police at all, but as the word went out on the grapevine and people began to come and ask for help, he interviewed each one from scratch and tried to assess whether they were in need, the reasons for their being in need, the possible sources from which they could get help, and the best way of seeing that they got the help they most needed. We were determined to avoid the use of Winnie Mandela as a welfare worker for the fund, although I had nothing against her personally. In some ways I considerably admired her, and I helped her on several occasions to visit her husband on Robben Island, but I did feel that if she was involved in the administration of the money, it would be asking for trouble from the authorities. So we used the African priests on our staff to do home visits when these were necessary and we co-operated a great deal with other welfare organizations. Often we would take on people referred to us by other organizations because their own terms of reference did not stretch to cover a particular category, and equally, when people came to us for help and we knew that Ekutuleni or the Quakers or someone would be able to help, we referred them on. The great joy of our set-up was that we were not a committee and did not have rules or terms of reference. We could give help where it was needed and to the extent that it was needed, and although I did consult Alison Norman if I felt we were going rather way-out, she always left things entirely to my discretion.

I suppose that we were rather amateur in our investigations.

We sometimes found that our applicants were milking several cows – though the others were generally generous individuals rather than agencies, since the various funds had a pretty good communication system between themselves. Sometimes it was almost impossible to assess how serious the need was. For instance, at the beginning of 1971 the Archbishop of Canterbury himself wrote asking me to try and find out what had happened to an African woman called Mrs Dhlamini and her two children because friends in England were anxious to help her and could not get any answer to their letters. I asked Father Rakale, CR, the senior African priest on the cathedral staff, to make enquiries, and later replied to the archbishop:

... Mrs Dhlamini is a divorcée of about 40, with two daughters aged 20 and 18, the former of whom does domestic work and gets R16 per month, including her keep, and the younger has an illegitimate baby at home. They pay a rent of R6 per month. She was, as you know, one of the nineteen detainees and since coming out of prison has not been able to find a job. The few detainees who do find jobs find very often that the Security Police make it impossible for them to keep the job.

Mrs Dhlamini's home is very simple, reasonably furnished, clean and tidy, and Father Rakale was very impressed by her as a person and her pride in her family and her home. She and her one daughter and grandchild live on approximately R10 a month and clearly she needs assistance. I think it might be worth while letting these people who want to help her know that if she gets too many letters from England it may well be the cause of more persecution for her, and certainly nobody who writes to her or sends her anything should be a person who is in any way connected with Anti-Apartheid, D. & A., Amnesty, WCC, or any other organization of which the government of this country disapproves.

If I can be of any use in passing things on to her, I, of course, will be only too glad to do so ...

This letter was written eight days before my arrest. When the Security Police saw it later, they roared with laughter and said that Mrs Dhlamini was one of the most notorious 'shebeen queens' (illegal liquor-sellers) in Soweto. Whether this is true, I just don't know, but the incident illustrates both the requests for information that we used to get and the difficulty of being certain that we gave the right answers.

It was our general policy not to give money direct to the applicants but to pay rent direct to the municipality, school fees to the schools, and so on. Our reluctance to hand out actual cash became rather notorious and caused a good deal of complaint from the more politically minded Africans who felt we were not treating them as responsible human beings. It was, however, a matter of self-protection (and of protecting the recipients as well). We felt we had to make sure that the money was spent on the purpose for which it was asked and that it did not get used for illegal political activity.

I felt rather strongly that the children of the men in prison were potential leaders of a free South Africa and as such should have the best education which we could manage to get for them. For this reason we sent quite a number of them away to boarding-schools and some to schools outside the country in Swaziland and Lesotho. This latter gave rise to the accusation that I was favouring the more prominent political leaders by giving their children a better education. We also paid the fees for a number of children to go to the ordinary schools in the African townships of Johannesburg and provided for their school uniforms by sending them with a letter to one of the two main outfitters in Johannesburg who catered for this trade – a firm which carried a bigger stock than its rival, was cheaper, and gave us a discount. Later I was told that this owner was a 'listed' communist and it was implied that using his services was all part of the 'plot'. So whatever we did was wrong.

We were always aware that some of the people who came to us were informers. (It is extremely difficult for an African not to be an informer, if the police happen to want him as one. Co-operation can mean being allowed to get a house and a job. Refusal may mean imprisonment, with hard labour for yourself and starvation for your family.) John Turnbull could generally guess who the informers were because of their tendency to ask questions, their vagueness about how they had heard they could get help at the cathedral office and their general 'smell'. But we were never certain, and we never refused help which we would otherwise have granted just because we suspected that the person was an informer. (A good proportion of the people we suspected did in fact turn up as state witnesses at my trial.) Sometimes it was glaringly obvious. For instance, there was a woman who refused to talk to anyone but myself and insisted on seeing me privately. She wanted me to pay the fares for the children of a South African exile to fly from Botswana to Lesotho, and she assured me that if I gave her the money for this it would be repaid to me from the ANC in London. I was absolutely certain that if she had been a genuine member of the ANC she would not have been so foolish as to broadcast the fact and I told her, truthfully, that I had no connection with the ANC and would not accept money from it for any reason at all. So she went away dissatisfied.

We never went into the political background of the people whom we helped. What mattered was the need of their families, and not who they were or what their relatives had done. In fact it was only when I read my indictment that I knew what many of them had been charged with. I am often asked why we put a special emphasis on helping political prisoners and their families and my answer is that it was because most of the other welfare organizations were too frightened to do so. It was clearly shown at my trial that in many cases, if we had not helped, no help would have been available. However, many of the people we aided were not 'politically' involved, although they were all, in one way or another, victims of apartheid. For instance, there was a former school-teacher who had had to leave his job because he was not qualified to teach under the requirements of the Bantu Education Act. He had a large family and we helped him with rent and school fees until he got another job at a much lower salary and then we still went on helping with his children's education because education was so important to this family and we felt they would make good use of it.

Other organizations often referred people to us because they were restricted in the amount of relief that they were allowed to give. Very often such referrals were for school uniforms. School fees in the schools in the Soweto area are fairly moderate but there are not enough schools for the children who want education and education is not compulsory. The result is that many headmasters refuse admission to children without uniforms and these cost R60 (about £35) per child. For a family to provide this from inadequate wages is often simply impossible.

Sometimes it was a question, not of school uniforms, but of simple survival. Very many of the political prisoners' wives had no income at all. Some of them had themselves been accused of political offences but not convicted, and they were all suspect because of their husbands' activities so it was very difficult for them to get jobs. Often when they did get jobs they lost them again remarkably quickly, and we always suspected, rightly or wrongly, that the Security Police or their agents informed their employers that these people were better not employed. The same was true, to an even greater extent, of prisoners who had been released or were under house-arrest and who found it almost impossible to get work.

One rather tragic case of this kind where we tried to help was that of a nurse who had been imprisoned for some political offence. When she was discharged after serving her sentence she was struck off the Nursing Register by the South African Nursing Council, so that she had to become a domestic servant. She was also banished back to her home-town where the chances of her finding a job were almost nil. I paid for a lawyer to help her in her appeal against the decision of the Nursing Council because I could not see how a nurse's political opinions could make any difference at all to her nursing qualifications. The appeal was turned down – and she was forced to give evidence against me at my trial. She did not want to in the least, but you don't get much choice. If you have been imprisoned as she had, you are under suspicion all the time. If the state wants you to be a witness, you are a witness, and that is all there is to it.

We often paid train fares for wives or other nearest relatives to go down and visit their menfolk on Robben Island. Such visits were a biggish undertaking for the women concerned because the journey to Cape Town took a couple of days and this meant taking four days off if they were employed. They were allowed only a visit of half an hour (speaking through glass, of course, and very strictly supervised), and then they had to take the long train journey back. We paid R30 for each journey, which barely covered the train fare, and the women paid for their own food and other expenses. I felt that these journeys were of very great importance, although the effort required was so great and the visit so short. They assured the men on the island that they were not just depersonalized numbers, that they still had families who loved them and kept them in mind, and they assured the women that they still really did have husbands who were alive and needed them.

The Ntuti family is one vivid example of the sort of problems with which the men on Robben Island were faced. Shumi Ntuti wrote from Robben Island to the Council of Churches in Johannesburg asking if someone could find out what had happened to his family, from whom he had heard nothing. The request was passed on to us and we investigated. We found that his wife had deserted, leaving their eleven children (of whom the oldest was thirteen) to fend for themselves. The eldest girl, Catherine, not surprisingly went on the streets and had become completely uncontrollable. The next daughter tried to cope but was herself sick. Shumi Ntuti's parents were still alive, but his mother was an old-age pensioner and his father was paralysed and unable to work, so they were also in need of help. We wrote to Shumi Ntuti breaking the news of what had happened as gently as possible and telling him that we would do our best to see that the family got the food, clothing and schooling that they needed and that we would try to get help for Catherine. We continued to write to him from time to time, giving him news of his family and assuring him of our concern.

Of course, old age or sickness often added to the hardships which people suffered. There was one elderly lady who was a close relative of Chief Albert Luthuli. She and her husband were well-educated and had been people of some standing in the community. But they had got into trouble for their political beliefs and the husband had been put under house-arrest and had lost his job. There was no prospect of getting another so he applied to have his restriction order altered to enable him to start a farm in one of the few areas where it is still possible for Africans to do this. Permission was given and the couple sank all their assets in the venture, but it was a disastrous failure and they lost everything. The old lady earned what she could by giving lessons in African languages and they hardly ever asked for help, but we knew that sometimes there was nothing to eat in the house at all.

In another case the husband was on Robben Island and the wife had ulcerated legs and was in very poor health. There were a lot of children and the two sons who were of working age could not get jobs. This family also were starving when we got to know them and they could not even receive letters or money-orders because they lived in the country and there was no postal delivery in their area. Of course they had no money to hire a post office box.

Sometimes it was difficult to know who really needed help and who could help themselves if they tried hard enough. For instance, there was Wallace Serote, a young African poet who had been arrested with those who were afterwards known as 'The Twenty-two' and charged with terrorism. Serote spent seven or eight months in solitary confinement, and then, he thinks, agreed to turn state witness. He is quite uncertain about this (one gets very uncertain about what one has done in solitary confinement), but he was certainly moved from Pretoria to the police cells in John Vorster Square and kept for several more months there, and then he was just released. When he came out of prison, he seemed to me to be a broken man – more or less punch-drunk. I sent him to a psychiatrist who thought 'he wasn't too bad', but he certainly did not seem fit to do anything much.

So I agreed to give his father, who ran a rudimentary garage, R30 a month to employ Wallace, although Wallace would not do anything much except to say that he wanted to write. Eventually he was offered a scholarship to Columbia University but could not take it up because he was refused a passport. What has happened to him now I don't know.

Another example was a man who worked full-time on inter-race relations. He was suddenly banned and went to the United States on an exit permit where he got a professorship at some university. Soon after this the Institute of Race Relations asked me to pay the fare for his wife and children to go over to the States. It seemed a bit curious because if the man had a professorship, he ought to have been able to afford to get his own wife and children over, but I was assured by the Institute that he had not got the money. I impressed on him that, though I would advance the fares, it was only a loan, but of course I never saw it again. If I had got the money back, I would have been able to help more people – and this sort of thing kept on happening.

Sometimes we felt that relatives could have done more. For instance, there was an old man of eighty-two who had been put under house-arrest for five years. He told me that he had two sons who were both qualified doctors working in England but who never sent him a brass farthing. He would have starved if he had not come in every week to get a food-parcel from us. He was a delightful person, full of great and deep biblical faith, and although he was not very well-educated he spoke beautiful English and was always talking about God. We enjoyed his visits to the office. (This old chap got permission to go for a holiday on a farm, but was told he would still have to report daily to the police-station. The nearest one was eight miles away and he explained that at his age he could not possibly manage this. He was told, 'If you can't walk sixteen miles a day, you can't go on holiday.' So he had to stay at home.)

As I have said, one of the great advantages of our set-up was that we had no terms of reference. If I had been a 'proper charity', I am sure that I could never have persuaded the trustees that I should finance the publication of a book, for instance, but that is just what we did over *The Discarded People*. This was a very thorough factual study of the living conditions of the thousands of Africans who had been displaced from their ordinary homes because the areas in which they had lived were declared 'white', or because they could not get passes to stay in a city. These people were and still are sent to camps in the middle of nowhere to live under appalling conditions of deprivation – *The Discarded People* is a very apt title. The author, Cosmas Desmond, was a magnificent young Franciscan priest who needed money to tour the country and investigate the camps. I advanced R3000 from the fund (which has been repaid), and he produced a complete documentation which was published by the Christian Institute in South Africa and has since been published in Britain by the Penguin African series. Cosmas is now (predictably) under house-arrest.

Another advantage of being so flexible was that I could use the account for money from other sources. Sometimes this was necessary because we were asked to act as administrators by other charities. For example, when 'The Twenty-two' were being tried for terrorism, the World Council of Churches provided funds for the support of the accused people's dependants but did not have the means of seeing that this was properly and fairly allocated, so they gave us the resources and we took it on. (It was meant to be a temporary arrangement, but in fact we got left with the baby.) I also became a regular recipient for money sent by student organizations overseas to the National Union of South African Students, and again used the Fund's accounting system to cope with this. The student organizations wanted to use a middle-man because they were afraid that money sent to NUSAS might be confiscated by the government, since NUSAS was always in political hot water. Before I took over the forwarding of this money, it was handled by an organization whose chief was so frightened by the size of the sums involved that he put the whole lot in a savings account. This was in January and NUSAS needed the money to pay the annual correspondence school fees for the education of men serving sentences for criminal and political offences, which was what it was intended for. I had to lend NUSAS R3000 from the Fund until they could eventually get their own money released, and after that it seemed simpler to handle the whole thing myself.

Another activity which it would have been difficult to explain to a committee was building a wall. This was for Helen Joseph who became a member of the cathedral congregation while I was dean. She was under house-arrest, which in her case meant that she had to be at home, alone, from 6 p.m. to 6 a.m. and throughout weekends and bank holidays. She had got into trouble originally because she had toured the Republic trying to find the people who had been banished (i.e. regarded by the authorities as 'troublesome' and sent to live in some remote area where they had neither friends nor work). She toured the whole country in her not very adequate car and then she set up a small organization to try and help the banished people with the bare essentials of life and the knowledge that there was at least someone who remembered them. She also wrote a book about these people called *If This Be Treason*★ which is now banned in South Africa (that is, it is a legal offence to have it in your possession). When this book was published, Helen was placed under house-arrest. She had been tried previously with many others on charges of treason and been acquitted, but you do not have to be convicted of anything to be put under house-arrest. This is done at the discretion of the Ministry of Justice on the advice of the police (as was openly said at my trial).

While Helen was in jail awaiting trial she met Hannah Stanton and some other Christians and was very much impressed by some quality in them that she wanted for herself. She had been confirmed as a child but had relapsed completely from the faith and wanted thorough preparation and instruction before she came back to it. I used to see her every Friday from 7 to 8 a.m. because this was the only time when she did not have to be either at work or alone at home. When she had undergone what she considered

★ Published by André Deutsch in 1963.

to be sufficient instruction (which was a good deal more than I considered necessary) she came back to receive Holy Communion again on the feast of St Peter's Chains, which she thought was a most suitable day. For a long time she could only come to Holy Communion on weekdays but I led a deputation of two or three members of the cathedral congregation to the Minister of Justice, Mr Pelser, and we got permission for her to come to Mass on Sunday. There was always a queue to speak to her after the service as she was only allowed to talk to one person at a time and had very little time to spare before she had to be back at home, but it meant a great deal to us and to her that she was able to be there.

Some time after this the house next door to Helen's was bought by a policeman. The houses in this area are very small, with tiny gardens, and they are right on top of each other. As soon as we heard that a policeman was coming to live next door, we all began to speculate as to whether he had bought it as a purely private matter or whether he had been instructed to do so, so that extra surveillance could be kept on Helen. We never knew the answer, but as soon as he moved in, Helen was subjected to minor acts of persecution. For instance, the policeman had a young son who used to get up in a tree in his garden and aim a presumably perfectly harmless toy gun at Helen. When one has been under the strain of house-arrest for so many years, things of this kind become intolerable, so we used the fund to pay for a high wall which prevented complete oversight of her garden and gave her a little privacy. (Helen's original banning order was for five years, but while she was serving it, she had the incredible courage to write another book, *Tomorrow's Sun*,[*] the manuscript of which she smuggled out of the country. Probably because of this the banning order was renewed and she was only released after eight years, when she was found to be suffering from breast cancer. Since then she has shown no sign at all of being less outspoken than she had been before.)

Even though I had all the advantages of not having a com-

[*] Published by Hutchinson in 1968.

mittee, I did of course make constant efforts to put the welfare work which I was doing on a more permanent footing. Obviously Alison Norman could not go on financing it for ever, and my term of office as dean was due to finish in 1972. In other parts of the country 'Dependants' Conferences' had been set up to fill some of the vacuum which had been left by the banning of Defence and Aid. However, the work they could do was very limited because they were only allowed by their terms of reference to give each family the bare minimum for survival and they were not permitted to help discharged prisoners, who were often the people most desperately in need. In spite of these limitations on their activities, I did do my utmost to get a Dependants' Conference going in the Johannesburg area, but nobody seemed to be much interested, perhaps because the job was already being adequately done. Later the rule about helping ex-prisoners was relaxed, and when Jean Webb and John Turnbull both left their work for the fund, and I was clearly going to be either in prison or abroad, a Dependants' Conference really did get going. Like the ones in other parts of the country, this is financed by the World Council of Churches and is administered in Johannesburg by two people who did a great deal to get it off the ground, Josie Emery and Ann Hughes, under the chairmanship of Professor Henderson.

Apart from giving help of orthodox and unorthodox kinds, I was also involved to some extent in financing legal aid, though of course our resources were not great enough to do this on any considerable scale and most of the cases which I helped were minor ones where an attorney (solicitor) or junior counsel could give the necessary defence. My own attorney, Raymond Tucker, gave me a lot of help in this way (with the ironic result that he was listed as a 'co-conspirator' at my trial because I had paid him from Alison's money), but I also met other lawyers through this work, and particularly Joel Carlson.

In the Transvaal area almost every African who got himself into political trouble went to Joel for legal advice and help and he briefed counsel in cases ranging from the big treason trials to very minor affairs. The strain of this work on him was very considerable. There was always uncertainty about whether the money for big defence cases could be found and he had a lot of difficulty in getting secretarial staff because the Security Police used to warn them not to work for him. Bullets were fired through the windscreen of his car while it was in his garage and through the front door of his office, and his wife and children were victimized in various ways. Not surprisingly this preyed on his nerves, and although he was a non-practising Jew, he used to come to me to get things off his chest. At times he would come and talk almost every day and I would find him waiting for me in my office or when I got home in the evening. Apart from paying for some of his smaller cases, I did not give Joel much active help except once when he had difficulty in communicating with the people abroad who were raising money for one of the big trials and I got Alison Norman to help re-establish communications. He was very grateful for this.

When Joel was attorney for most of 'The Twenty-two' who were tried under the Terrorism Act in 1969, they gave him handwritten accounts of the torture which they had undergone, and he succeeded in bringing these out of the prison. These were utterly horrific documents, and it was because of them that I later remarked that Colonel Swanepoel was 'a sadist who ought to be shot', and that Mr Justice Theron was 'a moron' when he ruled that it was 'not urgent' to hasten the hearing of an application for the protection of these people from further torture. When I reread these statements now, I cannot think why my language was so moderate.

David Motau, for example, wrote:

I was taken for interrogation on 16th May at about 11.30 a.m. They ordered me to stand on the top of two bricks. I was made to carry another brick with my hands high up. I did not stand firmly on the bricks as they were smooth. As my hands became tired an African policeman beat me at the elbows with a rubber stick . . . and on the feet. He tied my face with an old cloth. The white policeman said that I would not go out of Compol★ without making a statement. 'We will make you talk.'

When the second shift of interrogators came, he was hung up by the neck with his toes just touching the bricks. The torture continued for three days and nights, the police working in shifts.

I was not allowed to sleep or rest, I was punched on my cheeks and mouth and kicked. When they ate, they gave me some food, and I was given a small tin to urinate in. I only began to talk when after a long time they asked me about a meeting. . . . I realized they knew.

Another man wrote that Swanepoel had told him that he would stand on the bricks until he spoke, however long that was. In fact he lasted for three days – until he could not distinguish between night and day, and then, while he was still on the bricks, they dictated to him what they wanted him to say.

Women were treated in the same way:

They closed the windows, I continued screaming. They dragged me to another room, hitting me with their open hands all the time. In the interrogation room they ordered me to take off my shoes and stand on three bricks. I refused to stand on the bricks. One of the white Security Police climbed on a chair and pulled me by my hair, dropped me on the bricks. I fell down and hit a gas pipe. The same man pulled me up by my hair again, jerked me, and I again fell on the metal gas pipe. They threw water on my face. The man who pulled me by the hair had his hands full of my hair. He washed his hands in a basin. I managed to stand up and then they said, 'On the bricks.' I fell. They again poured water on me. I was very tired. I could not stand the assault any longer. I asked to see Major Swanepoel. They said, '*Meid, jy moet praat*' – 'Girl, you must talk.'

Age was also no protection from this kind of treatment. Douglas Mvembe was 73 and unable to balance on the bricks, but they handcuffed him and tied him up with a rope through the handcuffs so that his feet just touched the bricks, and later

★ The police headquarters in Pretoria.

they tied him up with his hands outstretched, as if he was on a cross. At night there was a terrible heat above his head; sweat poured down and blocked his ears so that he could not hear what they were saying. 'I would thirst and ask for water. . . . After many pleas for water they would give me a drop and then withdraw the mug from my mouth.' After three days, this old man was prepared to say anything they wanted him to, but he still had the incredible courage to refuse to sign a statement.

I felt these accounts of torture to be of such importance that I sent them to Alison in England so that she could try and get them published. The whole transaction was very near the edge, legally, and I was seriously pressed about it at my own trial. It would have been much more difficult for me if Carlson had not already left the country on an English passport (his South African one having been impounded) before I was brought to trial. We had in fact light-heartedly agreed that if one was arrested, the other had better get out and I was thankful when he did so, though of course my dealings with him were only a minor part of the work which made Carlson so unpopular with the Security Police.

There were other personal activities which had nothing to do with giving money or legal aid, and it was one of these which first gave me positive proof that my telephone was being bugged. A priest whom I had heard of, but never met, rang me up from the Free State to ask my help. A Coloured child had just been born to an African mother and a European father in his parish. Of course this meant that they had both committed an offence under the Immorality Act, and the priest was anxious to get the baby adopted before its mixed parentage was discovered. I pointed out that it was extremely dangerous to discuss this kind of thing over the telephone and asked him to come up and see me. In the meantime I did manage to find a home for the child in a Coloured family through one of our Coloured priests. Next day the Security Police called on the priest in the Free State and their first question to him was, 'What have you got to do with this man ffrench-Beytagh?' They were not in the least interested in the immorality case – that was a matter for the uniformed branch, who did subsequently see me about it, though they apparently decided not to prosecute. It was obvious from this that my telephone was being tapped, and we also knew that informers came to the Friday-night gatherings at the deanery and to the cathedral services. Letters were always being held up, and the police admitted at my trial that they had bugged both my office and my flat, as well as opening my mail.

Another area of personal, though reluctant, political activity came from my involvement with Ken Jordaan. For a long time it was a purely pastoral relationship. Ken Jordaan, like myself, had had a rather chequered career and not much formal education. He had moved around frequently from town to town and job to job and there were chronic family crises. His wife Sjoukje, who was several years older than him, was a very stable person who stuck to him and their children through every upheaval.

I first came to know the Jordaans when they were commended to me as church-people who were arriving from Bloemfontein to make a new start in Johannesburg. Ken joined a big tea company and by sheer hard work he did extremely well, eventually becoming sales manager, or something of the kind. He was a ruthless character, very strong-willed in some ways, though terribly weak in others, and he had a force and an obstinacy that could override a great many difficulties.

It soon became clear that the Jordaans were amongst the liberals in the cathedral congregation. I think this was much more due to Sjoukje's influence than to Ken himself, but he certainly joined in with her. Even in his job with the tea company he took particular trouble in his sales promotions with his African clients, and was acceptable to them. They also had Africans into their flat for study groups and so forth, although they were not particularly active politically.

Ken was a practising Anglican of the Catholic type, although I think he had been brought up as a Roman Catholic. He became a server at Mass and, because his position allowed him to get to work at a reasonable time, he used to serve regularly on a weekday. He was never popular with the other servers because he was an arrogant man, and could not stand the kind of sloppiness and lack of obligation which sometimes occurs amongst a group of altar-servers, but he was faithful and did his duties, as far as I can remember, without any failure at all. Apart from this, he did not take a prominent part in the cathedral life. He never became a member of the church council and I cannot remember him making speeches at vestry meetings or anything like that.

In 1967, or thereabouts, Ken came to see me about what he believed to be a vocation for the priesthood. I then got to know him rather better as I had to have several interviews with him to try and understand his spiritual life and assess whether his vocation was genuine. It was an astonishing story, rather like my own, of a man who had come out of considerable difficulty and darkness into the Christian faith and then fairly suddenly felt the call to the priesthood. After I had done my best to satisfy myself about him, I passed his application forward to the bishop together with a *curriculum vitae* which I asked Ken to write out. He did not give a full account of his background when he did this, and I had to point out one or two omissions to him which he duly rectified. They didn't cover anything very serious and he would have done better to have put them in from the beginning, because the contrast between the darkness of his past and the obvious courage with which he was overcoming his difficulties could only have been of credit to him. Quite naturally he was anxious to make a good impression, and didn't realize an even better impression would have been created had he been completely honest in his statement to the bishop. However the bishop did see him and agreed tentatively that Ken should go to a selection conference. This is an annual affair when several senior priests and laymen get together for a whole weekend with those who are offering themselves for ordination to try and decide whether or not they are acceptable candidates. Ken was scheduled to attend the next conference which took place while I was in England on leave in 1968 so I never got the whole story. All I know for certain is that Ken rang up St Benedict's House, where the selection conference was taking place, on the morning that it began, and said that he had changed his mind and would not be coming as a candidate. I never got to the bottom of why he changed his mind so suddenly but I am still convinced that at that time Kenneth Jordaan really had been seriously considering the priesthood as a vocation.

After I got back from England and heard about the abortive selection conference I hardly saw anything of Ken for some time. Then suddenly there was a dramatic change. He came one day to see me, by appointment as always, and he seemed to be almost a different person. He was phrenetically disturbed and angry about the inadequacy of the Church and its inability to affect national politics. He proclaimed that the country's apartheid policy was so thoroughly evil that it was clearly antichristian and that it must be changed as soon as it was possible to change it. He did not believe that the Church's policy of trying to change attitudes was good enough. He wanted action. The kind of action that he proposed appalled me. He suggested that one of the great men of South Africa was Tsafendas (a Greek who some years before had stabbed to death the then prime minister, Verwoerd, inside the House of Assembly in Cape Town). This, Ken said, was the only kind of action which was likely to liberate the black people of South Africa. He himself was a skilled scuba-diver and he made some wild suggestion that he could use this talent to place limpet mines on South African warships in Cape Town.

All this shocked me considerably, and I had to think how best to deal with it. It was a long interview, although I had not meant it to be so: clearly the man was so phrenetic that something needed to be done. It may well be said that I should have gone straight to the police and reported these things, but I was extremely fond of the Jordaan family, if not of Ken himself, and I did not fully believe that he had thought out these ideas rationally at all.

The line I took with him was that he was an Afrikaner and although there were very few Afrikaners who were liberals there were eminent exceptions. These men, people like Beyers Naudé and Fred Van Wyk, were of enormous value just because they came from an Afrikaner background, and I suggested that Ken could play the same role. This was nowhere near good enough for Ken. He said that like the rest of the Christian Church these men were much too pacific in the way they handled things.

My next suggestion to Ken was that he should use his Afrikaner nationality to infiltrate the Nationalist party, if he could. There were already one or two Nationalist members of parliament who had helped us with such things as the re-classification of people from Coloured to European status, and getting housing permits, and so forth. To have another member of the Nationalist party who could help us in things like that would be invaluable. Also I suggested to him that if one was ever to topple the government one must learn where the power really lay. (I had learnt this at the Urban Training Centre in Chicago.) Power normally lies where the money is and if we could find out where the money came from for the Nationalist party propaganda and its political organization, we might be able to bring pressure to bear in some way on those who supported it financially. I suggested to him that work along these lines might be much more effective in the long run than going about shooting people, or sabotaging ships, neither of which in my opinion comes within the scope of what is permitted to a Christian, except under the conditions of a just war or revolution.

Quite surprisingly quickly Ken Jordaan got hold of this idea, which seemed to appeal to him. Almost before I knew where I was he had joined the Nationalist party, and within a few months had become quite prominent in one of the local branches. I knew that he was a good businessman and a competent organizer, but I was astonished at the rapidity of his rise to a branch-secretaryship in a small district of Johannesburg. (Of course the reason for this becomes very clear as I look back from this side of the trial and know that he was at that time a member of the Security Police, who can bring great pressure to bear within the Nationalist party at almost any level, and certainly at the level of a minor branch.)

This achievement did not satisfy Ken at all. He said that if he was to be really effective in infiltrating the whole apartheid set-up he must infiltrate into its heart. This he believed to be the Security Police, and he may well have been right. This idea frightened me almost more than anything he had said before. When he talked wildly of shooting prime ministers and sabotaging ships it was all so far away as to be quite out of the question; when he talked about the Security Police who were round us all the time, his ideas became much nearer reality and scared me very considerably. I wanted no possible involvement with the Security Police. I had learnt a good deal about them and their activities from Joel Carlson and various political prisoners. I believed, and still do believe, that they are an extremely efficient and well-informed body, and I did not think it possible for anybody, even an Afrikaner like Ken, to infiltrate them. They themselves are so used to infiltrating organizations that they must be well aware of all the possible techniques and I believed it would be not only highly dangerous but completely impossible to do so.

In an effort to convince Ken that I was not just a gas-bag, and that it would be dangerous for me as well as for him if he got into trouble with the police, I told him something of the work that I was doing with Alison's money, but it did not make much difference. He persisted in trying to get to know the Security Police socially and succeeded in having drinks with them in their own canteen, playing snooker with them, and so on. I could not understand it at all, although of course I can now. His talk got more and more provocative and my association with him became something of a nightmare. I tried to give him innocuous things to do such as finding out the figures for the immigration of artisans into the country, the source of Nationalist funds, and similar information, but he complained of being more and more frustrated at not being given something 'active' to do. (Later it became apparent that he was convinced that both Alison and I were members of some revolutionary organization and was naturally frustrated at not being able to get in on it. But since I never knew that this was what he thought, it never occurred to me to assure him that he was mistaken.)

Ken's general style is best conveyed by quoting part of a letter which he wrote to me in May 1970 when I was on leave in England:

Now will somebody please tell me why? Why do I have to be an exemplary Nat.? What do we hope to achieve thereby? And since all these things which I have done and achieved have been at your behest – then why am I not given support? You will see from the enclosed press cuttings that the ruthlessness of Nat. rule does not diminish. We have now reached the stage where it is not permitted to even peacefully protest the collapse of the rule of law. And in all these circumstances, London, in their ineffable wisdom say that 'In view of the Portuguese situation' they are unable to help – shades of Munich. It wouldn't surprise me if the guy's name is Chamberlain. I certainly feel prompted to take up your suggestion and come to London, if only to tell those buggers what I think! However, I would point out that I would not come cap-in-hand. There are also American and Russian (for that matter) embassies in London. I will go into the matter and let you know what (if anything) I can wangle. In the meantime please tell those flipping Englishmen that my attitude is a simple one – they sit in the comfortable safety of their island and utter pious platitudes, but it is us in South Africa who fight.

In fact, as he admitted at the trial, Ken never did succeed in provoking me into doing or saying anything illegal, but he did induce me to take part in one bit of deception which I now very much regret. It was obviously a shock to some of the more liberally minded members of the cathedral congregation when he suddenly switched from being liberal to joining the Nationalists and so I helped him concoct a letter to the parish magazine which said that although his political convictions had changed completely he still intended to remain a member of the Anglican communion. This was certainly being an accessory to a lie and I regret my part in it.

I shall never understand Ken but I cannot bring myself to hate him, and I am sorry that he has made such a mess of things, and brought so much suffering on his wife and children. I am certain that his original conversion from a rather sticky past to practising Christianity and candidacy for the priesthood was perfectly genuine and I do not know what happened to make him switch to joining the Security Police and acting as an *agent provocateur*. Possibly he was pressurized because of his Afrikaner background into making the first step and then thought he might as well go the whole hog. He was never a personal friend whom I met for a drink or a casual conversation. Our meetings were in the office by appointment and were always rather formal, so I do not have the sense of being betrayed which I might otherwise have felt. I can only hope that this episode will not have destroyed him completely and that he will find a way back to a life which he can lead with some sense of integrity and fulfilment.

CHAPTER SEVEN

Arrested

One of the perks of being a clergyman of the Church of South Africa is that every five years you get six months leave on half-pay. In 1970 my long leave came round, and I went to England. I was always most thankful to get away from South Africa and its tensions, but equally, towards the end of my leave, I was tremendously anxious to get back to work, to the cathedral, which I loved, and to my friends in Johannesburg. This desire to get back was also tinged with a good deal of anxiety – mostly connected with whether or not I would be allowed back into the country. I had reason to believe that the Security Police were, to put it at its mildest, interested in me, because I knew of the tap on my telephone and suspected with a good deal of reason that some of my mail was being opened. Also I was never quite certain whether or not what I was doing for prisoners and their dependants was legal. There had been times when people had arrived in Johannesburg and been put straight on a plane back to London, and I always feared that this might happen, so the few days before I left and the journey itself were pretty anxious times. However, I did get back perfectly safely, very well rested and glad to be home, at the end of September 1970.

In almost no time at all I had settled down in the secure framework of my rule, my friends, and the life of the cathedral. The work for political prisoners had gone on admirably in my absence. I had signed one or two cheques while I was in England and sent them back so that money was available, and John Turnbull and Jean Webb had continued their work as almoners of the fund without any hindrance at all. There were always, of course, one or two people of whom they were slightly suspicious. It was never possible to do this work with complete confidence and knowledge that everything was safe, but there had been no particular alarms and we were all glad to be back in the usual routine.

One action on my part may have done something towards precipitating trouble. In November I took part in a provincial synod which debated the grants made by the World Council of Churches to various African organizations which were engaged in guerrilla warfare and other activities in different parts of Africa. These grants were not very substantial in terms of international finance, and the WCC had specifically said that they were not to be used for guerrilla warfare itself but to help those whose lives were being affected by the struggle for African freedom. They were supposed to be used for the support of the children and widows of men who had died in the fighting, medical assistance, resettlement of land gained from the Portuguese in fighting, setting up schools, and similar activities. Obviously, the organizations concerned could use the grants for military purposes, whatever the WCC said, but I felt that it was not fair to assume that this would happen. The white South African people as a whole did not agree. The grants were condemned on all sides because they were said to be in direct support of military action against the white régime of South Africa, and one after the other, the ruling bodies of the South African Churches agreed to withhold their subscriptions to the WCC because of this issue.

When the question of the Anglican contribution was raised at this provincial synod, I felt very strongly that we should continue our membership and pay our subscription as we had done for many years. Talking about it during the recesses before the motion came up, I found that Senator Edgar Brooks agreed with me. Edgar Brooks is a great man; he was a member of the South African senate for many years and still takes an active interest in politics as well as being a prominent Anglican layman and a scholar of some repute. We decided together to oppose the motion to withhold the Anglican contribution to the WCC, or at least suggest that the motion should be amended so that the contribution could still be paid, even if the Church expressed its uneasiness about the possibility of the money being used for military purposes.

Edgar Brooks, as usual, made a magnificent speech, which was not only reasonable, but forceful and passionate as well. I found it difficult to follow because he had made all the main points. The result was that my own speech was a rather impassioned but not very compelling call to the synod to be aware of the violence amongst which it lived and asking it to refuse to follow the lead of the other Churches in trying to wash its hands of any contact with violence. I did not know at the time that part of this speech was being televised by the BBC and was later to be screened several times, sometimes rather cut and out of context. When it came to the vote, only two others supported Edgar Brooks and myself in opposing a proposition which not only condemned the WCC's action but refused to renew the synod's subscription to it. I imagine that this incident and the resulting publicity may well have been the last straw as far as the right-wing terrorist organizations and the Security Police were concerned.

I suppose that the first indication that things were going to change was the destruction of my car. I was living at the time at the deanery in Houghton which is one of the rather richer suburbs of Johannesburg. It was a double-storey brick house with a very pleasant garden and a brick garage in which the car was kept. The garage door was hung on a runner and had to be pulled from the side of the garage around to the front and then bolted from the inside. One evening when I came home from work I found that this door was off its runners, but with some help from one of the servants I managed to get it back and the garage was locked as usual. On the next day the same thing happened and this time it was fairly late. I couldn't get the door back on to its runners by myself and there seemed to be no particular point in calling anybody out of bed – so that night the garage remained open, and nothing happened. Very stupidly, I forgot to get it seen to the next day, and again had to leave it open the following night.

At about half past two in the morning I heard a very loud banging on the french windows which open on to the garden at the back of the house. This not only woke me but also Mr and Mrs Maasch, who also lived there, and we all rather floundered around as one does when one is first woken from a deep sleep. We couldn't at first find the key to open the glass door where one of the neighbours in his pyjamas was gesticulating wildly outside and shouting something we couldn't hear. When we finally let him in he told us that there was a fire in the garage, which lay between his house and ours, and he had already telephoned the fire-brigade.

All that could be seen when we rushed out was a real inferno of flame and black smoke. We saw it first through the side door of the garage, and it was clear that the whole back of the car was fiercely ablaze. Even if the fire-brigade had been there, the car would have been a write-off. By the time they arrived, the flames had reached the front of the car and burnt out the front seat and the dashboard. The engine seemed to be fairly intact. The fire-brigade put out the fire, pulled the car out into the road, made certain the garage was safe, and then left. By this time, of course, a crowd had gathered from neighbouring houses, and I tried to clarify just what had happened. At least two of the neighbours said they had heard three loud explosions which had woken them up. They had looked out to see what had happened and saw the garage doors open and the car ablaze. Why nobody living in the deanery heard these explosions I cannot say except that we were fast asleep. Without my suggesting anything of the kind, bombs were mentioned by the neighbours as being a possible cause of these explosions.

By the time all this was over, it was getting on for half past three in the morning. My usual rising time was soon after four, so there was no point in going back to bed. I was fortunate enough to be able to borrow a car from one of the neighbours, who possessed several cars, and I went off soon after four to the

CID at Hillbrow police-station to report the incident. I mentioned the possibility of bombs and sabotage, but the detective didn't seem very interested. He asked if I had any reason to suspect any particular person, to which I could only reply that I had had anonymous letters threatening me on various occasions over the past few years and suggest that a bomb might have come from the same source. Having made my report, I went off to church to say my prayers and Mass as usual, and then went home for breakfast. During the day, various police people arrived, including some fairly senior men. They didn't take the trouble to come and talk with me or anybody from the house at all, but we did go out and try to find out what they thought. It became clear by the end of the day that they had decided the fire had been caused by some sort of electrical fault and the 'bombs' had been the two back tyres and the rear window of the car exploding.

I am in no way an expert on this sort of thing, but I find it difficult to understand why an electrical fault should start at the rear of the car rather than at the front. What I do know is that the assessor from my insurance company must have reported that the car was maliciously damaged, because the company refused to insure me again. In the end, I had to persuade the company which dealt with all the diocesan insurance to take me on – and very reluctant they were to do so. The car which had been burnt was a very smart Citroen which I had coveted and saved up for over a number of years. I was paid out on the assessed value at the time of the fire and had to replace it with a small 'Beetle' Volkswagen, which I resented a good deal.

The incident of the car frightened me considerably. I realized how isolated the deanery was, since the gardens in the suburb were big and the houses were far apart. I was also very aware of the attacks which had been made on Joel Carlson and I no longer felt safe sleeping on the ground floor. Rightly or wrongly, I decided it was time I moved out, and I took a flat in one of the biggest blocks in Johannesburg. As it turned out, this was one of the most foolish things I could have done, since, unlike the deanery, the flat was often empty and it was easy for my enemies to plant the subversive leaflets on me which gave the Security Police their chance. But I do not think I could possibly have foreseen this at the time.

There were two more warnings of what was about to happen which did disturb me. Perhaps I did not take them as seriously as I ought to have, but in any case I do not think there was much I could have done. The first came from Jean Webb, one of the almoners for Alison Norman's money. She told me one day that her husband had been called into his manager's office and been warned from a source that the manager could not disclose that Jean should be discouraged from working for me because 'they are going to pounce on him in January'. I simply could not see why the Security Police, from whom this warning must have come, should tell me about their intentions, and I discounted it as an attempt to frighten me out of the country. I sent Jean off to see Raymond Tucker, my lawyer, so that he knew about the incident, and left it at that.

The second incident is rather more difficult to substantiate because I must protect the person who gave me the warning. He was an official in one of the banks in Johannesburg who came to me in a very distressed manner because the bank had had a confidential query from a state department about any accounts which were held in my name in any bank in South Africa. The official concerned was of course required not to disclose such information, but because he was a personal friend of mine, and a Christian, he felt that he must tell me. I was grateful for the information because it was quite clear that things were beginning to close in, but again I was not prepared to be frightened out of the country. It was simply a question then of waiting and wondering what was going to happen. I did not have long to wait.

On Monday 18 January I had to go to the annual archdeacons' residential conference to make plans with other senior clergy in the diocese for the coming year. It was well known that this conference took place every year and the dates of my absence were always published in the parish leaflets on the Sunday before, so anybody could have known that I would be out of my flat for these three days. The conference finished with lunch on the Wednesday, and as soon as it was over I went back to my flat, but only to drop in my bag with my clothes and dash straight off to the office. I was dressed as I had been for the archdeacons' conference in corduroy pants and open-necked shirt. (January a hot month and if you are spending long days talking it is best to be as easy and informal as you can be.)

I was expecting guests in the evening and wanted to go off to the office to clean up the work of the last couple of days which I knew would be waiting for me and to get back before they arrived.

I finally got back to the block of flats at about half past four, which is the normal time for offices to close in Johannesburg. I would have expected there to have been a number of people about at that time, but the place seemed deserted. Just as I pressed the button for the lift door to close three or four noticeably large men got into the lift with me. Quite where they emerged from I don't know, but I presume they must have been lurking around the garage and somebody must have seen me approach and given a warning. I remember noticing that none of them pressed the lift button as they would have done if they had been going to different floors, but even then I did not register anything except mild curiosity. When we got to the fifth floor, on which I lived, these men all got out with me, and as I turned to walk along the passage to my flat, they followed. As I got to the flat door, one of them turned to me, and without asking my name or identity said, 'We are police officers.' As far as I can remember, that was all he said. I asked if they wanted to see me, and when they said they did, I opened the door and asked them to come in.

The smallest and oldest of them, whom I subsequently found was Colonel Greyling, handed me a paper and said, 'We have a warrant here to search your person and your premises.' I can only assume that this was in fact what the warrant said – I was too shocked to read it properly. Once I had handed it back he started to search my person. I did not have to take off any clothes, but he felt me all over pretty thoroughly and accurately, which I found a rather degrading procedure (but then I don't like tailors measuring me for the length of my trousers either). He took everything out of my pockets, including my rather bulky diary, which contained my daily intercession list and a whole lot of other things. (Luckily, only two or three weeks before, I had torn out of this diary all the English engagements I had undertaken. It was a looseleaf book and I had just got around to putting in the new year's refill. I was very thankful about this later.) Then they started to search my flat.

They insisted on searching my bedroom first. As it happened, I had chosen for my bedroom the small back room and kept the main, double room, for guests. I took them into the bedroom where I myself slept, and I honestly believe that they were expecting to find something there. They took immense trouble with the one cupboard which was in the room. This was a big, built-in cupboard which had a cavity between it and the wall. On this cavity they spent a great deal of time. One of the policemen climbed up and shone a torch right down into the hole. They also reached right down into it, and seemed disappointed that there was nothing there. The rest of the search in my room seemed curiously disinterested. They did take all the bedclothes off the bed, but they only fiddled in the drawers without emptying them, and although they turned up the sides of the carpet they did not look in the centre.

Then we moved into the big front bedroom and here again they immediately went to the cupboard (though being a spare room there was very little else to search except the dressing-table and two beds). The left-hand side of the cupboard, which they searched first, simply had odds and ends hanging in it and a box which some of my stereo equipment had come in. The right-hand side had a top section for suitcases and similar items in which was a big, empty cardboard box, which I had used when I moved to pack things in. From behind this they produced another box, about the size of a shoe-box and coloured with a blue, wavy pattern. As soon as this was brought down to eye-level and they could see what was in it, there was great excitement amongst the police. One of them said something about 'another Blaxall', referring to an old Anglican priest who had been sentenced several years previously for some kind of treasonable activity. I got up to see what the excitement was about, because it was quite clear that they had found something which they regarded as being very, very important, and I had a quite definite impression that they had expected to find it.

As soon as I could see what was in the box, I recognized anti-government leaflets of a kind I had seen reproduced in newspapers which had been sent to me from New York. Some had been published by the African National Congress and some by the Communist party – and they were quite clearly dynamite.

Once they had discovered these pamphlets, I realized that the whole thing was extremely serious. Until then, although I had felt a considerable degree of shock, I had also felt rather thankful that things were at last coming to a head. In some ways I was almost flattered at getting all this attention from the Security Police, and I felt myself completely safe, knowing that I had nothing of any moment at all in my flat. As soon as these leaflets were found, however, the whole atmosphere changed completely. I was warned by Colonel Greyling that anything I said could be used in evidence against me, and one of the men was sent to use my telephone, evidently to ask for reinforcements. They must have been pretty well prepared to come, for I think it was only a quarter of an hour or so before another posse of Security Police arrived, led this time by Colonel Coetzee. He is a very notorious character, much younger than Colonel Greyling, but he was clearly in charge as soon as he got there.

I cannot remember any more searching of the main bedroom. I suppose they must have done, but I was much too shocked and shaken to worry about that. The next thing that I remember with any clearness is sitting at my own desk in the living-room while the search there went on. There was of course by now a much bigger party searching and they took a great deal of time. They went through every book on my shelves, for instance, and took away some of them. One was *The Foolishness of God* by J. A. Baker, an Oxford don – which perhaps they took because I had been so impressed by it that I had underlined it a great deal, but perhaps because in their curious, twisted way they may have thought it was some sort of anti-God book. They also took a book of photographs of Rodin's sculptures which Alison Norman had given me for Christmas a couple of years before. Colonel Coetzee told me that they were taking it because of Alison's signature on the flyleaf, so I realized then that the whole question of Alison and her money was going to be raised.

By this time it was 6 p.m. or later and I asked if I could have my usual 'sundowner'. They agreed, and I poured myself one of the biggest brandies I have ever had in my life. I did not offer a drink to any of them. When I wanted a second one, I was not allowed to have it, so I was very glad that I had made the first as strong as I had.

They took away all my very carefully prepared Lent course which I had been working on in the early part of January, and a lot of other sermons and notes, including a sermon prepared for the coming Sunday. I told them they were taking my sermon for Sunday and they said, 'You won't be needing that anyway.' Then I was told by Colonel Coetzee to put one or two things together in a bag, because they would be taking me away. The impression I got was that I might be kept overnight in prison, but certainly no more. I did not even realize that I was being formally detained – only that they wanted me for questioning. I was worried about the guests I was expecting and I asked if I might leave a note for them on the door referring them to Laura Clayton, my secretary. They let me write the note, but I found it was never pinned to the door. Presumably they just wanted to ease me out with as little trouble and fuss as possible.

When they had finished their search and collected all the things they wanted to take away, they took me down to the cathedral offices – making quite sure that no one saw me on the way. By this time it was getting dark. A further contingent of searchers arrived, making about sixteen or seventeen in all. In this new group there was a man whom I instinctively feared. He was a very good-looking, blond young man who could have played one of Hitler's officers extremely well. He never smiled at all, and I remember thinking to myself, 'Well, I hope I don't have anything much more to do with him.' He turned out to be one of my chief interrogators.

They had been searching these offices for a long time, when one of my expected guests, not finding me at home, came down to the parish office to see what had happened. He knocked on the door, which was just slightly opened by a Security Policeman, and was told that he could not come in. He naturally went to Laura Clayton, my secretary, who lived upstairs, and explained to her that there was something very funny going on in the offices. She came down, but could not get in until the police realized that they needed her to get the keys to the files. Later, she got permission to go upstairs, where there was no phone, and fetch me a cup of coffee and a couple of buns, because of course I had had no food since lunch-time. It was just as well, since I got no other food that evening.

This great posse of policemen searched the offices for a long time. They took away dozens and dozens of files, and went through almost every file, paper by paper, but it was surprising what a lot they missed. What they did not realize was that all the records of the money I was dispensing were kept in a different office along the passage where Jean Webb worked, so they were looking in entirely the wrong place if that was what they were after. I think this puzzled them a good deal, but as they never asked me where these papers were, I naturally did not offer to tell them. (Later, in prison, they did ask me and I sent a note along to John Turnbull asking him to hand them over. He did then give them all the original receipts and so forth, but managed to hold on to the index cards on which all the information was summarized. The result was that we were able to go on helping people almost without a break.)

Once more there was a long receipt to be signed for all the files which they took away. Then I was taken off to John Vorster Square, the police headquarters. The move was done with considerable secrecy. The stairs were cleared by men going down first, and a police car was parked immediately outside the side entrance of the office-block. I was in the back seat with Colonel Greyling and whisked off almost before I knew what had happened.

At John Vorster Square, I was taken to the security floor. The ordinary lifts do not go there at all – there is a special one, controlled from outside, which takes you straight up the centre of the building and into the Security Police section. There you have to pass through an electronically operated door controlled by a man on duty. It really does seem to be secure.

There was a long conference, during which I was left in a room with a series of young security men to guard me. They changed every twenty minutes or so, and I just sat in silence for what seemed like a couple of hours. Possibly the conference was about whether or not they were going to hold me. Certainly the man who was officially in charge of the whole investigation – Colonel Botha – was there. I could hear them having cups of tea or coffee, but I had nothing at all.

While I was sitting waiting, I was wondering what on earth was going to happen, not so much to me (I had done most of the thinking about that in my first fears in the flat), but as far as the parish was concerned. Would Laura be able to fix up the Masses for the morning? And had she been able to get hold of the bishop? It was only afterwards that I learnt of the great many things that had happened as soon as I left Darragh House – how Laura had got hold of the bishop, the various newspapers and the clergy, and how they had all rallied together in the most extra-ordinary way that night. Before midnight, the whole town, indeed people all over the country, were aware of what had happened. They had a Mass at the cathedral late that night, with I don't know how many people present, who collected most miraculously out of nowhere. Already a great wave of prayer and love from so many people had begun to roll. Next day, churches of many different denominations tolled their bells for ten minutes at midday, and later there was one of the biggest protest meetings that has ever been held in Johannesburg. It was a most magnificent example of how a danger brings people together – from every faith or none at all, and from all parts of the world.

Of all this, of course, I knew nothing at all. I just sat and waited. At last the conference was over, and I was taken away to the cells by a couple of policemen. These were in a different block from the police headquarters, so I was taken down outside the building, through some back corridors and in through the main charge office. Behind this there was a short passage, a steel grille and gate, some stairs, yet another steel grille and gate, and finally another reception office. I imagine that this one dealt with people who were going to the cells, whereas people who were not being detained were charged downstairs. Here I was divested of everything I possessed except my clothes. (Incidentally, in my flat I had asked Colonel Coetzee if I would be allowed to smoke and he had said, 'Oh, yes, of course you will have cigarettes', but clearly this had been sheer bluff to keep me quiet.) My cigarettes were taken off me, but so was everything else – money, washing gear, medicines, pills, the lot. I was left simply with the underclothes, shirt, trousers, shoes and socks in which I stood up. They took my belt, of course, but as I haven't got a waist anyway, my trousers still stayed up.

The Security Police were clearly handing me over to the ordinary uniformed branch who were in charge of the cells, but it was also clear that the uniformed police were subject to the Security Police and did exactly what they were told. The uniformed policeman who took my clothes and gave me a receipt for them was quite a pleasant English-speaking man – an unexpected person to find in such a place. It was only when I got the receipt that I realized I was being detained under the Terrorism Act, because it was headed '*Wet Op Terrorisme*' (Act of Terrorism). That again gave me a very considerable shock.

When all this was completed, there was a further handing over of keys and I set off, escorted by police and Security Police, on the last lap to my cell. There was a further set of iron grilles, more stairs, and, after a sharp bend, a long corridor – about thirty or forty yards, which stretched in front of me. On each side were cell doors, each with an individual number and a peephole. A few doors were labelled with such signs as 'Immigration – Immigrasie', so I suppose that illegal immigrants were held and investigated there. The passage seemed like one of those long disappearing corridors that one sees sometimes at the beginning of a television mystery show – for ever receding. At the end I could see two rather forbidding yellow doors and it was to one of these that I was taken. As I approached it, with its single ominous eye of a peephole, I glimpsed the number, 211. Then I was thrust through the door and the grille inside and left alone in the darkness on the damp concrete floor. (It was only damp because it had just been scrubbed, but at the time it felt clammy and forbidding.) A little light filtered through the windows and I could see the cell walls well enough to make my way around, and finally, when I had said some rather distracted prayers, to bed.

CHAPTER EIGHT

Prisoner under interrogation

On that first night, a policeman came in every hour or so and switched on the light until I was fully awake, and then put it out again. Why, I don't know, except to see that I did not get a good night's sleep.

When it was morning, and I could look around, I found that the cell was a largish concrete box, about seventeen feet square, and in it was simply a lavatory pan, an iron bedstead with a mattress and blankets, and two concrete blocks – one of which could act as a table and the other as a seat, though they were both on the same level. There was a big iron grille against the door so that the warder had to open the cell door first and then the inner steel guard, presumably in case the prisoner tried to attack. There was absolutely nothing else at all.

Early that morning (and every morning afterwards) I stood in front of a piece of wall between the two barred and grilled high windows, which was the nearest thing to a cross that I could find in the cell. I faced it as I would an altar and said what I could remember of the Mass. Later when I had my Office Book (a book of Common Prayer, with the daily Bible lessons for matins and evensong), I could read part of an Epistle or Gospel as well, but from the first morning I said the Creed, and prayed generally where the Prayer for Church comes, and made a short confession; then I said the *Sanctus* by heart and made a spiritual communion. This is something I have never really experienced before, though I have read about it and advised people to do it. But I can say with complete certainty that the communion that I received then was as real as any communion that I have ever received sacramentally. I find this a bit difficult as I have been a sacramentalist all my life; I believe wholly in the real presence of our Lord, his Body and his Blood, by the means of bread and wine, and I was not making any attempt to use bread or wine in prison. It was a purely spiritual communion, but I believe it to have been an absolutely valid one.

At breakfast-time a policeman walked in silently with two pieces of dry bread, a hard-boiled egg, and a cup of horribly sweet coffee. Then I was left again until midday when another policeman came in with coffee, two more bits of bread, and two very tiny bits of skinny, fatty, bony meat which looked as if it was meant for dogs. There was no water in the cell, and if I wanted some to drink I had to shout for it. Sometimes I got it and sometimes I did not.

After breakfast and doing my usual intercessions I just sat on the bed, waiting and wondering. It is hard to describe the emptiness of having absolutely *nothing* to do. I did manage to find some bristles on the floor which looked as if they had come out of a broom, and plaited a small mat with them. It was only about two by three inches, but it took quite a long time getting it exactly right. (I put it into my Office Book as a marker later on, and they did not take it when I left, so I shall keep it for the rest of my life as a reminder of that time in solitary confinement.)

Some time in the afternoon, the cell door opened, and there walked in a senior uniformed man with gold braid on his cap and two men whom he introduced to me as doctors. They were Professor Rose, the professor of forensic medicine at the university, and the senior district surgeon of Johannesburg. Apparently what had happened was that Richard Llewellin, the senior curate at the cathedral, had very sensibly got hold of my own doctor, Dr Miller, and he had made some representations about the state of my health to the powers that be. So the doctors were sent to see how true this all was and what was necessary for me. The policeman also had with him my Office Book. He referred to it as my Bible and said the bishop had sent it in, and I was to be allowed to use it, and for this I was extremely grateful. Here again I gather Richard Llewellin had got permission for its use.

When the doctors started to talk to me about my health I suddenly found myself weeping: whether this was through self-pity, or just over-nervousness, I don't know. I strongly suspect that the coffee had been drugged, otherwise I cannot imagine why I should have been so emotional. The doctors treated me with extreme kindness and took a good deal of trouble with my blood pressure and the general state of my health. They immediately prescribed medicines for me, having learned from Dr Miller the prescriptions I was on, and they tried to alter my diet. From then on I no longer had dry bread, but I imagine there is no real provision for special diets under these conditions and what happened after this was that meals were sent up to me from the police canteen. They were pretty unsuitable meals, consisting largely of eggs, which I am not supposed to have, and I was only allowed a spoon with which to eat them, but certainly my conditions from that time on were a great deal better. The doctors also allowed me to have four cigarettes a day, although I was not allowed to have any matches, so I was completely dependent on a policeman coming in to get a light.

It was a tremendous help to have my Office Book and to be able to keep to my ordinary rule of saying matins and evensong every day, as well as to use it for my act of spiritual communion. Also, of course, I did my usual intercessions every day.

I have always said to people when they are feeling 'down' about their religion that if they can only go through the motions and do the things that their rule obliges them to, they will come out all right. This was my experience at this time – not because I had any conscious feeling of the presence of God, but because, by doing what the rest of the Church was doing, I was joining in something much bigger than myself. Underlying my panics and weeping-fits and fear, there was a sense of immense strength upholding me, and surrounding me like a wall. Later, of course, I found that Christians all over the world, including many religious communities, had been praying for me. I did not know this at the time, but I did feel quite certainly that I was surrounded and protected by a wall of prayer.

About the middle of Friday, the cell door opened again, this time with a Security Policeman there also, and I was told that I was 'wanted'. What I was wanted for, I had no idea. By this time, since I was not allowed to shave, wash, brush my hair, or clean my teeth, and had to eat with my fingers, I was in a pretty filthy state. They took me down the steel stairs and up on to the inter-rogation floor, where I had been on Wednesday evening. (I always had what was perhaps a not entirely irrational fear of walking down these stairs in front of the two Security Police who always accompanied me. I believed, in common with a great many others, that when the Iman Haroun fell down some similar stairs to his death in a Cape police-station, he was, in fact, pushed, and I felt very strongly that the same thing might quite easily happen to me. It never did – but this shows the state of fear into which one gets.)

After a wait, I was taken into an office where Colonel Botha sat behind the desk and Colonel Greyling sat on one side of it. There was a fourth man in the room, whose face was slightly familiar, and whom in my muddled state of mind I couldn't place until he was introduced to me as the British consul, Cecil Smith. I was overwhelmed with relief at seeing him. He asked if he might be allowed to interview me alone but this was refused and so we had to have our interview with the two security men present.

My one great anxiety was that people outside might not know that the communist leaflets found in my flat had been planted on me, and, without any questions being asked or any further introduction, I immediately started to tell Cecil Smith he must make it known to the public that I was completely innocent of this charge. I was so emotional in trying to convey the urgent importance of people knowing that I was not guilty of this charge that again I felt myself all choky and weepy as I had done in the presence of the doctors. Cecil Smith seemed rather astonished at hearing anything about leaflets, and the police then told me, in front of him, that no news had been given to the newspapers at all about the reasons for my detention; I was the first person to mention these leaflets, and if any publicity arose it was my fault and not theirs. I, of course, had presumed that if there was any knowledge of my detention, the reasons for it would have been published and I was so anxious that people should not believe this of me.

Cecil Smith immediately started to make requests for the betterment of my condition in prison, and he had brought with him several packets of cigarettes and some books for me to read. I explained to him that I was not allowed to have books and that my cigarettes were rationed to four a day. I told him that what I was much more in need of was my toothbrush and my razor, and to be allowed to wash and have some clean things to wear. Smith then made requests along these lines for me to Colonel Botha, who was ostensibly in charge. It was very noticeable that at each request Colonel Botha looked over to Greyling, who either nodded or shook his head as the case might be, but they both claimed ignorance of the conditions under which I was being detained. I do not believe they were in the least ignorant, but the act was played through to the full. The uniformed policeman in charge of the prison, who had the previous day been in to see me with the doctors, was summoned, and had to stand at attention in front of the desk while Botha enquired whether it was true that I had not been allowed to wash, shave, brush my teeth, have full access to drinking water, etc. Instructions were given that I should be allowed these facilities, and indeed have my clothes washed, but how this last was to be done was not made at all clear. (In the event, on about the day before I was released, some of my clothes were washed by a Chinese prisoner on the instructions of the policeman in charge.)

In the course of this interview, Smith did manage to convey to me (probably without giving a great deal of pleasure to the Security Police) that my detention had made world headlines. This did bring me a very great sense of relief – not only at the knowledge that the British authorities were taking trouble on my behalf (as they continued to do throughout the whole trial), but also because thousands of people were aware of what was happening to me. I was certainly not alone and hidden away in some obscure hole where I could easily be forgotten. (This again was another of the irrational fears that had been haunting me.)

The visit must have lasted about twenty minutes, and when the British consul had gone Colonel Botha said that I could either make a statement about what I had been doing, or I could sit and answer the questions which they wanted answered. I explained to him that I had no idea what the Security Police were after, so there was no point in making a statement and I would much prefer to answer their questions. I was immediately taken away to another room, which I was to get to know very well during the next few days. The whole interrogation took place here and it started within a few minutes of the British consul's departure. I had no idea what to expect; I had heard so much of people having to stand on bricks and other kinds of torture, so I was pleasantly surprised when I was told to sit down. I was warned that I was under oath (although I did not have to swear an oath) and immediately Natie van Rensburg started to ask his questions. He sat in front of me and wrote in longhand on foolscap paper, and on either side of him sat Robbie Bouwer and Dick Visser.

Visser was the one whom I had found so intimidating when they were searching my office, because of his silence and apparent arrogance. He was a very tall, extremely handsome young man who combined the look of a Nazi officer with that of a British public schoolboy. When I got to know him, he was not as frightening as all that and seemed quite a simple single-minded sort of man. For example, during one of the 'soft-sell' periods, when Visser was the only person left with me, he talked about his house in the southern suburbs (the poorer area of Johannesburg) and about his children, and then got extraordinarily angry with me because on his way to work every day he passed a lot of advertisement hoardings and not one of them was in Afrikaans – they were all in English. I answered that I supposed most of the buying public in Johannesburg was English so this seemed sensible, but that didn't help at all. He just went on frothing at the mouth because there was not an equal distribution of the two languages (as there would have been, of course, if they had been official notices).

Van Rensburg led the questioning and wrote down the answers in longhand – a time-consuming business. He was a dark little man with a moustache – apparently in his late thirties or early forties – and rather sardonic-looking. He was said to have been one of the men who had followed me in England and I was asked if I recognized him. Of course I didn't, since I had not realized in England that anyone was following me. Van Rensburg was also a family man. When they started to question me on the Friday night, because the British consul's visit had induced them to hurry things up, he had to cancel a date with his wife and said, 'This is the sort of thing that happens to us policemen.' His English was very good, but of course the interrogators spoke Afrikaans amongst themselves and talked too fast for me to catch much of it.

Bouwer was a pleasant-looking, middle-aged chap. He again was a family man and a churchman. He had undergone a partial gastrectomy for an ulcer and proudly pulled up his shirt to show me the scar during one of the breaks. But when they got into one of their vicious shouting rages, he was in some ways the worst of the three.

Apart from these three main interrogators, others came in from time to time. One was called Dircker – a huge fellow, one of the biggest men I have ever seen. I used to think of him as the 'heavy comic', in so far as I was capable of seeing anything as comic at the time, because he used to bring in papers from the office where they were investigating my files and do an act with them. For instance, in one of her letters Alison Norman mentioned the work she was doing at LSE, and he wanted to know what LSE stood for. So I said 'London School of Economics', and this brought an absolute uproar because they considered the London School of Economics to be the centre of all communist work in England and presumably throughout the world.

In the same vein was an incident concerning John Lascelles, who had been a church-warden of the cathedral in Salisbury. His name cropped up in the correspondence that they were investigating, and Dircker came pounding in, waving a paper with his name on it, and demanding to know who he was. It happened that John, after leaving the Rhodesian Selection Trust, had gone to work for the World Bank. As soon as I mentioned this there was an uproar. 'You communists get into the United Nations in the highest positions', etc. The idea of John Lascelles, with his name, background, and indeed his whole character, being a communist, really made my imagination boggle.

Another time he brought in a piece of paper with the words 'Seven Seas' on it. I had no idea what this meant but they verbally beat me over the head and said I must know and it was probably some communist organization which covered the whole wide world. I went back to my cell wondering what on earth this was about and then it suddenly occurred to me that Alison had been on a charter flight when she came to South Africa on holiday and this might be the name of the charter company. The next morning I suggested this, but by that time Visser, who apparently had met and followed Alison, had realized it himself. (From a note made on one of the letters they apparently also supposed that a Thai girl-friend with whom Alison had once gone on holiday must be a communist agent.)

Colonel Coetzee, who seemed to be in practical charge of the whole investigation, came in from time to time. He was a good-looking, suave man with an attractive smile and a frightening underlying bitterness. He does not have Swanepoel's reputation for sadistic physical cruelty, but there is a quality of cold-blooded bitterness about him which I found very frightening. One day during the tea interval, when he was alone with me, he suggested that if the bishop went to see the Attorney-General or the Minister of Justice it was quite possible that some bargain might be reached by which I should be released. When the bishop and my counsel investigated this later, everyone denied any knowledge of it, and it now seems an obvious lie – but it wasn't obvious to me at the time. Why Coetzee should have concocted this story, I do not know, but I suppose the object was to unsettle me by giving me a bit of hope and than smashing it down. (Coetzee later also told me that his superiors were inclined to believe that the pamphlets were planted on me, but he himself was perfectly convinced that I owned them myself and I deserved everything that was coming to me.)

A further technique was for one of the investigators to pull a piece of paper out of his pocket and quote it as being evidence of something that I had said or done. For example, they shouted at me that I had been preaching revolution and produced a report from an informer that I had said there was going to be a revolution and it would be a very good thing. This was a total misunderstanding of what I had in fact said, as the evidence in court showed later. But at the time I could only deny it.

Quite early in my interrogation they showed me photographs of myself and Alison Norman walking together on holiday, and it was clear that I had been closely followed during my leaves. I told them as clearly and honestly as I could remember all the people I had met when in England but I had never been anywhere near the ones they were really interested in like the African National Congress or the Pan African Congress or the Anti-Apartheid organization. (When they went out of the room for tea on that occasion they left, very obviously, a paper with two names on it – one of a person I had not met and one of somebody whom I had forgotten to mention. I told them about the one I had forgotten when they came back and they seemed to accept it.)

It was very difficult to know just what the interrogation was really all about, since there seemed to be no real plan to it. They switched from subject to subject, and from one date to another, and one incident to another, so I never knew what to expect next. Perhaps this was the plan, in the hope that I should get muddled in my answers. The general outline of a day's questioning was almost that of an office routine. We made a start at some time between eight and nine in the morning and would deal with one

subject, and then there would be a break for tea when the interrogators went off and I was left either with one of them or with
a substitute guard. They would come back at about 10.30 and
start perhaps on an entirely different line in the questioning.
Again there would be a break, slightly longer, at lunch-time,
and I would have my lunch brought to me in the same room.
After lunch perhaps another entirely different line of country
would be tackled, and there would be afternoon tea at about
three o'clock. The last session varied very much in length. On
at least one night it went on until quite late, but I think it is only
fair to point out that it was repeated to me, on several occasions,
that if I felt tired I could call a halt to the questions. I never did so.

Each day, and sometimes more than once a day, as van
Rensburg completed a number of pages, these were handed to
one of the junior Security Police who took them along the
passageway where they were transcribed into a typewritten
document. From time to time, I had to sign several pages of the
statement, which was emerging as a true record. In fact van
Rensburg was pretty accurate, though he made one or two
attempts to slip a nuance into my answers which I felt was pretty
unfair. When I pointed them out, these nuances were immediately
corrected, and I can say that they did record my answers on the
whole perfectly satisfactorily, though obviously I should like to
have enlarged upon some which seemed over-simplified.

It is worth while re-emphasizing that on no occasion did I
undergo any physical torture. No one touched me or beat me,
nor was I made to stand during my questioning, nor was there
any arc-lamp or anything of that sort. I sat facing my three
interrogators across a desk and that was the normal method of
procedure.

The only real physical discomfort was that on two nights out
of the eight my cell light was left on all night. When this happened
I could get very little sleep because it was a centre light, high up
in the ceiling, and I could not get out of its reach. I used to put
my shirt round my head to try and keep it out, but I kept looking
out of the shirt to see if it was still on! I complained about this

and they said it was a mistake, but I am sure it must have been deliberate.

There was one technique which I did find very frightening. This was vicious verbal violence. On these occasions all three of the interrogators would get up out of their chairs and walk around screaming, shouting, and swearing at me. Having been a sheep-shearer up the Waitaki river, I have a pretty extensive vocabulary myself – but these men knew the lot, and used it. These attacks generally came after Dircker or one of the other officers had brought in one of his bits of paper, or after one of the interrogators had produced a special question from a paper in his pocket. To some extent they must have been timed and rehearsed, and I must say I found them psychologically a considerable shock and very difficult to withstand. My interrogators were utterly irrational and it was simply no good trying to argue or be reasonable about the subject of the tirade. For example, on one occasion two or three of them shouted at the same time, 'You don't preach Christianity, you preach shit', and this was repeated over and over again.

During another shouting tirade they all screamed that both Alison Norman and I were 'highly trained communist agents'. I did try to respond reasonably to this by pointing out that I could not have been very well trained if they had successfully unmasked me, and by asking how, when and where I could possibly have been trained. They knew my history for the last twenty years, and they had my passport, showing that I had never been further afield than England, France, and the United States. But they only answered that I could easily have gone to Russia without my passport during one of my leaves.

I don't know why this irrational, screamed-out type of accusation should be psychologically hard to stand, but I can only record that I found it so. One feels completely helpless and has no idea of what is going on. There seems to be no real purpose to it so you can't defend yourself against it and I suppose that is why it is so difficult. There were opposite times when their questions seemed perfectly reasonable and they seemed prepared to listen to the answers. Then I would be lulled into thinking that I was really getting somewhere at last, and they were really listening and there was some hope of proving that I was innocent. As soon as I began to feel a bit like this there would come another of these violent outbreaks. By the end of the interrogation, I was getting used to the pattern of this and might have been able to stand up to it better had the interrogation gone on longer. However, they might well have made the 'hard-sell' periods even harder if this had happened.

I have been asked by a number of people whether I find it hard not to hate these men. I can make no claim to be anything at all special, but in fact I find it very difficult to hate them, or anybody concerned with the case. I think this is because I cannot help seeing them as human beings, rather than as interrogators or prosecutors or judges or whatever their professional guise might be. In the tea intervals I had come to know just a little bit of the family lives of men like Dick Visser and I couldn't help all the time seeing the ordinary family men behind their angry, shouting, vicious faces. (This is also particularly true of Henry Liebenberg, the prosecutor at the trial. He put me through a pretty grim seven or eight days of cross-examination, and I think he was extremely unfair in some of the things he said and some of the assumptions he made. But again, he was a small grey-haired man, with what I thought was rather a pleasant smile, and I could never help seeing him as the head of a typical Dutch-Reformed family in his family church, and pottering about his garden and his home. I felt very much the same thing about Mr Justice Cillié who found me guilty.)

I believe that with all these men I could under different circumstances have found some common ground, perhaps not as friends, but as men who could respect and understand each other. When one can see this sort of thing in other men it becomes impossible to hate, although I don't want to deny that I felt angry with them, frightened of them, and from time to time disliked them and their methods more than I can say.

One morning, when Dircker was the officer who came over

to fetch me from my cell for interrogation, he took me down to the office on the first floor of the cell building and went through some kind of 'ceremony' which I did not understand clearly at the time. He said he was releasing me from being held under the Terrorism Act and that he was re-detaining me under the Suppression of Communism Act, and he asked me if I understood this. I said I understood the words, but I simply didn't understand what the whole thing meant at all, and to this day don't quite know what it was all about. All I know is that when I appeared in the magistrates' court I was charged under the Suppression of Communism Act with the possession of the leaflets, but this charge was subsequently dropped and I was charged finally with ten counts under the Terrorism Act. What made them change their minds in midstream during my detention, and then change them back again, I simply do not know. I don't think it had any effect on my morale at all. I did have a sudden leap of hope when Dircker said he was releasing me under the Terrorism Act, but that was only momentary, because he wasn't really releasing me in the true sense of the word; all I knew was that I was still being detained in exactly the same circumstances and conditions as before. The name of the Act under which this was happening to me seemed to be of no importance whatsoever.

Another incident occurred because, as it happened, I had my fifty-ninth birthday in prison – six days after I was arrested. Barbara Waite, a parishioner who was always endlessly kind to me, cooked me a birthday meal – a rather special job – and got permission to send it in. The meal was duly delivered to the police, but I certainly never saw it, so some of the police must have enjoyed my birthday celebration considerably. However, to my astonishment, I *was* allowed to have a birthday card which the bishop had sent in. It was an ordinary card and had been signed by about fifteen people who work in and around the parish and diocesan offices, clerks and secretaries, and so on. The reason why I was allowed this soon became obvious. The interrogators took the card and sat in front of me and questioned me about each of the people who had signed the card. They wanted to know exactly who they were and what they were about and what they did. So each of these people is now on file in police headquarters – because they signed a birthday card.

On the second Friday morning – nine days after I was arrested – I did not get much religion done because they came for me much earlier than usual. They took me over to the questioning room, and I had the most awful fear that they were going to take me out and kill me. There was a suit waiting for me to get dressed in, but that didn't reassure me, because it seemed to me, in my irrational state, that this meant they were going to pretend that I had been killed trying to escape or something. (It is difficult to describe the curious contradiction between this superficial, and yet very taut fear, and the depth of real assurance that whatever happened did not really matter very much – I only wish the depth had come through and been able to appear on the surface. I think I would have been a much more convincing witness to the faith if that had been so.)

I told the policemen about my fears, and in the lift going down to the garage level, they joked amongst themselves in English about how they were 'the exterminators'. I suppose I ought to have been reassured by this, but I did not feel any reassurance. It seemed the kind of grim humour that they might well have really meant. When we got to the garage and the lift door was opened, there was a car outside with two women in it. This caused a good deal of consternation. One policeman got out of the lift and we stood inside with the door closed while he got the car removed. Later he explained in Afrikaans to his colleagues that they were a couple of police wives waiting for their husbands to come off duty. Obviously the policemen were afraid they might have been journalists, waiting to try and get a word with me or a picture of me as I was being taken off to court. The car into which we got was a minibus. I was seated surrounded by three or four policemen so that no photographer could possibly know I was there and the car was driven directly into the bowels of the magistrates' court where the black Marias normally discharge their prisoners. I was taken through this underground courtyard into a cell, where I was left alone. Fortunately I somehow had some cigarettes with me and I smoked a couple while wondering what was going to happen next.

At last a uniformed policeman came for me and I was taken again through passageways, past a whole lot of African prisoners, and up stairways, and suddenly found myself in the magistrates' court. The magistrates' bench was empty and I could only see a few people along each wall. I recognized one of them as being a journalist member of my congregation, and smiled at her, but I had no idea that behind me, where I thought there was a wall, there was in fact a completely packed court of my friends and interested people. The only other people I recognized were my own lawyer, Ray Tucker, and Joel Carlson. There was a third man whom I subsequently found was Ernie Wentzel, who became my junior counsel, and it was he who made the plea for bail on my behalf.

The whole hearing was taken up with the reading of the charge and long selections from the subversive leaflets. This was obviously for press purposes, to show how devastating the material in the leaflets was. The only charge against me was under the Suppression of Communism Act for the possession and presumably the distribution of these pamphlets. Nothing was mentioned of Alison's money or the other matters about which I had been questioned. Ernie Wentzel then made a speech asking for my release on my own recognizances and the public prosecutor asked for a bail of 5000 Rand. I was astounded at the amount, and wondered where on earth the money would come from. Ernie Wentzel got up and said that an amount of this kind was much too great, pointing out that I was a fairly well-known citizen and hardly likely to abscond, or be able to abscond even if I wanted to. However the prosecution insisted that this was the amount of bail, and that my passport should also be impounded, and that was that. I was then told by Ernie Wentzel that I must go with the police while the money was arranged, so I turned round to go down the stairs and for the first time saw the great crowd of people behind me. I was literally taken aback and again became extremely emotional.

I could not distinguish the faces clearly, but I think the first person I saw was Laura Clayton, and then the bishop and John Turnbull and Barbara Waite, but apart from them there seemed to be a sea of faces. The magistrates' court isn't very big, but it was packed to the doors. I had no time to speak to them, but it was a tremendous relief and joy to know how many friends I had with me. I was taken away to sit in a room with a policeman and Ernie Wentzel while bail was arranged by Raymond Tucker. In fact Raymond Tucker had found out the night before how much bail would be required, and he had taken the trouble to get this money out of his own personal bank account and had had it transferred to a bank near the magistrates' court, so that it was immediately available. Five thousand Rand in notes takes a good deal of counting, and we must have sat in this room for about an hour before Raymond Tucker came with a note saying the bail had been paid and that I was free to go.

With Raymond and Ernie I walked out into the corridor and there I was simply amazed at what was going on. The corridor was jammed full of friends, both from the cathedral and outside it. Then of course there were the flashing bulbs of the still cameras, and the moving cameras, and the TV cameras, and I had to walk down this very long passage, with all these bulbs flashing all the time, and feeling completely lost, not knowing whether to laugh, or to cry, and utterly overwhelmed with relief, and with a sense of being loved and mattering which I suppose is one of the deepest emotions a man can have.

As far as I can remember I wasn't asked to make any comments. I was simply hustled through the crowd by the bishop and one or two others so that I could get down to the car, where Barbara Waite was waiting to take me to the bishop's house. I was pretty overwrought by the time I got there and they sat me down and gave me a couple of very stiff brandies. (I do not generally drink brandy in the middle of the day, but I must say I welcomed these very much.) I was very glad of the chance to talk firstly and privately with the bishop and the two lawyers, but while I was talking to them, Dr Miller arrived. He gave me a pretty thorough examination, and prescribed a dose of Librium, which some of my other medical friends afterwards told me was calculated to put a calving cow into a state of tranquillity. I was extremely glad of the brandy and Librium and a good lunch, but even with their help the future was so full of questions that I could not relax much and by three or four in the afternoon I was up and answering questions on television programmes.

I cannot remember much about the next few days. I was being heavily drugged with Librium and I don't think I realized that I was actually in a state of considerable emotional shock. Two things I do remember. The first and best was the Mass I said next morning – the first day after my release. This was what I really was – a priest – in spite of all that the Security Police might say. There was a good crowd there, but even that was not what mattered. What did matter was the tremendous deep and glorious gratitude that I felt to God because I had come through without a complete collapse, because I was free again, and particularly because God was *there* and I was in his presence.

The other occasion that I remember was a party which I threw in my flat a day or two later for some of those who had helped me behind the scenes. I won't mention names – there were the bishop and my lawyers, and so very many other friends. But for me it was the complement to my first Mass – an attempt at thanksgiving to my friends as that Mass had been an attempt at thanksgiving to God.

I felt so deeply overcome with love and gratitude that both were beyond any words that I could use.

CHAPTER NINE

On remand

The experience of detention changed me in a number of ways. In prison I had been given a new awareness of the glory of God and an almost completely satisfying knowledge that God *is*. (This is described in more detail in the diary which I kept in prison and in full which is printed at the end of this book.) This awareness gave the practice of my faith a fresh depth and vision which strengthened me during the fifteen months of strain and tension which followed. Equally, I had had a new experience of the meaning of 'the Church'. The solid wall of prayer which had sustained me in prison, the glorious wave of love which met me when I came out, the courage and loyalty of my own parishioners, and the support of all sorts and conditions of folk from all over the Republic and, indeed, the world – all these brought a humbling and deeply moving realization of what it means to be a part of 'the body of Christ'. When my lawyers and doctors told me that they could not understand why I did not collapse I knew where the strength to keep going came from.

But although love had a new meaning for me, I had also grown to understand and experience hatred. As I said in the first paragraphs of this book, it was in prison that I had suddenly glimpsed in a new way the reality of the insanity and evil which is at the root of apartheid, and I knew that my feeling about it was no longer fear or anger or dislike, but hate. If I could find a stronger word to express this emotion, I would use it. Hatred is a theological word; it is the antithesis and complement of love. If you love something or someone very much, you must hate that which destroys the beloved, and the Bible is very clear about the many things that God hates. (I think that Christians are far too apt to try and escape from the need truly to hate evil, so that their love is also wishy-washy and weak.)

However, from my long hours of talking with my Afrikaner interrogators, I had also come to understand and appreciate much more deeply the reasons for their hatred, not only for Africans but for the English too. For the first time I realized that we English have the same unconscious arrogance towards the Afrikaner as we and they have towards the African, and indeed we may well be partly responsible for the Afrikaners taking out on the Africans the treatment which they have received from the English. Again and again during my interrogation the treatment of Afrikaner women and children in British concentration camps during the Boer war was brought up, and my interrogators claimed that 20,000 of them had died there. Later I asked another colonel from the Security Police about this figure and he said that it was 27,000. What the rights and wrongs of all this were, I do not know. Certainly the Boers themselves had a scorched-earth policy which left their women and children in a dangerously vulnerable state and perhaps such camps were inevitable. But I do know that the memory of this suffering, in all its horror, lies burning and deeply bitter in the Afrikaner heart.

The story of the Afrikaners' rise to power again as a people in the fifty years between the end of the Boer war and 1948 is a magnificent one, and 'even the ranks of Tuscany could scarce forbear to cheer'. But it has been a growth behind walls of bitterness and pride, in a laager no less real than the enclosed circle of ox-waggons behind which the old Afrikaner pioneers defended themselves against Zulu attacks. And, for this, casual British snobbery, greed, and unconcern must bear a considerable share of blame. Almost until the end of the second world war, English-speaking people dominated the commercial life of the big cities (remember Dick Visser's fury about the posters in Johannesburg), and they excluded Afrikaners from almost any social contact. The Country Club in Johannesburg would not at one time admit Afrikaans-speaking people. It is no wonder that Afrikaners withdraw from contact with a European culture which for half a century rejected them, and that they have developed a collective paranoia which feeds on the rejection which it invites. A man who has been deeply hurt emotionally closes in on himself and then comes to believe that the whole world is against him, and he also takes out his hurt and anger on anyone weaker than himself. The same can be true of a people, and the English-speaking population must bear a deep responsibility for their own share in creating the South African situation.

While I think I had grown internally in freedom and understanding, externally I felt something of a prisoner. This was not just because I was on bail awaiting trial and had surrendered my passport, but also because of the measures which my friends had insisted should be taken to protect me from the various threats against my life which were made by right-wing terrorists.

Only a few days after I came out of prison, I got the fright of my life when I opened the door of my flat and saw three Security Policemen standing there. They said they had been sent by the British ambassador, who had asked for police protection on my behalf, presumably because he had heard about these threats. They asked quite politely if they could come in, and enquired if I really needed or wanted this protection. I pointed out that it would be extremely foolish of me to say that I did, since presumably they could protect me quite adequately by putting me back in prison, and their leader, who was a colonel, said that this had occurred to them too! In the end it came down to whether I objected to police protection. I said I did not object in the least and we settled down to have a drink together. (It was on this occasion that I tried to check how many had died in the Boer war concentration camps and was told 27,000.) Whether they did provide protection I do not know, but I never saw any sign of it, or noticed anyone following me. They certainly went on bugging my flat until 17 May, because they admitted this at my trial, and I believe myself that they went on until the day I left South Africa, though they denied this.

However, whatever the police were, or were not, doing, the

lawyers insisted that I should not be alone in my flat or outside it. This meant that a whole series of young men from the cathedral congregation took it in turns to spend a week guarding me. It was pretty tough on them because it meant that they too had to get up at 4.30 a.m. and come down to the cathedral with me, and it also meant that they took the burden of the threatening and obscene phone calls which used to come through at odd hours of the day or night. Sometimes these were very unpleasant indeed and I was most grateful that I did not have to cope with them myself. In addition to this constant bodyguard, some friends of mine also insisted on my having a bullet-proof screen installed in the flat so that I could not be attacked by someone firing through a window. I must admit that I felt a lot safer when it was there.

One of the first things we had to do was get hold of a senior counsel to take over my defence. I already had an attorney, Raymond Tucker, whom I had known and liked for a long time and who had helped me enormously with legal advice for Africans in trouble and in advising me about my own legal position in the work I was doing with Alison's money. While I was in prison Ray and my assistant, John Turnbull, had chosen Ernie Wentzel as my junior counsel because I had to have a barrister when I appeared in the magistrates' court. Ernie was a delightful person, solid, cheerful, and immensely reassuring. He had been a prominent member of the Liberal party and had himself been detained in the early 1960s. (When the police-station where he had been held was demolished he went and bought the iron gate to his cell and now has it as his garden gate, complete with its number.)

The three of us met together, and after some discussion we decided to ask Sydney Kentridge to take on the burden of the defence. I gathered at the time that he was in some ways loath to do this. He had defended people in many of the great political trials in South Africa and he found that he got so personally involved that such cases were a tremendous strain upon him. He is a brilliant lawyer and can make a perfectly adequate income from practice in chambers so I felt very privileged and fortunate when he agreed to take on my defence.

The four of us met for the first time at a secret meeting-place in a flat belonging to a friend of Raymond Tucker. I am not quite sure of the reason for this secrecy but they insisted on it. It was the first time I had met Sydney Kentridge and I found him a forbidding figure. He looks rather like the pictures I have seen of Disraeli – handsome, but seemingly cold and intellectual. He is certainly intellectual, but he is anything but cold and I came to be extremely fond of him. He, like Raymond Tucker, is Jewish, while Ernie Wentzel is a lapsed Anglican, but these differences in religions seemed, if anything, to cement our friendship. I grew to like and admire all three men more than I can say as well as to be most grateful to them for the tremendously long hours of work that they put in, night after night, on my defence.

Life went on for six months in an extraordinary nightmarish half-and-half existence. Twice I had to go back to the magistrates' court because the period for which I had been remanded was over, and each time the public prosecutor asked for more time for further investigation so I still did not know what I was going to be charged with, apart from having the planted pamphlets in my possession. On the second occasion Ernie Wentzel asked for an assurance that the next remand appearance would be the last before trial, and pointed out that it was usual for investigations to precede an arrest and not the other way round. We were promised that this would be the last time and bail was renewed until 30 June.

Although I did my best to carry on with my ordinary work during this period, I relied tremendously on the cathedral staff. Richard Llewellin, my senior curate, was a tower of strength, but in May the government refused to renew his residence permit and he and his family had to leave. (All foreign clergy coming into the country now have to get a permit to stay that has to be renewed each year, which is an admirable way of muzzling them. I was exempt from this rule because I had been there for so long.) Richard's work was taken over by Neville Palmer, who had, in theory, retired from full-time ministry at the age of sixty and had been devoting himself to the chaplaincy work in the city nursing homes. He was an utterly reliable and devoted person and a magnificent organizer, who in spite of age and ill-health got through an immense amount of work. Then there were Leo Rakale and Dick Yates – but if I go on mentioning names, I shall never stop.

I was, I am afraid, sometimes extremely bad-tempered. There was one occasion when the diocesan trustees were opposing our plans for Darragh House because they claimed that the Church should not be involved in a commercial venture, and I was very rude indeed. I can only hope that people understood and forgave me for it. Perhaps my state of mind is best expressed in a circular letter which I wrote at the end of May when I had just been remanded for yet another month. The letter started by explaining what was happening and went on:

I have come through the time of waiting extraordinarily well from a health point of view: and I've little doubt but that I shall continue to do so. I would have expected to be prostrated by coronary attacks, perforating ulcers, and all the sorts of psycho-somatic goings-on to which my flesh is particularly subject! But I have survived even this particular week, which included the resignation of the senior church-warden, and the organist having a coronary thrombosis! Even my blood pressure, and so on, are not really as bad as they might be. I know that this is partly because Bill Miller, my doctor, sees me every week and doles out the requisite quantities of 'muti' at the correct moments. But what is abundantly obvious is that the great amount of real strong prayer that is being made on my behalf, around the world, is literally holding me up in every sense of the word. It is almost palpable and solid and I just do not sink as I might have been expected to do. My own prayers are not doing an awful lot because I get too easily distracted by thinking about the case, the future, and so on, instead of about God, but I do the best I can. I'm not setting the Thames on fire in the parish because I wrongly allow all this business to distract me too much: but at least I keep things going with the help of an admirable staff, both clerical and lay. And one curious thing is happening, which I don't quite understand. I'm doing most of the preaching in the cathedral, because there are so many other things that I cannot do, and these sermons all turn out to be very much the same – which must be a bit boring for those who have to listen to them. They are all about the love of God, and the fact that love is the only thing that matters in, or out of, the whole wide world. If I had the right words I could probably get it into one sermon, and then get on to some teaching or something. I haven't those words, so I just go on and on about it. Perhaps one day I'll find the right words that will convey what I want to say about God and his love: but somehow I do not think I will.

And then there is, of course, the love of persons. I have been given so much love by so many people that sometimes I can hardly bear it. It is shown to me in so many ways and I cannot, again, find the right words with which to return such love and show my gratitude for it. The Church in America, for instance, sent out this week three men to be with me at my court appearance this morning; Bishop Creighton of Washington, representing the presiding bishop of the Episcopal Church in America, Judge Booth of the New York Criminal Court to watch the legal side of things, and Dean Sayre, also of Washington. The deans of all the cathedral churches in the USA and Canada got together and commissioned Dean Sayre to come to be with me and this, which is more than just a gesture, is an action which makes me feel very, very humble indeed – and deeply appreciative of their concern and care for me.

Care and concern are both practical applications of love, and it is this care and concern which you have all in your different ways expressed, which I am trying to acknowledge in this letter. I still don't know about the future and what it holds, but why should I care, and why should I be concerned – in the sense of worrying – since you all do so much of that for me?

These circular letters were the only way in which I could possibly respond to all the assurances of love and support that I received from all over the world. And of course it was Laura Clayton who coped with all this as well as with all her usual secretarial work. I owe her more than I can possibly say.

As I mention in that letter, my health did stand up to the strain remarkably well, and this was due, not only to the prayer of many people, but also to devoted and skilled doctoring from my GP and medical specialists, which went far beyond any professional obligation. The only thing which really went downhill was my psoriasis, which is a skin complaint I have suffered from most of my life. It is caused by psychological factors, so that wasn't surprising. I did also have a brief recurrence of the 'fugue', or whatever it was, which had occurred before when I was at school and in New Zealand. As far as I can remember, Barbara Waite (who is another person to whom I owe more than I can say) came into my flat to cook my supper one evening, and found me lying on the couch in my sitting-room. I was not unconscious or asleep, I was simply catatonic, or almost so. I came out of it later that night to find Ernie Wentzel and a psychiatrist called David Weinbren by my bed. I had never met Dr Weinbren before nor have I seen him since, but I shall remember his immense kindness and patience with me that night as we talked about what had happened for an hour or more. As I have said, I suppose it is some kind of subconscious contracting-out when things get too much for me, or perhaps some kind of safety-valve, which guards me against real mental illness.

At long last, on Wednesday, 30 June 1971, I went back to the magistrates' court for the last time. The spectators' gallery was well filled before nine o'clock, but fortunately the bishop and one or two others were allowed into the well of the court, so I felt closely supported.

Before the court opened Colonel Coetzee told me that I was again 'formally' in detention under the Terrorism Act – which did not do my blood pressure any good, but at the time it did not mean much to me. Then, a few minutes later, when the court started, the prosecutor stood up and withdrew the case against me. There was a happy gasp from my friends in the gallery – some of the more innocent ones really thought I was going to be set free. But then he announced that I was being charged with ten counts under the Terrorism Act.

The indictment was over forty pages long and was not read out in court, but the prosecutor did say that the charges were very serious and pointed out that the Act carried with it the possibility of a death-sentence. I felt I had to pinch myself to see if I was awake or having a nightmare. It seemed so utterly unreal that a perfectly ordinary sort of person like myself should find himself facing what could be a capital charge. But the immediate effects were only too real. Because of the nature of the charge the prosecutor asked for bail to be raised to R10,000. Ernie Wentzel opposed it on the grounds that I was hardly likely to run away – or be able to if I wanted to – and the court was adjourned. In an unbelievably short time the court was sitting again, and Ernie whispered to me that unless we paid up I would be remanded in custody, so there was nothing else for it. The diocese put up the extra R5,000.

Then the work began in earnest. The same afternoon the lawyers and I set about examining the indictment and working out what 'further particulars' we needed to ask for so as to get an absolutely clear idea of exactly what I was supposed to have done. There followed what seemed to me a long succession of almost interminable interviews. Again and again I had to go to Ray Tucker's office and make a statement in reply to his slow and careful questioning. He wrote down the answers in longhand and when the statement had been typed it was sent to Ernie. Then I had an interview with Ernie while he went through it word by word and often amplified it until finally the statement was ready for Sydney Kentridge's appraisal. Then I had to go to Sydney's house, normally with the other two, and Sydney started working through the statement in minute detail. He was quite ruthless in identifying the gaps that I had left and things that I had forgotten and demanding the reasons why I had done this or that. I was extremely grateful to him for this since it forced me to get the facts really clear in my own mind, but it was pretty hard going at the time. Once, for instance, I said that I thought something I had done was 'OK' and he stood up and almost screamed at me, 'What do you mean, "OK"?' He would have no truck with anything that wasn't quite exact and accurate. He wanted precise detailed facts and he wanted them clearly presented in a coherent and unemotional way – and as my tutor had told my bishop, my brain is quite exceptionally muddled, it was not easy to satisfy him. But I was encouraged by his insistence that if what I had told him was true, I was innocent of the charges and I ought not to be timid about replying to questions in the witness-box. Although the sessions were pretty hard work, I enjoyed the hospitality of these meetings in Ernie's and Sydney's homes and I felt a growing confidence in the whole team and the way in which they worked together so confidently.

The main part of the indictment is published at the end of this book and I shall only summarize it here. Although there were ten counts, there were really four main charges. I was accused of:

1 Possessing for distribution, and/or distributing, communist pamphlets advocating violence.

2 Advocating violence on various occasions and inciting people to take part in it.

3 Encouraging Ken Jordaan to commit sabotage and infiltrate the Security Police. (There was no mention at this point that Ken was a policeman himself.)

4 Receiving money via Alison Norman from the banned International Defence and Aid Fund which was used to further the aims of the ANC by relieving its members of anxiety about the welfare of their families.

All these activities were alleged to be directed towards the implementation of the ANC's plan to overthrow white government in South Africa, and therefore 'the said accused did, wrongfully, unlawfully and with intent to endanger the maintenance of law and order within the Republic, participate in terroristic activities'. The main indictment ran to nine pages – with two annexures listing 141 people or bodies as 'co-conspirators'. These included the ANC, the South African Communist Party, Canon Collins, Jordaan, and 130 recipients of the money I had paid out. (Among these, ironically enough, was my own solicitor, Ray Tucker, whom I had sometimes employed to defend Africans in the courts.)

CHAPTER TEN

Trial

THE SETTING

At long last, on 2 August 1971, the trial began in the Transvaal Supreme Court under the judge president, Mr Justice Cillié. I thought that at least the waiting was over – which goes to show how wrong I can be.

Like other treason trials, it took place, not in the ordinary court-room in Pretoria, but in the 'Old Synagogue'. In earlier treason trials this had been necessary because there had been something like a hundred accused and there was not room for them in an ordinary dock. In the Old Synagogue they could occupy the whole of the floor while the public sat in the gallery. In my own case I was, of course, the only person on trial and there did not seem to be much point in not using the ordinary court, but for some reason the authorities thought otherwise. It was a curious building, looking more like a mosque than a synagogue from the outside, with its two onion-shaped turrets. But inside its former use was obvious and during the trial I often thought of the Jews of Pretoria, who for so many years had offered their prayers here, and it seemed somehow blasphemous that so much injustice had been committed in a place where the God of justice had been worshipped.

At the beginning of the trial, an application was made to have it transferred to Johannesburg, on two grounds:

Firstly, that all the 'crimes' that I was supposed to have committed had taken place in Johannesburg, and trials are normally held in the city where the alleged crime has been committed (though there is, of course, a special provision in the Terrorism Act which says that they can be held anywhere –

presumably in order to keep them secret or make demonstrations difficult);

Secondly, that my health was very poor and I ought to be in constant reach of an intensive-care unit. This meant that all the evidence from doctors about the state of my heart and so on had to be read out in court, and it scared me stiff. I had known for years that my heart was a bit dicey but I had never envisaged myself dropping down dead at any moment and it was most alarming to hear that this might happen.

The application to transfer the trial to Johannesburg was refused, both at the beginning of the trial and when it was renewed later on. We were not told why. Perhaps the authorities were anxious to prevent demonstrations from Africans in Johannesburg who could not take time off to come to Pretoria, though as the court was almost empty on some days and no one ever showed any wish to demonstrate this seems unlikely. There were some libellous suggestions that the judge and the Security Police were interested in the considerable travel and subsistence allowances which they got for coming to Pretoria every day, but I have absolutely no reason to believe that this was true. In any case, it did add to the hardship of the trial because Johannesburg is 36 miles from Pretoria and we had to leave soon after 8.30 to make sure of getting there at 10 a.m. The travelling added nearly three hours to the day.

The judge, Mr Justice Cillié, rather embarrassed me because he looked so like me. He is portly, grey- to white-headed, and wears horn-rimmed spectacles. I could easily visualize him helping his wife with her shopping on Saturday morning, and there was nothing vicious about the way he conducted the trial, even though I seldom agreed with his decisions. He was also intelligent and asked some extremely shrewd questions when my cross-examination was over. On the other hand, I understood that he had had very little experience as a senior counsel because he had been promoted almost immediately from being a junior counsel to the judiciary, and it seemed regrettable that he chose to sit without assessors who would have helped him to weigh the evidence.

Also I was told that he was a personal friend of the prime minister and that one of his first jobs as a judge was in a delimitation committee which re-allocated constituency boundaries with the practical effect that many more Nationalist MPs got into parliament. None of this increased my confidence in him, particularly as he chose to sit without assessors.

The chief prosecutor, Henry Liebenberg, was a short man with a tiny little voice and an incredible capacity for asking the same question over and over again – apparently under the impression that he was pursuing a ruthless cross-examination. Ernie Wentzel told me on one occasion that one of the arts of cross-examination is to ask a really telling first question, so I was all keyed up for Liebenberg's first question to me. When he said, 'Can you hear me, Dean?' in his little voice, I felt completely floored. I got very angry with him at times, when he would go on and on making 'suggestions' without a jot of evidence, or try to get me and other witnesses to comment on letters without showing us the text, or refer to his suppositions as if they were facts. But I could not bring myself to hate him. He was doing a professional job to the best of his ability and I did not have the feeling that there was any personal animosity in it, though I did find it difficult to get used to the way he and my own counsel were apparently on the friendliest of terms as soon as a formal court session was over. I understand that, having got a conviction against me, Liebenberg has been appointed assistant attorney-general in the Cape, and there is a rumour that he will be a judge himself very soon. If this is true, I hope for the court's sake that he is less repetitious on the bench than he is at the bar!

The assistant prosecutor, Dennis Rothwell, was a very different type. He was a good-looking, youngish man with a dark moustache (I am told that his nickname is 'Clark Gable') and an air of looking round for applause when he made a point. He seemed a good deal too pleased with himself, but he was much more thrusting in cross-examination than Liebenberg and I was rather relieved that I did not have to cope with him instead of with Liebenberg's painstaking, plodding repetition.

Throughout the case there were a good many Security Police-men present, and almost all the time at least one of my three interrogators sat opposite me while I was giving evidence. It was a very threatening reminder that these men, who once had me completely in their power, could take charge of me again if they chose to do so, and no court could stop them. If you have been tortured, especially, it must be terrifying to have them there, and it was bad enough for me. To balance this, however, I had a great deal of personal support. I was allowed to sit with my lawyers, which was a great comfort, and many of my Johannesburg friends made a tremendous effort to come over as often as they could, not to mention the people who chauffeured me and organized lunch and Thermos flasks and so on, throughout the trial. The British consul also came often, which really did make me feel that the British government was concerned for my interests, and Bishop Howe, the Anglican executive officer twice took time from his very busy schedule to come out to the trial as the Arch-bishop of Canterbury's representative. The Church in North America sent no less than three representatives at different times, as I have mentioned earlier in the circular letter which I quoted, and for these very practical expressions of support I was deeply grateful. But I often thought of the contrast between all this help and interest which I was enjoying and the situation of the Africans who were being tried for terrorism in Pietermaritzburg at the same time – and about whom nobody seemed to care at all.

One question which was brought up early in the trial was how Alison Norman could give her evidence. She was, of course, the principal defence witness, and Ray Tucker had already been over to England to get a long affidavit from her about the source of her money and other matters. She had said that she would come over to give evidence if she received a satisfactory guarantee that she would not be arrested, since she was of course, according to the state, my principal 'co-conspirator'.

There was a great deal of toing and froing between my lawyers and the legal officials, including the Minister of Justice, about the terms of this safe-conduct, but of course it was impossible to make it absolutely watertight without, as Ernie said, 'giving her a licence to shoot the prime minister'. In the end, everything seems to have got a bit confused. Alison told her own solicitor in London that she would accept the safe-conduct offered, but either this message did not get through or it did not arrive in time, since my lawyers thought that she had finally refused to come and Judge Cillié granted a formal request that evidence should be heard on commission in England. (The prosecution also hoped to call witnesses there, so they were co-operative about this.) Alison, of course, was very thankful since she had good reason to think that the Security Police were liars and was under a lot of pressure from her family and her own lawyers not to put her head in the lion's mouth.

The upshot was that Ernie Wentzel, Liebenberg and Rothwell went over to England. (Kentridge went also for a couple of days and then came back because there were, in the end, no prosecution witnesses for him to cross-examine.) Alison gave evidence and was cross-examined on it for four days before a commissioner in barrister's chambers, and this evidence was later 'read into the court record' verbatim – a necessary but most tedious business. I shall refer to it where it occurs naturally in my own account of the trial.

It would, I think, be boring to give a chronological account of what went on. The main interest of the trial lies in what it shows of the state's determination to fit anything which I said or did into a preconceived mould; in the activities of the Security Police, many of which were admitted openly for the first time; and in the contrast between the view taken of the evidence in the trial court, and that taken by the appeal court, a contrast which I think is very significant for the future of South African justice. Legally the trial and appeal were also of considerable importance in that they defined much more clearly the meaning of the Terrorism Act and considerably narrowed its field of reference.

In order to illustrate these points as clearly as I can, I have taken in turn the three main subjects of the trial – my relationship with Jordaan, my alleged propensity for violent revolution, and the source and use of Alison's money – and have tried to show in each case the sort of evidence given, Cillié's verdict, and the appeal court's judgement, given six months later by Ogilvie Thompson and two other appellate judges. I have also included the appeal court's comments on whether my admitted activities could be called treasonable in terms of the Terrorism Act and on the conditions under which people accused under the Act have to prove themselves innocent rather than the state having to prove them guilty.

Since the trial lasted forty days, with three thousand pages of court records and an incredible mass of letters and other documents handed in as evidence, it is obviously impossible to cover everything (the appeal court judgement alone ran to about forty-two thousand words). I have done my best to be fair, but I am afraid that my selection may be rather biased since Kentridge's cross-examinations are a great deal more quotable than Liebenberg's sledge-hammer techniques, and I must admit that some of the comments of the appellate division do give me considerable pleasure.

JORDAAN

The first state witness was Louis (Ken) Jordaan. Our first intimation that Jordaan was involved in this whole business was when Ernie Wentzel flipped through the thick wedge of the indictment as it was first produced in the magistrates' court, and caught sight of Jordaan's name in block capitals. (He had not been mentioned all through my interrogation.) After my release from custody, he had been importunate in asking for interviews with me and on two occasions he had tried to get me to break my bail by offering to smuggle me out of the country, once to Lesotho and once over the Botswana border. Luckily I neither wanted to let my friends and the Church down, nor did I think his schemes had the slightest possibility of success. Apart from that, I had become a bit suspicious that he was more than an extremist crank because in one of these conversations his phraseology had been remarkably similar to something the Security Police had said to me, and I did just wonder if he wasn't a good deal more friendly with them than he had told me he was. So when his name appeared in the indictment and he later appeared in the witness-box, I was shocked and saddened but not totally surprised.

Jordaan said that he had gone to the police headquarters in John Vorster Square early in 1969 (i.e. some time after he had decided not to offer himself for the priesthood) and offered his services as a police reservist 'because he was anxious to join the police reserve'. He had been interviewed by a recruiting officer and later been sent for by a Lieutenant Bean who had questioned him about me and agreed with him that he should be appointed a constable and attached to the Security Police. After that he had made regular reports to the police about anything that I did and said (and quite a lot which I did not). I have already described what I had in fact suggested Jordaan could do in the way of infiltrating the Nationalist party, supplying figures on immigration, etc. But in his evidence-in-chief he alleged that not only had I been the initiator in encouraging these activities but I had also encouraged him to infiltrate the Security Police. In addition I had told him that I was 'a distribution point' for ANC funds and had advocated the wildest schemes for sabotage; and while on holiday in England I had spent four hours in a lavatory discussing guerrilla activity and other subversive matters. By the time he had finished it sounded as though I was mad, rather than bad, but certainly a very dangerous character to have around. Several of my congregation looked at me very askance after that first day's evidence.

Apparently Jordaan had made rough notes of his conversations with me, written them up (sometimes days later), and then taken them to police headquarters, where they were typed and he signed them. He was told by the police to destroy his rough notes, so there was no means of checking how accurately his reports reflected what he had originally written – let alone what was originally said. Several times, he said, he had tried to use a hidden tape-recorder when talking to me, 'but it never worked properly'. Jordaan relied entirely on his written reports when giving his evidence and could not remember anything which was not in them, while insisting that what was in them was entirely accurate even when it was manifestly out of context, incomplete, or confused. Sometimes he produced the most bizarre 'slants' on what had actually been said, because he was determined to fit everything and anything that I had said or done into his image of me as an important figure in some tremendous subversive organization. His general image of me became clear when Kentridge asked him if he saw me as a type of general in the anti-government movement and he said, 'I can't say he ever told me that he would direct the operation. I could not describe his position as that of supreme commander. However, I seriously believed that he would occupy a senior position. It was my opinion that he would co-ordinate the activities and funds of organizations such as ANC and Frelimo.'

Everything had to fit into this pattern. For instance, I had described at a deanery party how a Negro doctor whom I had met in the United States was talking in fantastic terms of rescuing prisoners from Robben Island by submarine. (I was trying to illustrate how much hostility there was to South Africa in the States.) Kentridge pointed out that there was nothing to suggest that I had been involved in this and Jordaan answered, 'It seemed to me that the dean was involved in the plan', though he agreed the scheme was utterly impractical. Another time I had given a light-hearted description of how 'cloak-and-dagger' (i.e. Security Police-minded) people were becoming in England, whenever they discussed anything to do with South Africa, and had illustrated this by describing a meeting with some people who wanted to talk about what could be done to help the South African situation. They had insisted that this should take place in a jewellery factory in Soho. The meeting had gone on interminably – so much so that half-way through we all had to adjourn to the public lavatory down the street (the factory facilities not being up to much). This rather absurd incident became, in Jordaan's report, a four-hour meeting with terrorists in a PK (South African slang for a lavatory). As Alison said later in her evidence, 'it all sounds quite unnecessarily uncomfortable'.

Jordaan had met Alison when she came over to South Africa and Rhodesia on holiday in January 1970. She had spent most of her time with relatives but did have a week staying at the deanery and talking to various people because she wanted to try and understand the whole situation at first hand. After meeting people like Cosmas Desmond and Helen Joseph, she said that she would like to meet someone who could give her a real idea of the Nationalist Afrikaner point of view. The only person I could think of was Jordaan, and he had, as he admitted, been pestering me to let him meet her. They met and talked for over an hour, mainly about Nationalist politics, but Jordaan left with the impression that he had been probed by a 'very skilled interrogator', and had passed some kind of test which had resulted in his being admitted to the inner reaches of an organization in which Alison was a high-ranking member. (He had also managed to convince himself that she was 'Lady Alison Norman'.)

The allegation that I had distributed funds to Frelimo turned out to be derived from a reference which I had made, in a letter to Jordaan from England, to the effect that people there were not interested in helping resistance inside South Africa any longer – they thought it was of more practical use to help the Frelimo guerrillas. And so it went on.

One of Jordaan's allegations, on which the trial judge convicted me, was that I had told him I was working with the ANC. There were four reports to this effect. In the first I was supposed to have said that my function at that stage 'was merely to act as a distribution point for ANC funds'. This I could only deny, though, as the appeal court pointed out, it was not even alleged in the indictment that I had distributed ANC funds, and there was absolutely no evidence that I had done so. The second statement came only in the second and later version of a report which had two versions. No evidence about how this happened was produced. It alleged that I had said that 'in the present circumstances – the oppression and so on – one was forced to work with an organization like the

African National Congress, because they were the only really effective opposition in the country'. Again, I could only deny that I had ever said this.

Jordaan's third report connecting me with the ANC ran, 'He also said that he was connected with Winnie Mandela. It was very difficult to negotiate with members of the African National Congress because they had always been suspicious of white people. However, Janet Llewellin had been able to secure contact with Mandela.' Here Kentridge argued, with considerable force, that the word 'not' had been left out before the word 'connected', which would make much better sense of the whole paragraph. (Jordaan had admitted making a similar mistake in an earlier sentence of the same report.) Jordaan denied this, and I am sure that I had never said anything of the kind to him at all. I had never met Winnie Mandela and, as I have explained, had tried to avoid all contact with her, and the state could not produce any effective evidence to the contrary. The last sentence of this bit of Jordaan's report was complete nonsense. Presumably he meant Jennifer (not Janet) Llewellin, who was the wife of my senior curate, and she had never had any contact of any kind with Winnie Mandela. The prosecution never tried to show that she had.

Jordaan's last report in this connection said I had told him that the African National Congress was 'scraping the bottom of the barrel' and that 'Winnie Mandela was now forced to recruit sixteen-year-olds for guerrilla fighting' (which makes it difficult to believe that I could ever have said that the ANC 'were the only really effective opposition in the country'). Since Carlson had told me this, I might have mentioned it to Jordaan, but of course it did not, as the prosecution claimed, prove that I had an intimate knowledge of the affairs of the ANC and therefore must be associated with them.

Again and again Jordaan alleged that I had suggested what he, in fact, had been pushing at me, and in the end he admitted this.

Kentridge: You used to initiate conversations about revolution and violence? – I made myself available. I said that I knew nothing about demolition.

Kentridge: I am suggesting that you first raised the question of
    sabotage. – The accused raised the question of sabotage.

Kentridge: I am putting it to you that you spoke of it first. – I
    did speak of sabotage.

Two incidents when he had shown me a gun (which had scared
me stiff) were brought up. Jordaan said that he had thought I
might have brushed against the tape-recorder and become
suspicious so he had produced the gun instead – presumably to
reassure me! He was of course asked why he had offered to help
me jump my bail and leave the country and he said that he had
wanted to give me the impression that he was my agent and would
carry out my instructions.

Kentridge: In January the dean was detained. After he came out
    of detention you offered to get him across the border. – I
    offered to give him a lift to Ficksburg.

Kentridge: To get him over the border? – To convey to him
    that I was his agent.

Kentridge: No, to attempt to get him into further trouble. –
    No.

Kentridge: If he had said yes, what would you have done? – I
    would have told him he must reconsider his action.

(The spectators roared with laughter at this point and were
reproved by the judge.) Jordaan later said that if I had persisted
he would have arrested me as I crossed the border but that his
reason for making the offer was that he had hoped I would send
him to London as my 'agent'.

Kentridge, in his cross-examination, brought out very clearly
what a world of fantasy Jordaan seemed to be living in, in so far
as my activities went, and how he had done nothing to test the
reality of his preconceptions.

Kentridge: Over the whole eighteen-month period that you had
    discussions with the dean you asked no questions to elucidate
    your reports? – No, I did not want to probe too deeply.

Kentridge: Perhaps if you asked one or two straightforward
    questions instead of drawing inferences in your reports this

whole bubble would have burst and you would have been out of your job as a police spy? – No.

By the time Kentridge had finished with Jordaan, it seemed to me that his evidence had been blown to smithereens.

Kentridge: Yesterday you objected to my calling you an *agent provocateur*. Do you still object? – Yes.

Kentridge: I think it is clear from your reports that for a period of eighteen months you were urging the dean to commit an unlawful act. – I wanted action.

Kentridge: There was no response from the dean to your suggestion of sabotage on South African warships. The dean did not assist you in your plans for sabotage. – He did not.

Kentridge: You offered to help him escape; he rejected it. – (No reply.)

Kentridge: You showed him a gun; he did nothing. – Yes.

Kentridge: You offered to photograph documents and he rejected that. – Yes.

Kentridge: Over the long period of time that you enjoyed the dean's confidence can you tell us of one unlawful act committed by the dean? – No.

Cillié, when giving judgement on the part of the indictment relating to Jordaan, found that it was not proved that I had told Jordaan that I 'had large sums of money available to finance activities directed against the state' or that 'boycotts could be effective as a means of undermining the authority or safety of the state' – as the indictment alleged. Cillié also accepted that I had not meant it literally when I told Jordaan that Swanepoel should be shot, and that it was not proved beyond reasonable doubt that I had said that I could arrange for him to have training in sabotage. (Cillié in fact agreed that it was Jordaan 'who usually initiated discussions about this matter and asked for such training'.) However, Cillié did hold that it was proved that I had told Jordaan 'that there should be an organization in existence to control and direct the commission of acts of violence in the event of it being resorted to', and that Winnie Mandela was recruiting youths in furtherance of ANC aims; also that I had acted as a distribution point for ANC funds, and that I had told Jordaan that overseas organizations were going to support Frelimo rather than activity within the South African Republic.

As well as these specific accusations in the indictment, Cillié also found it proved that I had encouraged Jordaan to infiltrate the Security Police, 'but the extent to which it was to be done is never certain, and it is possible that it might not have been intended to be more than a social infiltration'. He concluded:

Jordaan is to be believed beyond reasonable doubt on the major issue, namely that he had been incited or encouraged to take part in acts which were in support of the aims alleged in the general conspiracy; in particular, the court believes that the accused had told him that he had money to be distributed and that it was on behalf of the African National Congress.

The appellate division tore to shreds both Jordaan's evidence and Cillié's assessment of it. Ogilvie Thompson said that Jordaan had lied about his reasons for joining the police and was biased in his reports as soon as he had done so; also that his attempt to provoke me into doing something illegal had been in the nature of a trap and that he was over-anxious to please his superiors in the police.

The appeal judgement points out several flat lies in Jordaan's evidence and says they 'clearly demonstrate, not only his unreliability as a witness, but also his readiness untruthfully to involve the appellant with the African National Congress'. It concludes that Jordaan's allegation that I had told him that my function was merely to act as a distribution point for ANC funds 'becomes in the circumstances highly suspect', and could not be said to have been proved beyond reasonable doubt. 'In fact', the appeal judge said, after considering further allegations, 'there is on Jordaan's evidence no satisfactory proof whatever of any association between the appellant and the banned African National Congress.'

The judge commented on the vagueness of Jordaan's reports when there was a suggestion that I had been doing something illegal, and his failure to find out more about the sabotage training which Jordaan said I had offered him, and he said that Jordaan's denial that he had hoped to get me into further trouble by offering to help me to escape 'was plainly false'. However, I came in for a considerable rocket over the letter to the parish magazine which I had helped Jordaan to write, and it was said that my conduct over this 'can only be described as highly reprehensible' for a man in my position, but the judge did not think that this and other subterfuges 'were of any significant importance in relation to the charges preferred in the indictment'.

The appeal judge concluded:

I come to the conclusion that Jordaan was a wholly unsatisfactory witness and that the trial court erred in accepting his testimony where it conflicted with that of the appellant . . . the evidence of this single state witness – contradicted as it is by that of the appellant – cannot, in my judgement, be accepted as adequate proof of any of the 'acts' averred in paragraph (8) of the indictment. The appellant's conviction in relation to that paragraph must accordingly be set aside.

It is, I am told, most unusual for the court of appeal to overturn findings of fact made by a trial court. It is still rarer for the court of appeal to disagree with the trial judge on the credibility of a witness. But in the case of Jordaan's evidence, the appeal court did both these things. I find it a terrifying thought that, if the generosity of people all over the world had not enabled me to go to appeal, Cillié's judgement would have gone unchallenged and I would have been in prison for five years. But it is still more terrifying to wonder what will happen to South African justice when the present members of the appeal court retire.

'VIOLENCE'

The state's evidence that I had tried to promote violent revolution rested on the fact that very subversive communist pamphlets (including receipts for Molotov cocktails) had been found in my cupboard, and on various statements which I was supposed to have made in public writing and speaking, as well as in private conversation with Jordaan.

There was not much dispute about finding the pamphlets. The police did try to make out that I must have known what was in the box because, they alleged, I had said 'Those are not mine' while I was still sitting on a chair and before I had seen inside the box. Kentridge pointed out that in the course of giving his evidence, Colonel Greyling had moved from being very vague about what had actually been said when the pamphlets were found, to being absolutely certain about the exact words. Kentridge also pointed out that the prosecution had put in as an exhibit a photograph of the cupboard in my own room, and not the one where the pamphlets had been found, and that another witness, Major Viviers, had positively identified the wrong photograph.

However, the real question was whether an unauthorized person could have gained access while I was away at the residential archdeacons' meeting or while I was in my office. The defence brought a witness who said that he had been admitted to a relative's flat in the same building by one of the African cleaners who had a passkey, and no difficulty had been made about whether he should be allowed to go in. I myself told how I had met a meter-reader coming out of my flat who said, 'The "boy" always lets me in', when I asked him how he got there, and how my own African servant, Mrs Kota, who came every morning to clean and cook breakfast, had lost her key some time before and been given another one. The prosecution called the caretaker, Mrs van Houte (an over-dressed woman who wore vast wigs), and she said that of course no unauthorized person could have got in. She was, naturally, backed up by the two African cleaners who would have been much too frightened to contradict her. (For some reason Mrs van Houte felt it would support her evidence if she produced all the keys for the entire building in the witness-box – the biggest bundle of keys you can imagine – and this caused a good deal of amusement in court.)

Cillié found that the prosecution had proved that no one could have got into my flat, and therefore that I had knowingly had the pamphlets in my possession and must have been plotting revolution, but he said it had not been proved that I had tried to distribute them (for which the state produced no evidence at all). Just having the pamphlets in my possession was not by itself an 'act' in terms of the Terrorism Act and so he acquitted me of this clause in the indictment.

The appellate division analysed the evidence and commented that Cillié's 'conclusion that the possibility of an unauthorized person gaining entry to the flat is so remote that it can be ignored would, with all respect, not appear to be warranted'. The appeal judge then reviewed the evidence that the police had been immediately interested in a particular cupboard, that my car had been burnt and three insurance companies had refused to reinsure a new one, and that I had received various threatening letters, including one which said, 'We got rid of Joost de Blank and you are the next one to go.' He concluded:

> The possibility that the pamphlets were indeed 'planted' in the appellant's flat can, in my opinion, hardly be said to be an unreasonable one. . . . In my judgement the state's contention that appellant was knowingly in possession of the pamphlets was not established with that degree of proof which is required in a criminal case.

I was naturally questioned a great deal at the trial, by both Kentridge and Liebenberg, about my attitude to violence and what I had written and said about it.

One of the state charges was that I had 'written notes for purposes of propagating the need for a violent revolution within the Republic in order to overthrow the present state'. This rested on some notes which I had made on a paper called 'The Just Revolution', by a Lutheran, Dr Gyula Nagy, which was published by the Theological Peace Conference, held in Sofia in 1966. These notes I later expanded into an article for the parish magazine, which read as follows:

REVOLUTION

A revolution in this Republic of South Africa seems to be a very remote possibility. That it is a possibility is clear from the fact that we have on our statute-books a good many laws

directed against those who might foment rebellion. It may even
have been closer than most of us realize if we are to judge by
the veiled comments made by various Ministers that they know
more about subversive activities in this country than it would
be good for the general public to know.

The whole matter of what is, and what is not, a just revolu-
tion has been and is being discussed by Christian theologians.
It is very relevant in a good many different parts of the world.
I quote two comments made recently by a Lutheran theologian,
Dr Gyula Nagy, in a document concerning 'The Just Revolution' issued by the Theological Commission of the Christian
Peace Conference in Sofia in 1966. This is what he has to say:
'Revolution should be defined as an inevitable historical process
causing the radical and abrupt alteration of unjust conditions
which, in their petrified state, would resist any other means.'
And 'there can be no doubt that Christians, in their conscience
and in the sight of God, may reach a decision that involves
them, under certain conditions, in a struggle against an
obsolete, essentially impossible and unjust economic, social or
political order.'

When I was asked why I had written this, I replied:

To make people think. There are Christians who consider in
some parts of the world that there comes a time in the history
of races and people when revolution is a necessary thing, tragic
as it may be.

I went on to explain, in answer to a further question, that I did
not think that the conditions for a just revolution applied in
South Africa 'at present or in the foreseeable future' because 'the
end result would have to be better than the present situation'. I
continued:

I don't believe the African people could run a better country
than is the present situation. I mean, it will be an awful
shambles. Secondly, there must be less harm done during
revolution than would be done by letting the present system
continue. I don't believe that would be. And the third point is
that there must be a very good chance of the revolution being

a success. You may not do a sort of do-or-die attempt. You must have a reasonable and good chance of success and there is no chance of success at present.

Kentridge: And is that your understanding of Christian doctrine on that? – That is my understanding of the Christian doctrine on the just revolution, yes.

The appeal judge commented:

The views expressed by appellant in this passage were repeatedly reaffirmed by him under cross-examination. He throughout maintained that the three conditions mentioned by him in that passage do not exist in South Africa, and that he is wholly opposed to guerrilla warfare or terrorism.

This was in very marked contrast to Mr Justice Cillié's judgement that:

If the accused over-emphasized the question of justification for violence and ignored the Christian belief in a change of heart to such an extent that he never mentioned it, then he has only himself to blame if some people think that it does not exist for him, and others that the only solution that he sees is the use of violence.

The prosecution placed a lot of emphasis on my relationship with an American called Bill Johnston in its attempt to prove that 'it is an inescapable inference from all the evidence that the appellant regarded revolution as both inevitable and desirable'. Bill Johnston was the president of a very anti-apartheid organization in the States called 'Episcopal Churchmen for South Africa'. I used to send him newspaper cuttings and he sent money for the relief of need from time to time. In November 1967, he had sent me a copy of an ECSA bulletin which contained an article on the seventh anniversary of Sharpeville by Dennis Brutus, who himself had been a prisoner on Robben Island and had later left South Africa on an exit permit. The article described his experiences on Robben Island and said (of course, addressing Americans):

We will fight and there are men all over Africa who will fight alongside us. . . . In my country, you see, constitutional change by peaceful means is not possible. If we resort to violence, it is because no option remains.

I had replied to Bill Johnston:

I do congratulate you on the last issue of ECSA, which is pretty strong meat, particularly Dennis Brutus's stuff; it makes good reading here and will do so until somebody clamps down, which I think isn't improbable.

Under cross-examination I agreed that I found Brutus's address 'good reading' because of the anti-South African material, but in spite of Liebenberg's constant suggestions to the contrary, I did not agree that this meant that I endorsed the present use of violence as a means of bringing about constitutional change.

I do not have to agree with everything that I read, but this [i.e. Brutus's address] is very strongly put. I have made it very, very clear what my position is about violence and the awful tragedy I think it would be, and I feel we are very close to it. . . . I hold that we have not reached the point where violence can be justified. I have made this very clear.

Liebenberg: You say you don't agree with Dennis Brutus's statement here that there is no option but to resort to violence? – No, I don't agree with it, but I say that is precisely the position that it is very hard to see what alternative there is. But I believe there is an alternative.

Liebenberg: Yes, what is the alternative? – Reconciliation.

Liebenberg: Yes, but if there is no prospect of reconciliation? – But it is always possible. I mean, if you are a Christian there must be a prospect of reconciliation – love is all-powerful. But I cannot see love growing in men's hearts, that is the tragedy.

The appeal court concluded that my 'undoubted sympathy with the anti-South African sentiments expressed in the ECSA magazine' was 'not necessarily incompatible with disapproval of a resort to violence' and did not think that the state had proved its case in that regard. The court was no more impressed by a private letter I had written to a young man in my congregation in which I advocated a 'really organized passive resistance' as being incitement to violence, nor did they think that my writings in the *Parishioner* over the previous six years were 'consistently though subtly advocating violence'. 'On the contrary', the appeal judge said, 'these writings, while uniformly critical of the government policies, not infrequently counselled the opposite of violence.' And he illustrated this from an article which I had written in the *Parishioner* in 1966.

BAD GOVERNMENT—ACT!

I know that there are a very considerable number of church-people who, although they are not as rabid as I am, are very dissatisfied with the way in which this country is administered by the present government. They are, however, citizens of the Republic and quite naturally don't wish to be disloyal.

Many of them feel hopeless in the face of such things as bannings and detentions and don't know what they can do. It is, of course, extremely difficult to know what to do, and still to remain a loyal and orderly citizen.

However, I am quite sure that there are things that Christians can do. The relevant text in the Bible – at least as far as I am concerned – is 'and, sitting down, they watched him there'.*

It is much too easy to sit down and just watch something evil happening. It seems to me that one of the practical things that Christians ought to do is join at least one – if not more than one – of the various groups which in different ways are trying to achieve some better conditions in this country than prevail at the present moment.

Of such groups I would suggest that membership of the Institute of Race Relations, the Christian Institute, the Black Sash, and the Penal Reform Association, would give opportunities to Christians to increase their knowledge of what the situation is at present, of which many people are extremely ignorant. It would also give the opportunity to work together with other people of like mind for an improvement in the different spheres with which these groups are concerned.

* Matthew 27:36.

I am sure that there may be other groups also, but it seems to me that those that I have mentioned are each of them doing valuable work in different ways and I should be glad to put anyone into touch with any – or all – of these organizations if you don't know how to get hold of them.

As far as I can judge, from my knowledge of them, none of them is a political organization in the usually accepted sense of that word, but they are concerned in different ways with improving the conditions under which people of this country labour at present.

The appeal court went on to summarize my views on violence very fairly as follows:

The appellant undoubtedly often expressed the view that violence might well erupt from the non-white population of the Republic. At times he added that, in such event, Christians, and more especially non-white Christians, would be faced with a difficult dilemma as to what course they should follow. In my opinion, however, the evidence fails to support the state's contention that appellant advocated a resort to violence. After carefully considering the evidence and the arguments addressed to us, I am disposed to think that a fair summary of appellant's general views on violence, as reflected in the record, is that he believes outbreaks of violence to be highly likely, if not inevitable; that he considers that such outbreaks are liable to occur sooner than many people think; and that the whites of the Republic should be induced – if not through love then through fear – to realize this danger in time to avert it. In my judgement, however, the state's contention that in general – as distinct from the specific 'acts' forming the subject of paragraphs (7) and (8) of the indictment – appellant positively desired, and actively advocated, violence is not established.

In spite of Cillié's notion of my views on violence, he did acquit me of items 2–6 and 10 of the indictment, either because the state brought no evidence of its charges or because police spies had manifestly misreported and exaggerated what had been said at meetings or because the Security Police had read meanings into what I had said or written which were just not there. For instance, item 10 of the indictment alleged, 'During the period 4.8.1967 to 21.1.71 in Johannesburg, the accused discussed or was party to a plan to commit acts of sabotage at buildings or installations to the prosecutor unknown.' This turned out to refer to a tape-recorded description of a drive I had taken round Hillbrow in the early hours of the morning, right back in 1966. This recording had been made because the cathedral staff were concerned about the people who have very lonely all-night jobs, firemen, care-takers, nurses, and so on, and it seemed worth while to spend a bit of time finding out just who was up all night and whether they needed help. The police pounced on this tape when my office was searched and they seriously put it forward as evidence that I was plotting to sabotage the Hillbrow Tower (the equivalent of the Post Office Tower in London) and other targets, which made them look pretty foolish.

Cillié's judgement on this point was that the reason I gave for having made this recording 'cannot reasonably possibly be said to be untrue', and 'for that reason' he accepted it (a most negative way of putting things). The appeal court judge dryly remarked that, without expressing any opinion of Kentridge's criticism of the wording of Cillié's judgement, 'this tape-recording affords an apt illustration of how incidents, in themselves insignificant, are susceptible of being misconstrued'.

Another example of this was the evidence of a Security Police-man, Sergeant Kennedy, about a conference he had attended which had been organized by the South African Council of Churches. As the Council's general secretary, Bishop Bill Burnett, later described, the subject of this conference had been 'The Generation Gap', and it was an attempt to get younger and older people together to work out the problem of the relationship between freedom and authority. It had started with a film-strip showing photographs of student demonstrations and then there had been a long and dull address by an American sociologist, followed by discussion in groups.

On the second day the young people, led by a student called Kaplinsky, had taken over the conference and changed the structure of the discussion groups to include one on race problems. Burnett had resigned the chair to Kaplinsky, because he felt he was not in control of the meeting, and because the take-over seemed to be a practical and interesting demonstration of the struggle for power which, as Burnett said, is exactly what the 'generation gap is about'. Kaplinsky had then made a speech, which Burnett described:

A rather arrogant sort of speech . . . in which he was saying there must be change and giving the impression that young people like himself were likely to be the cause of such change, that they would be the initiators of it. And the rejoinder of the dean, as I recollect it, was an attempt to tell him that he was rather a young puppy and arrogant, and that any change which would take place would take place almost certainly without him, and that it would probably be violent change.

(I had probably said that it would be a good thing if people like him realized that any change in South Africa would be a violent and bloody thing.) Burnett felt there had been some satisfaction among the older members of the audience that someone had been able to stand up to Kaplinsky's steam-rollering tactics and put him in his place.

Kennedy had attended on behalf of the Security Police, dressed in a blue safari suit, with a comb in his sock – dress, as Burnett said, 'unique on that occasion'. The organizers had checked that he was not in fact a delegate of the parish that he said he had come from and everyone had been certain that he was from the police, but this is too common at meetings in South Africa to bother about, and we had just carried on.

Giving evidence, Kennedy said:

The purpose of the conference was to discuss the generation gap between youth and the adults in this country. I do not believe, however, that this was the real purpose behind the conference. *Liebenberg*: What was the purpose? – I feel that the purpose had a political motivation to incite members to demonstrate and to protest and to be pressure groups against this government.

He went on to describe what had happened at the conference, reasonably accurately. He described how Kaplinsky had advocated a new structure in the country and how he had said there could be a revolution, without necessarily having bloodshed or violence.

The accused stood up and disagreed with him. He stated that there was going to be a revolution and that it would be a revolution of violence and bloodshed and that it would be a good thing. There was about a hundred people and the reaction was cheering, laughter and applause.

Kennedy later said, when cross-examined by Kentridge, that this very staid audience of churchmen had allowed my saying that bloody revolution would be a good thing to pass without any protest and Kaplinsky had continued with his analysis of the generation gap.

In his judgement, Cillié said he thought that Kennedy was a reliable witness, although he might only have heard part of my statement. In any case, my remark was only an expression of opinion and could not be regarded as incitement, so he acquitted me on the charge of advocating revolution on this occasion without any finding on the actual facts.

The appeal judge commented:

The learned trial judge expressed the view that Sergeant Kennedy was a reliable witness. However, after due consideration of all the relevant evidence, the criticisms directed before us of Kennedy's evidence by defence counsel, and the evidence of the above-mentioned clergymen [Bishop Burnett, Mr Theo Kotze, and Mr Hamer], which cannot be rejected, I am of opinion that Sergeant Kennedy's testimony on the crucial point of difference between the state and defence versions about what the appellant said is not acceptable.

There were similar and even more contradictory and confused accusations that I had advocated violence at a deanery Friday-night 'open house' which a young African Security Policeman had attended, having previously joined my confirmation class on false pretences, but it would be tedious to go into this at length, and again I was not convicted on this charge.

However, I was convicted of the heinous offence of inciting members of the Black Sash to violence. I have already described how the Black Sash is an organization of white women who are specifically committed to non-violent protest and giving legal advice and help. They have regular monthly meetings with a speaker, and in December 1970, soon after I got back from my long leave, I had been asked to give them 'a pep talk'.

It seemed to me that the organization had got rather stuck and unimaginative about its methods of protest. Standing silently in mourning was all very well, but it did not really bother anyone very much. So, in an effort to get them thinking rather more aggressively, I had described some of the methods of protest which I had heard about when I did a course at the Urban Training Centre in Chicago three years before, such as putting rats in a councillor's house when the local authority had failed to clear a rat-infested Negro ghetto, getting Negroes to walk round and round the branches of a chain-store so that no customers could get in, in order to get a fair chance of promotion for Negro employees in the store, and similar activities. Also, as I so often did, I had tried to bring home to my audience how vulnerable the white position in South Africa is and had described how an African in Rhodesia had told me how easy it would be for African cooks to poison their employers' food. I had plugged my usual line about how volatile the situation was and how some chance incident, like a train crash, might spark off 'another Sharpeville' which would cause the rest of the civilized world to turn on us.

I felt that there were circumstances in which it was justifiable for a Christian to defend with violence someone that he loved – such as a father defending his daughter from rape – and similarly a Christian African might well feel compelled to go to the aid of his brother Africans if violence should break out. I had asked my audience, 'Where do you, as white people, stand, if violence should break out?' but had been able to give no answer myself. I had certainly not advocated violence, but had described, as I had previously done in my parish magazine, what I thought were the conditions of a 'just' revolution, and had said that I did not think they obtained now in South Africa and would not do so for a long time to come. I had ended by saying that we all had to try to keep and work within the law, but the time might come when we might have deliberately to disobey the law – as, for example, if it forbade people to meet in church to worship.

We ended with four versions of this talk: my own, which I have just summarized; those given by two members of the Black Sash, Mrs Gardner and Mrs van Heerden; and that of a Security Policeman, Warrant-Officer Helberg, who had been eaves-dropping from outside the house. Helberg's English was very poor and he had been put on the job because he was an electronics expert and not because he would be good at taking notes on an address given in English. His job had been simply to work a secret apparatus which could pick up what was said inside the house and record it. (The apparatus was not allowed to be described in court for 'security' reasons.)

Unhappily, as happened with remarkable regularity to police equipment when it was being used to pick up what I said, this mysterious apparatus had gone phut and not recorded anything at all. Helberg had only discovered this when he played it back afterwards and found that the tape was blank. The result was that he gave his evidence from a few notes which he said he had made to supplement his understanding of his tape. He had only been able to hear part of what was said and his notes were very brief. They started with the last remark that I had made, so they must have been made after I had finished speaking, though Helberg denied that he had written them when he discovered that his recorder had not worked.

He reported that I had said that after I became a Christian I was not peace-loving any more (in fact I had said that I stopped being a pacifist), that love and fear were the strongest emotions and could be used advantageously, and that although I had much respect for the Black Sash, they would make no progress if they worked within the law. He also reported me as having said, 'Another *good* Sharpeville would be the end of South Africa', and included my reference to the possibility of African servants poisoning their employers' sugar. He agreed with Kentridge that his notes (which were in Afrikaans) did not represent my exact words and that he could only remember what he had noted down.

Mrs van Heerden, who was a prosecution witness, was first presented to the court as a bona fide member of the Black Sash, but as evidence was later produced by the defence to show that she had been arguing in favour of Nationalist policies with colleagues in her office, this seems unlikely. Nor was there any explanation as to why the police had selected her in particular to go and give an account at John Vorster Square of what I had said. However, her account was not all that unfair, though it had considerable omissions and some distortion of what I had meant. For instance, she alleged that I had said, 'A revolution on behalf of the African people can be justified . . . it can be interpreted as love for the Africans', and not just that African Christians might be justified in supporting a revolution, if it started, from love of their own race. She also thought I had said 'One more *good* Sharpeville would be the end of this country', but under Kentridge's cross-examination, could not be certain it had not been 'one more Sharpeville'. She added, 'I think he did say that he didn't see how we [the Black Sash] could further our aims if we always worked within the law', but did not say she had assumed I meant they should go beyond the law.

The account of the defence witness, Mrs Gardner, agreed substantially with my own, though it, too, had some omissions, which were not surprising in view of the length of time which had elapsed since the meeting in question. She denied that I had told the Black Sash that they should go outside the law or use violence to achieve their ends. The cross-examination went (in part) like this:

Liebenberg: You say that by telling you about the difference between forms of protest used in America, the dean was not also suggesting that the Black Sash should work along the same lines? – I never got that impression. The impression I got was that the dean wanted us to examine our consciences.

She added that I had said I feared that a revolution would come in ten years and that violence would come to South Africa in the future, but not that the Black Sash should try to use violence.

Liebenberg: You are doing your best to protect the dean? – No, I have never met the dean before. All I am doing my best is to remember what happened at the meeting.

Asked whether I had been trying to influence the Black Sash in a subtle way to adopt the methods of Negro Americans, she said, 'If the dean was saying in a subtle way what he thought we should do, it didn't get through to me. I don't think he incited anyone.' She agreed with Mrs van Heerden and myself that I had posed a question as to where whites will, or ought, to stand if violence should break out and that I had made no attempt to answer it.

Cillié accepted Helberg's evidence, in spite of the manifestly unsatisfactory nature of his notes, and did not think the evidence about Mrs van Heerden's true political views was relevant:

Because she has not disclosed her true political views, it is argued that her evidence is suspect. However, it seems to me that there is a conflict about her true political views and I do not think that I should look at the evidence of a witness with suspicion because she says she holds one view and her employer says she holds another. This would be particularly dangerous when one realizes how easily political views and leanings are attributed to people.

I wish he had told Liebenberg that.

He went on to say that Mrs Gardner's evidence was confused and unsatisfactory (although my defence counsel said that she was one of the best witnesses they had ever heard):

She, like others, could not remember the details of some forms of protest discussed by the accused. My impression is that she remembered very few details and could not be relied on to give a good picture of what happened. Indeed there was some justification for Mr Liebenberg putting to her that she was protecting the accused.

Mr Justice Cillié concluded that I was guilty of inciting or encouraging an audience of Black Sash members to contravene the laws of the Republic, and convicted me on this count.

The appeal judge emphasized that my address must be considered as a whole in trying to determine whether I was guilty of this charge, and it was no good 'dwelling upon isolated passages' quoted out of context. For this reason he thought Helberg's evidence to be of very little use since his notes 'consist only of some twenty, mostly laconic, unconnected sentences', and the judge illustrated this by taking one phrase Helberg had written in his notes, '*Hy glo in revolusie*' ('I support revolution'), which out of context was damning but in context had quite a different meaning. The appeal judgement went on:

There is, I think, substance in the submission advanced on appellant's behalf that the trial court's finding of deficiencies in Mrs Gardner's evidence was not wholly justified. She was not a member of the appellant's congregation – indeed, she was not a church-goer at all – and prior to the trial she had never met or seen him. There would, therefore, not appear to be any reason why she should – as the trial court seemed to think – desire to protect appellant by giving favourable testimony. Her suggested evasiveness about what the appellant said regarding violence and unlawful action, mentioned in the judgement of the court *a quo*, could have been due merely to faulty recollection induced by the lapse of time. Moreover, she held an honours degree in English and was used to listening to and remembering lectures; and she had held office in the Black Sash Organization, having been the vice-chairman of its regional committee for two years. It is therefore probable, contrary to the view of the court *a quo*, that she would have been better able to understand and remember the substance, the import, and the effect on the audience of the appellant's address than Mrs van Heerden. Indeed, her testimony about what the appellant said on the topics she remembered seems more coherent than that of Mrs van Heerden. It is quite obvious, too, that the latter was mistaken about, or did not wholly understand, certain parts of the appellant's address. Thus, according to her, the appellant, *inter alia*, mentioned that he supported and had preached to the Bantu the doctrine of 'pie in the sky when you die'. If correct, that would mean that he had tried to induce their resignation to terrestrial woe by holding out to them the prospect of celestial weal in their life hereafter [I like that paraphrase]. The appellant does not deny that he mentioned that doctrine in his address; but he denies that he said that he on that occasion supported it or had ever preached it. This is inherently probable; for Mrs van Heerden's version would have been quite contrary to appellant's general philosophy that religion has to work towards achieving prosperity, both terrestrially and celestially.

After summarizing the various versions of what I had said, the appeal judge concluded that I was not guilty of having incited or encouraged the audience to violent revolution and that Liebenberg's contention was wholly untenable when he claimed that I had done so indirectly 'by subtly sowing in their minds the seeds of the need for violence and unlawful action for wider dissemination and burgeoning in due course'. The court added:

Apart from the appellant's sworn direct denial, it is in the highest degree improbable that he had in fact such an intention. For he could hardly have chosen a more infertile soil for sowing such seeds than an audience of women, including mothers and grandmothers, who were all members of an organization avowedly opposed to violence and strictly committed to working within the law.

MONEY

The last of the three counts on which I was convicted was of receiving money from the Defence and Aid Fund, via Alison Norman, and thereby of participating in terroristic activity with intent to endanger law and order. (In South Africa the ANC and Defence and Aid are thought to be virtually synonymous.)

To begin with, the prosecution made a determined attempt to show that the actual use which I had made of the money I had received was subversive. They brought a whole series of witnesses for this purpose. There were, for example, Mrs Mashaba, who was given a ticket once a year to visit her husband on Robben Island; Mrs Motsawaledi, whose husband was sentenced to life-imprisonment at the Rivonia trial, and who got a ticket to Cape Town and school fees paid for her seven children; Mr Nkadimeng, who had served a sentence for ANC activities and had been sent to us by the Quaker Relief Organization for help with his children's school-books, and so on and so on.

The main point that the prosecution seemed to be making was that many of these people had previously been helped by D. & A. and that many of them had been in trouble for political offences. But as I had openly taken over the D. & A. list (though, as I have said, in the end we did not use it), and as I had never tried to conceal that I was willing and able to help people in political trouble, there did not seem to be much point in this. In fact, it rather backfired, because, as they brought witness after witness to testify, it became more and more evident that, what-ever the politics of the people I had helped, the money given had been spent on meeting basic human need and in most of the cases the families concerned (if they had political connections at all) were related to men who were already in jail or had been released and not to terrorists who were still active. The indictment shows that of the 125 separate entries in the list of 'co-conspirators' who had received money from me, 69 were men who had been convicted and were in prison or had been released, 22 were restricted (i.e. under some kind of house-arrest or banning order), and 6 were detained. Obviously none of these could have been taking part in terrorism. Seven had been acquitted, sometimes with legal help from me, and 21 had left the Republic without first being under some kind of police detention or imprisonment.

It was mainly members of this last group about whom Colonel

Swanepoel (the man whom I had described as a sadist) was called to give evidence. He alleged that quite a few of these were actively engaged in terrorist training-camps overseas, thereby implying that I was part of an active organization which maintained the families of men who went abroad to fight. Actually, as the indictment clearly shows, almost all these people had left the Republic *before* I started making any payments of this kind. However, as my concern was whether or not their families were in need and had no other source of support, this distinction made little difference to me either way.

When Jean Webb, who administered the fund, was giving evidence, she said that after I had been arrested, as a matter of personal interest, she had sorted out the index cards of those who had been helped, and only a little more than half of them were 'political'. She gave a whole series of harrowing examples of people who had been helped who had had nothing to do with politics.

A determined effort was also made through some of the state witnesses to prove that I had been associating with, and actively helping, Winnie Mandela in what was said to be her work for the ANC. A letter was produced from Winnie to me, which read:

31st March 1967

Dear Father,
re: Mrs Rebecca Kotane

Bearer is in difficulties. She is one of us but her circumstances are slightly different.

I suggested that she should see you about her problems. She has been to see me about them on several occasions.

Thank you for your very kind assistance at all times.

Yours sincerely,
Winnie Mandela

I explained in my own evidence that I had never seen this letter, since routine requests were dealt with by John Turnbull and Jean Webb and we had had several similar ones from Winnie Mandela when we started administering Alison's money. 'One of us' I assumed meant that Mrs Kotane, like Winnie Mandela, was the wife of a prisoner. In any case we had asked for more information before we paid anything, and Mrs Kotane's 'problems', as a subsequent letter showed, were that she wanted help with her sons' school uniforms.

On one issue the prosecution did succeed in showing that money from the fund might have been used for 'ANC activity', though without our knowledge. This arose out of our efforts to help a group of women political prisoners in Nylstrom jail. I had been told, by very roundabout means, that these people were there, and had asked the local Methodist minister to visit the place and see if anything could be done for them. Then a Mrs Ndala had come to the office, claiming to be a relative of one of the prisoners, and bringing a note written by the prison matron saying that the women could be visited and some personal necessities, like soap and washing things, taken in. Mrs Ndala had four other women with her and we had paid for them to visit Nylstrom and had also given them money to buy toiletries. Later they had applied again, but as they had apparently not been allowed in the first time after all, John Turnbull had said that we would only pay when they could produce written permission to visit from the prison authorities. However, as well as visiting the jail and reporting back to us, Mrs Ndala and the other women had also apparently reported to Winnie Mandela, and at some point, so Mrs Ndala said, she had used R10 of the money we had given them to help pay for a journey to Cradock on ANC business.

Mrs Ndala was questioned by Kentridge about her danger in incriminating herself by admitting that she was an ANC member.

Kentridge: Have you been told that if you give this evidence you won't be prosecuted? – I was told I must tell the truth so there should be no case against me.

Kentridge: You mean if you didn't tell the truth there would be a case against you? – That is what I understood, my lord.

(State witnesses were very well-trained and always remembered to address the judge and not the counsel, which is more than I did.)

Later, after protesting that the witness had not been told of her right to claim an indemnity before giving evidence, Kentridge went on:

Are you giving this evidence voluntarily? – Yes.

Kentridge: How did you come to court yesterday? – By car.

Kentridge: Whose car? – I do not know whose car it was.

Kentridge: Well, who drove you? – A driver.

Kentridge: Was it a police car? – Yes.

Kentridge: When were you told that if you told the truth you would not be charged? – I don't remember whether it was this year or last year.

Kentridge: And who said that to you? – The police. I do not know their names. I was at John Vorster Square. I was under arrest because the police fetched me at home. . . . I thought I would be locked up in jail if I didn't make a statement. My husband was not questioned. It was said that I and my husband would be locked up when I was questioned by the police.

In addition to calling Mrs Ndala to show that I might have inadvertently contributed R10 to ANC travelling expenses and that Winnie Mandela, like us, was interested in prisoners and their needs, the state also called the nurse, Mrs Mpendu, whom we had tried to get reinstated on the nursing register. The burden of her evidence was that I and Winnie Mandela had both suggested that if she could not get reinstated she should leave the country. Since her qualifications would have been acceptable abroad this would seem to have been common sense, but Liebenberg claimed that two people having a like thought must have been in conspiracy even if they had never seen each other.

The final attempt to show that Winnie Mandela and I were in cahoots arose because I had contributed R500 to a collection which was organized via the Christian Institute to supply her with a car. This had been necessary because she was under house-arrest, which meant that she had to be back in her house in Soweto every night by a certain time, and the only work she could get was in Germiston, nearly twenty miles away. I was questioned *ad nauseam* about this car, and the third time I answered:

I wonder if I could put this on a record or something and play it over. I bought her a car so that she could go to work in . . . Well, I didn't buy her a car. I was willing to contribute towards the purchase of a car so that she could go to work in Germiston.

Liebenberg: Did it occur to you that there was a possibility that she might have used the car for political purposes? – No, it didn't occur to me, mainly because she was so restricted that I gathered she wasn't allowed to have gatherings and meet people, and so on. I don't know how she could do any work. But this obviously never occurred to me. But when I think on it now, this is why it would never have occurred to me.

Liebenberg: But do you really say that Winnie Mandela would have stopped her activities just because she was charged? – I am afraid I don't know anything about her or her activities.

Liebenberg: Yes, but it must have occured to you, Dean, that there is a possibility of that car being used for underground work? – I am afraid that I may be very jejune, but it did not occur to me.

Kentridge then intervened: 'I do think on a precise count that that is at least the third time on which my learned friend has been back to those questions about this motor-car and the R500.' And after some discussion even the judge said, 'Yes, I think you have asked the question a few times, Mr Liebenberg.'

In the end, the prosecution rather abandoned this line of attack and took the line that it did not matter two hoots what I had done with the money; they claimed that I had received it from the Defence and Aid Fund so I *must* have been intending to further the ANC plan and therefore been committing an offence under the Terrorism Act. Here, of course, Alison Norman's evidence was vital.

Alison, in her evidence, described her family background, which had left her very well-off in her own right, and with a lot of family money behind her, and how she had met me in Salisbury and come back to the Church. She was then taken through a long series of letters which the police had impounded from my files and which we had written to each other after she had returned to London from Rhodesia. These were mostly to do with religion but some related to the £8000 which she had given me in Salisbury to administer for her, and to offers of financial help she had made to me in Johannesburg before D. & A. was banned. There followed a letter which was not in my files, but of which she had kept a copy as an explanation to her executors about the Johannesburg account in case she should be killed suddenly. This letter was the one she had written to me asking whether she could give me financial backing for carrying on the work which D. & A. had been doing.

Alison then described how, in addition to sending her own money, she had also collected several thousand pounds from two friends who were interested in helping this cause, and she called her stockbroker to give evidence about shares sold from her account and transmitted to Johannesburg. She also tried to get her bank (a Martins branch of Barclays) to testify, but was told they did not do this as a matter of policy unless they were subpoena'd under English law, and of course the English legal system had nothing to do with this case.

Both Alison and I were questioned over and over again about referring to 'friends' or 'your friends' in our letters to each other, and about occasions when letters and papers had been sent via a third party, or a false name had been put on the envelope. I must admit that this did look like 'conspiracy', but the trouble is that a system like the South African one drives you into being conspiratorial even when you are not doing anything illegal. We all knew that letters were constantly being stopped and read, and sometimes never reached their destination, and it had seemed only sensible to evade this as far as possible. Some of the stuff that I had sent Alison was legally dicey – particularly when it related to information that Carlson had given me. There were, for instance, the reports of prisoners being tortured and there was also information about a Tanzanian citizen Joseph Shayo who had been kidnapped by Swanepoel on the Caprivi Strip in 1968 and held incommunicado since then. I thought his own country should be told that a citizen of theirs was being held without trial, and had tried to get the British consul to act on his behalf. He had been unable to do so, so I had asked Alison to try and get her friends to do something about it.

Liebenberg referred to this when cross-examining Alison:

. . . Again, I would suggest to you that this would be an appropriate case to refer to this central bureau which could take it up through the channels of the Anti-Apartheid, of the African National Congress which had its headquarters in Tanzania, and to deal with it very, very simply. – Well, that is not, in fact, what I did.

Liebenberg: I suggest to you that 'our friends' there refer to this mysterious group of people comprising the Anti-Apartheid, the African National Congress, Christian Action, Defence and Aid. – A large collection is it not? In fact, I think he was referring to my friends generally, the people I was in contact with in England, anybody I thought would help, probably thinking in particular of anyone with legal knowledge on this question.

Liebenberg: Why would the dean have any objection to going to Canon Collins and the African National Congress people in London in a matter like this? – I do not know about the dean, but I, as I have said a great many times before, kept off any kind of contact of this kind because I did not wish to be implicated with them. What I did in fact was that I tried to get hold of the person I referred to in my evidence on Saturday [Lord Campbell], and he was not available and I went to the Tanzanian embassy myself.

Liebenberg: That is what I do not understand. There is an organization which can deal with a problem like this very easily, and yet you prefer to go about it in a roundabout way on your own? – Yes.

Liebenberg: Why did you not use the source available to you?

> That is what I do not understand. – I have explained it so
> many times, Mr Liebenberg.

We seldom mentioned names in letters because it might well have brought unwelcome Security Police attention on to the person or organization concerned. Alison was particularly thankful that we had been careful about this when Eva Auerbach, who was one of the people who had raised money for us, decided to come and live in the Republic. It would certainly have been assumed that she was a 'Defence and Aid agent' from the word go, if we had put her name in our letters. (As it happened, she contracted cancer soon after getting there and has since died.) Because of all this, some of these letters did sound a bit conspiratorial, though it was a very far cry from this to proving that Alison's money came from Defence and Aid.

Often Liebenberg invented a 'fact' to see what reaction he got. For instance, he said to Alison: 'We have evidence that the underground African National Congress in Johannesburg applied to the dean from time to time for advances of money in order to pay for their trips throughout the country when they went about organizing' (which was a gross distortion of Mrs Ndala's account of how she had got R10 from us). He also said he 'seemed to recall' that Alison had been thanked for a donation of property to Christian Action in the newsletter of another organization called 'The Servants of Christ the King'. Alison replied that this was quite impossible and Liebenberg said, 'I will try and find it, if I can. If I do not, it is just too bad.' That, of course, was the last she heard of it. Liebenberg also asked Alison why I should have Canon Collins's name and address written down in my diary, but did not bother to mention that it had obviously been written years before D. & A. was banned – it was left for Alison to ask to see the entry and point this out herself.

Alison, like me, got extremely tired of answering the same 'suggestion', made without any evidence and repeated over and over again. When Liebenberg said for the umpteenth time, 'That sounds like Collins to me, Miss Norman', she finally lost patience and replied, 'Everything sounds like Collins to you, Mr

Liebenberg' – a point which Kentridge later took up in his closing speech. Also, when Alison, being questioned about Jordaan, said that she thought Jordaan was lying, and Liebenberg said: 'Are you not just drawing inferences without any definite proof?' she could not resist replying, 'Mr Liebenberg, you have been doing that for the last two days.' To which he could only say, 'I am asking you.'

Liebenberg seemed to spend remarkably little time questioning Alison about her bank statements (all of which she put in as evidence) or about the sources of her money and, as the appeal court later said, 'Miss Norman's testimony . . . remained unshaken in all material aspects.'

So in the end, in spite of all Liebenberg's 'suggesting', the prosecution relied for any evidence that Alison was connected with D. & A. on the evidence of a Security Policeman, Major Zwart, who had given her a lift while she was on holiday in South Africa at the beginning of January 1970. Alison had come over on a charter flight and, as is the way with charter flights, it had been a week late going back. This had given her a week to spare, so she had sent a telegram to her cousin, Sister Phoebe Margaret of the Community of St Mary the Virgin, whom she had not seen for a long time, to ask if she could go and stay for a few days with her on a mission at Tsolo in the Transkei (one of the Bantustans). Sister Phoebe Margaret had responded enthusiastically and Alison had duly set off on what was nearly a twenty-four-hour journey, by overnight train from Johannesburg to Pietermaritzburg, and then a bus journey which would get her to Tsolo at about 5 p.m.

In her second-class sleeper she had found one other passenger, a youngish woman who seemed friendly enough. Alison can't remember her name, but she was referred to throughout the evidence as 'June'. Just before the train pulled into Germiston, June had left the carriage and come back later to say that she had run into a man whom she had not seen for years and would like to talk to. Did Alison mind if she invited him into the carriage, as his own compartment was crowded? Alison did not mind and the man had come in – a tall well-built chap who had been introduced as Mr Morley but who was in fact Major Zwart of the Security Police. He and June had talked for a time and gradually brought Alison into the conversation – asking what she, as a visitor, thought of South Africa, where she was going, and so forth. Alison had mentioned the prospect of a very hot and uncomfortable bus journey of eight or nine hours the next day and 'Mr Morley' had said that he was being met at Pietermaritzburg by his local representative with a car; the two of them were to drive down to Umtata and would be passing very close to Tsolo, and he had offered Alison a lift. Alison says that when she is offered a lift she is only concerned with two things: will the car end in a ditch and will she be fending off unwanted passes? 'Mr Morley' looked as if he would be a reliable driver and as there were going to be two men the second problem did not seem likely to arise, so she had accepted gratefully.

Next morning, the young man with the car was, as had been promised, at the station. But here the two accounts differ fundamentally. Alison says that all four of them, Zwart, June, herself and the young man, had gone to have breakfast together in the town (for which Zwart insisted on paying) and then June had gone off, ostensibly to meet relatives, while Alison, Zwart and the young man had set off for the Transkei. Alison does not remember much about the journey – it was hot and she had not slept much in the train. The three of them had talked about the scenery, the race problem, the political situation, an African millionaire in Umtata, the problems of the Bantustans and so forth, but as far as she was concerned the conversation was pretty desultory. She had slept some of the time and for some of the time the two men had talked in Afrikaans, which she does not understand, ostensibly about 'business'. Around one o'clock they had reached Tsolo, which was about five miles from the mission, and had stopped for lunch at the hotel there. (Alison was not expected till late afternoon and was not anxious to arrive unexpectedly before lunch with two unfed men in tow.) The hotel was an extremely scruffy one-horse place and the sight of it had turned Alison off any wish to eat, but she had probably drunk quite a lot of beer since it was a very hot day. They had hung around here almost interminably while the men ate and drank, and had finally left for the mission, where Alison was duly delivered to her cousin.

Zwart's version differs radically from this. He says that the car had been left for him at the station without a driver and only he and Alison had breakfasted together. On the way to the Transkei and in the hotel they had had a very serious political discussion during which he had convinced Alison that he was a dedicated member of the Liberal party and Alison had said, 'I am of the opinion that a revolutionary situation is developing. The government is smothering the political aspirations of the indigenous population.' She had added that 'it is necessary to show the African people engaged in a righteous fight for freedom that there are Europeans prepared to assist' and that 'Alan Paton had great political courage in the face of Fascist oppression'. (Zwart alleged that he had kept diving off to the gents in order to write down what she had said, and he asserted that these were her actual words, not a paraphrase of them.) He went on to claim that Alison had drunk two double brandies, as well as beer, at the hotel, and they had stayed till 4 p.m., while she tried to enlist Major Zwart as an agent of the Defence and Aid Fund and said that there were 'several prominent clergymen in Johannesburg who could protect him if he got into trouble'. Then they had gone off to the mission, picking up a male hitch-hiker on the way, so that there had been two men present by the time they got there. Also she had dropped a mysterious black notebook in which she had been writing in the car, and Zwart, on picking it up later, had found Canon Collins's name on the same page as my own.

As with myself and Jordaan, much of this was Alison's word against Zwart's. Alison could point out that she could not imagine herself being as pompous as Zwart described. 'Righteous' was a word which had lost its original meaning and was normally used for phrases like 'Don't be so bloody righteous', and she could not conceivably have talked about 'the political aspirations of the indigenous population'. She went on to say that she could not remember having drunk brandy at lunch-time in her life and if she had done so would probably have gone to sleep. Sister Phoebe Margaret was brought by the police from the depths of the Transkei to say, as the *Rand Daily Mail* headline put it, 'NUN: ALISON NORMAN DID NOT SMELL OF BRANDY'. (Alison got teased a lot by her friends about that.) The mysterious black book was identified as an intercession list (which it seems very unlikely could have been dropped as Zwart said it had been), and, along with my own name and that of Canon Collins, it contained the names of a whole series of clergy, organizations, and other people, many of which had nothing whatsoever to do with South Africa. But the major point at issue still remained. Zwart said that Alison had tried to enlist him as an agent for D. & A. and Alison could only say that, brandy or no brandy, this was totally untrue and impossible.

Cillié's judgement, as the appeal court later remarked, 'contained no explicit unequivocal finding' on whether Alison's money had come from D. & A. Cillié referred briefly to the money which she had given me in Rhodesia and help she had offered me in Johannesburg before D. & A. was banned and then immediately went on to discuss her conversation with Zwart. He pointed out that Zwart had given evidence in front of him, while Alison had refused to come to South Africa, and said that Zwart 'made a good impression on the court'. He concluded:

On a consideration of all the facts, I have come to the conclusion that Alison Norman's evidence in denying the conversation with Zwart is false and that Zwart's evidence is true. Therefore, the state has proved beyond reasonable doubt that she had said to him that she was an agent of the International Defence and Aid Fund for the distribution of funds and that she had not spoken the truth about it before the commission.

The appeal court took a very different view of the value of Zwart's evidence. The judge commented on the 'inherent improbability' that Alison would have said she was an agent of Defence and Aid. He went on:

It is difficult to credit that a woman such as the evidence

indicates Miss Norman to be, would, in the middle of a hot day, consume not only three beers but two double brandies as well, the latter, as Zwart pointedly mentioned, being pre-metrication tots. Moreover, if Miss Norman were indeed an agent for Defence and Aid, one would hardly expect her to communicate that fact to a chance acquaintance whom she had so recently met for the first time. However well Major Zwart played the part of the 'liberal, anti-government Mr Morley', it is not readily credible that Miss Norman – herself manifestly not unfamiliar with 'liberals' – would either have been so readily taken in by 'Mr Morley's' expressed sentiments, or (again upon the assumption that she was indeed a Defence and Aid agent) that she would have been so indiscreet as to endeavour to enlist his services upon such short acquaintance. That all the more so if she was in truth in contact with 'several prominent clergymen', to whom she presumably could have referred 'Mr Morley's' credentials.

In his judgement Cillié, JP, remarked that Zwart was 'a liberal who was in the correct position and the correct place'. There is, however, no evidence to support that view. The record contains no suggestion that distribution of Defence and Aid funds in the Transkei was envisaged at any time; nor did the herb-dealing 'Mr Morley' disclose where his headquarters were situated. That Miss Norman would have employed the somewhat stilted and stereotyped phraseology attributed to her by Zwart – who, incidentally, appears himself to be fluent in the English language – in his recorded notes of her alleged *ipsissima verba*, would appear to be somewhat unlikely.

In addition, Miss Norman's address, where it appears in Zwart's notes, has – contrary to Zwart's evidence – the appearance of having been written in later, and the sequence of events reflected in the notes is not entirely beyond criticism. Before her journey to Pietermaritzburg Miss Norman had met, and had had a discussion with, Jordaan. In his evidence Zwart maintained that he did not know June's surname and that, before embarking upon this assignment, he had been told nothing about Miss Norman's political views or of any suspected association between her and the Defence and Aid, and his instructions, he testified, were merely to ascertain what her movements were when she went to the Transkei. All this notwithstanding, it is somewhat surprising that, on his own admission, he addressed no enquiries to Miss Norman concerning the Defence and Aid organization after she had allegedly disclosed her agency, beyond asking her who the prominent clergymen were. Under cross-examination Zwart's explanation of his failure to do so was that Miss Norman 'was talking pretty fast at that stage' and that 'the conversation was going on at a rate where I could not ask her. It was just not possible.' Pressed further on the point, he replied: 'I didn't ask her and I cannot say why I didn't.'

The appeal judge went on to describe the direct conflict of evidence over whether 'June' had breakfasted in the hotel at Pietermaritzburg and whether there had or had not been a second man present throughout the trip, and he commented: 'Despite this sharp conflict on an obviously material point and although the state's case was not yet closed when Miss Norman gave her evidence, neither June nor the man who brought the car to Pietermaritzburg railway station was called by the state.'

With regard to the rest of Alison's evidence about the sources of her money, the appeal judge commented that, apart from my alleged admission to Jordaan and Alison's alleged admission to Zwart, the state had led no direct evidence to support their contention that her money came from D. & A.: 'The only direct evidence relating to the source of monies transferred to the Johannesburg account was that of Alison Norman, of her London stockbroker, Evans Lombe, and of appellant himself.' And after reviewing Alison's personal background and the evidence she had given about the money he said, 'Despite a meticulously detailed and extended cross-examination, Miss Norman's testimony as above summarized, remained unshaken in all material aspects.' He concluded:

In the light of the various considerations I have mentioned, the court below, in my judgement, erred in finding Miss Norman's aforementioned alleged admission that she was an agent of International Defence and Aid to have been duly proved beyond reasonable doubt.

The last plank of the prosecution's 'evidence' that I was conspiring with the ANC was hewn from my attempts to get the same sort of work as I had been doing in Johannesburg started in Port Elizabeth and Durban. The Port Elizabeth issue was very simple. Late in 1966, I had been in touch with a Mrs Crafer in Port Elizabeth about setting up a system for helping prisoners' dependants there, and I had written to Alison to ask if she could do anything about raising funds for it. Alison had written back in April saying, 'I have made enquiries and your plans for P.E. are thoroughly approved of.' Mr Liebenberg said, at length, that this was a clear reference to some controlling authority which could only be D. & A. Alison gave evidence that the 'approval' she had obtained was from Eva Auerbach, who was in touch with a group of rich Jewish people who had had experience of racial discrimination themselves, and were willing to give money to help others who were suffering from the same thing.

The dean was trying to extend the same sort of charitable activity to Port Elizabeth, and Eva thought that she and her friends might support this as a sort of separate thing. I couldn't undertake it; my resources were not great enough.

This had not come to anything because we had been unable to find reliable people to administer it, but eventually a Dependants' Conference was successfully established in Port Elizabeth. As the appeal court said, 'the correspondence relating to Port Elizabeth affords no support of the state's contention that appellant was handling Defence and Aid funds'.

The Durban issue was much more complex and related to my dealings with Mr Howard Trumbull, who had been treasurer of an American missionary society called the American Board Mission. His office in Durban had been searched in February 1971 and a lot of letters impounded. He himself had been deported in May 1971, so the only evidence available was the correspondence found in Durban and in my own files, and what I was able to say about it. (Why the police had not held him as a witness instead of deporting him if they considered, as they alleged in the indictment, that he was one of my 'co-conspirators' must remain a mystery.)

It all started with a letter which I had written to Trumbull in December 1967 saying:

I understand that you know Mrs Phyllis Naidoo and that you have also recently had a talk with Mrs McKee. I have asked the latter to obtain some more financial assistance for Mrs Naidoo from a source of which she is aware and I will myself be sending her a few extra Rand for Christmas.

I understand from other sources that Mrs Naidoo admits to helping various people who wish to travel some distance to visit their husbands in prison. I have a good deal of spare money which I am at liberty to spend on paying the rail fares for such people: and quite a lot of women from the Johannesburg area bring their visiting permits in to me and I am able to pay their fares. Can you yourself organize something like this for women in Durban if I was able to provide you with the money? I could either do this for individual cases or send you a lump sum if you are willing and able to tackle it?

I explained in evidence that the 'source' in the first paragraph of this letter was Diana King – a girl who had been my secretary in Salisbury and had since trained as a social worker in England. Her father was a Conservative MP and she had some fairly rich friends. She had agreed to try and raise some money for this kind of purpose, though she could not do it on anything like the scale that Alison Norman did. Sylvia McKee was the wife of a clergyman whom I had known in Rhodesia and who after a spell in the north of England had joined the staff of St Paul's. (This of course meant that they lived in Amen Court, which is the 'cathedral close' for St Paul's. To the South African Security Police, Amen Court was synonymous with Canon Collins and Defence and Aid. Later I had begun to wonder about this myself in connection with Sylvia.) My 'spare' money mentioned in this letter was of course from Alison.

Sylvia had visited South Africa in 1967-68 and had come to see me a couple of times, but we had not had monetary dealings of any kind. However, unknown to me, she had been sending fairly large sums to Trumbull during the first eight months of 1968. If I had known this, obviously I would not have asked Diana King to rustle up what she could, nor would I have sent Trumbull small sums from my own funds, which I had done from time to time.

The state case really rested on a letter which Trumbull had sent me on 22 January 1968, enclosing, he said, a copy of a letter from him to Sylvia McKee. This copy had not been found in my office files with the rest of the correspondence and I can honestly not remember getting it. Nor I am sure, had I made the suggestion about 'several thousand Rands' which it contains. The letter found in his files read in part:

Would it be possible for you or someone else in England to open a chequing account in my bank in Durban and give me a power of attorney to write cheques on that account only? I can forward you the necessary papers to sign. Then you could just transfer monies into that bank account.

Then, after going into detail about the people he wanted help for, it goes on:

I have been in touch with and saw Dean ffrench-Beytagh who suggested that you might want to send me several thousand Rands to help with such items as those above plus sending wives to see their incarcerated husbands, and studies and sports equipment for them.

Do you want me to continue to send details as above through the post?

Many thanks for your past help. Phyllis saw her husband this past weekend for an hour.

I had replied to Trumbull's letter on 25 January:

Thank you for your letter. I enclose R250 for immediate needs at your discretion, covering the things set out in the 3rd paragraph of your letter. I don't want individual receipts, but if you would, send me a receipt just for this amount and keep individual receipts for covering yourself.

I have written to my friends in England suggesting that it might be possible for them to have the same set-up with you as they do with me, which you mentioned in your letter to Sylvia. I hope very much that something will come of that. If you don't hear anything within a few weeks, let me know because I am going overseas at Eastertime and will try to follow this up.

Not surprisingly, I was hammered very hard about this whole issue when I was being cross-examined. It began inauspiciously with Liebenberg losing his temper. He had been using one of his usual techniques of assuming the existence of an 'organization', in Rhodesia this time, and then asking me why I had not worked with it. Kentridge intervened:

My lord, there is a good example, with respect, of an improper question. My learned friend says he can't understand how this witness could have worked in one group without knowing of the existence of another group. There is no evidence at all of the existence of another group and well my learned friend knows it. That is what is wrong with this sort of cross-examination.

My lord, it is only coincidental that it is the witness's ninth day in the box, but at this stage it is difficult to refrain from objecting. My learned friend feels I do it too often – I stand astonished at my own moderation.

Liebenberg: Well, I am sorry. If you have to stand there for ninety days it will make no difference to me. If that worries my learned friend, it certainly does not worry me.

(Next day he said, apologetically, that he had not meant this literally.)

Then Liebenberg went on to deal with the 'H. T.' (Howard Trumbull) exhibits in a cross-examination which covers the next sixty pages of the transcript. What I said was summarized rather caustically, but not unfairly, by the appeal court:

Appellant testified that he warned Trumbull against receiving money from Mrs McKee. This because 'she was connected with St Paul's Cathedral and therefore she might have connection with Canon Collins'. Appellant throughout his evidence maintained that he was unaware that Mrs McKee was sending Trumbull money, and that Trumbull had deceived him in this regard.

Appellant's testimony that he has no recollection of receiving any copy of a letter from Trumbull to Sylvia McKee, the general tenor of his evidence regarding his 'suspicions' concerning the possible origins of the money to which, during her visit to Johannesburg, Sylvia McKee gave him to understand she had access, and his inability to fix with any reasonable precision the time when he warned Trumbull against the possible dangers inherent in receiving money from Sylvia McKee is, in my opinion, all somewhat unconvincing. Nor did appellant furnish any very feasible explanation why, if, as he said, his initial request to Diana King was as early as 25th January 1968, it was only on 20th August 1968 that Diana King dispatched the first remittance to Trumbull. In this last regard appellant said that Diana had not complied with his January request and that 'we only established it when I went to England in May-June'.

However, the appeal judge went on to point out that Sylvia McKee had been sending money to Trumbull before I had given him any myself and she had apparently had some difficulty in raising the first £100 which she sent, which would indicate that it had not come from D. & A. 'There is a total absence of any positive evidence', the appeal judge said, 'to show that any money which Mrs McKee sent to Trumbull was indeed Defence and Aid money', and the state's inference that it was 'rests upon the mere fact that Sylvia McKee's husband was during the relevant period a minor canon of St Paul's Cathedral'. There are many other organizations in England, the judge said, 'who are willing, indeed anxious, to contribute to the type of activity in which Trumbull was engaged', and the fact that I had met Trumbull's various appeals for money seemed inconsistent with my knowing that he was getting it from Sylvia at the same time. The state had argued that Diana King had been substituted for Sylvia McKee as a means of channelling D. & A. money to Trumbull after his office had been searched in July 1970 but this was contradicted by a letter which I had written to Alison at the time.

Ogilvie Thompson continued:

In my judgement, the proper conclusion to be drawn from all the aforegoing is that the state's contention that appellant was knowingly administering, or directing the channelling of, Defence and Aid funds, derives no appreciable support from appellant's relationship with Trumbull as reflected in the H. T. series of correspondence.

Summing up all the evidence which the state brought to try and prove that I had been conspiring with the ANC, the appeal court judge finally concluded that:

The cumulative effect of the inferences sought . . . to be drawn by the state from the appellant's activities in relation to Trumbull and Port Elizabeth, and from the administration of the fund, does not, in my view, suffice to discharge the onus of proof resting upon the state.

He accordingly concluded that the state had failed to prove that I had received monies from the Defence and Aid organization, London, and therefore that it had failed to establish the main connecting link between me and the ANC plan. In consequence, it had not proved that I had taken part in a criminal conspiracy to overthrow the state by violence or intended to endanger the maintenance of law and order within the Republic.

THE TERRORISM ACT

The appeal court judgement dealt with one further issue which, it seems to me, is of vital importance for the future of any kind of political thought or protest, and of any effort to help the victims of apartheid in South Africa.

It all turns on the meaning of the Terrorism Act and the circumstances in which the accused has to prove himself innocent rather than the state having to prove him guilty. In most civilized countries, of course, it is a basic principle of law that the onus of proof rests on the prosecution. But the South African government found that this principle was too inconvenient to retain, because in spite of all the efforts of the Security Police, people who were accused in the big political trials kept being acquitted for lack of real evidence. So in 1967 the Nationalists introduced the Terrorism Act. This is so vaguely worded that it is extremely difficult to understand what it really means. Some of its provisions relate to people who have undergone military training outside the Republic or who are found with arms and explosives. But there is also a 'catch-all' clause which says that a person can be *presumed* to be guilty of terrorism if, 'with intent to endanger law and order in the Republic', he has taken any part in committing an act which had or was likely to have any of the following results:

(a) to hamper or to deter any person from assisting in the maintenance of law and order;

(b) to promote, by intimidation, the achievement of any object;

(c) to cause or promote general dislocation, disturbance or disorder;

(d) to cripple or prejudice any industry or undertaking or industries or undertakings generally or the production or distribution of commodities or foodstuffs at any place;

(e) to cause, encourage or further an insurrection or forcible resistance to the government or the administration of the territory;

(f) to further or encourage the achievement of any political aim, including the bringing about of any social or economic change, by violence or forcible means or by the intervention of or in accordance with the direction or under the guidance of or in co-operation with or with the assistance of any foreign government or any foreign or international body or institution;

(g) to cause serious bodily injury to or endanger the safety of any person;

(h) to cause substantial financial loss to any person or the state;

(i) to cause, encourage or further feelings of hostility between the white and other inhabitants of the Republic;

(j) to damage, destroy, endanger, interrupt, render useless or unserviceable or put out of action the supply or distribution at any place of light, power, fuel, foodstuffs or water, or of sanitary, medical, fire-extinguishing, postal, telephone or telegraph services or installation, or radio transmitting, broadcasting or receiving services or installations;

(k) to obstruct or endanger the free movement of any traffic on land, at sea or in the air;

(l) to embarrass the administration of the affairs of the state.

The appeal court judge pointed out how loosely this Act is worded and that it is not difficult to imagine actions which might 'cause serious bodily injury' or 'endanger the safety of any person' which had nothing whatever to do with terrorist activities. This, he said, 'can hardly be the intention of the legislature' so it must be shown that there was, *in fact, an intent to endanger law and order in the Republic*, and that any particular action *was likely* to have had one of the results listed, *not that it could, possibly, have had such a result*.

This seems to be of enormous importance in narrowing down the range of activity which the Terrorism Act covers. It is still bad enough, but it is not the complete *carte blanche* for clamping down on any kind of protest which, I have no doubt, its authors intended it to be.

This decision was reinforced by the appeal court judge's consideration of whether the 'acts' which I had admitted to committing in the administration of Alison's money were intended to endanger law and order and were likely to lead to one of the twelve 'results' which the Terrorism Act lists. He dismissed the evidence brought by various state witnesses that the Defence and Aid Fund and the ANC had an identity of aim, and that ANC members were encouraged by knowing that D. & A. was there to help their families, because all this evidence related to the period before D. & A. was banned and because no association between myself and the Fund had been proved.

> The state led no evidence to show that any member of the African National Congress, or any other political offender, terrorist or saboteur, entered upon, or continued to engage in, the activities of that body because of any assistance obtained, either by himself or by his family, from the funds administered by appellant. Knowledge that his family is receiving some assistance while he is serving a prison sentence (or while he is outside the Republic's borders engaged in terroristic activities) is no doubt some solace to the individual concerned; but that can hardly be regarded as an intended boosting of morale in such a degree as to qualify as promotion of the activities of the African National Congress.

It was, the judge said, too remote a contingency to be 'likely' within the terms of the Act.

The prosecution had argued that – regardless of the result that I had achieved – my use of the money showed that I *had the intent* to endanger the maintenance of law and order within the Republic. In other words, that my motives were really political rather than humanitarian.

The appeal judge pointed out that in her original letter to me Alison had asked me to help 'the sort of people who used to be helped by Defence and Aid, now that this has been banned, *and any others who are in need of help* and can't get it through the existing welfare organizations'. Jean Webb's evidence showed that the latter group had become more and more numerous. In fact over half the money had been spent on people who had nothing to do with politics. Also payment had been in kind wherever possible. The court concluded:

> The features mentioned above point away from the Johannesburg account having been administered pursuant to the conspiracy or in furtherance of the ANC plan, as contended by the state. The systematic provision of funds for the defence of

persons charged with certain categories of criminal offence – irrespective of whether such persons be rightly designated 'political offenders', 'saboteurs' or 'terrorists' – might conceivably not meet with universal approval; but that is of no moment in relation to the present case, for it is in itself manifestly not a contravention of the Act. Nor is it relevant that the solicitude consistently exhibited by appellant towards such persons may not be shared by everybody. The court is concerned solely with the enquiry as to whether appellant was rightly convicted of 'participation in terroristic activities' in contravention of the Act. It may be questionable whether in his administration of the Johannesburg account appellant was, as he asserts, actuated solely by humanitarian considerations or, to cite his own words, 'just doing ordinary work of charity'. The expansion of Miss Norman's original £2000 to nearly R50,000; the extension of appellant's activities, through Trumbull, to Durban; his attempted establishment of similar arrangements in Port Elizabeth; and the terms of his extensive correspondence with Miss Norman and others suggest that appellant may increasingly have seen himself in the role of the resident champion of those whom he regarded as the 'victims of apartheid'. It may be that appellant was in some measure motivated by the circumstance that, as he remarked in explaining why he continued living in the Republic: 'I have got to put it out that I am doing my best to try and work within the situation which I abominate.' Moreover, in order to 'work within the situation', appellant – who, as his letters indicate, was always conscious that his activities were liable to be regarded by some with disapproval, if not actual suspicion – was, as has been indicated earlier in this judgement, admittedly not above resorting to stratagems and to what he himself in a letter to Miss Norman described as 'probably a Jesuitical and legal nicety'. All this notwithstanding however, the totality of the evidence falls short, in my opinion, of establishing with the degree of proof required in a criminal case that in his admitted administration of the Johannesburg account appellant was, as contended by the state, acting pursuant to the conspiracy charged, or in furtherance of the ANC plan mentioned in the preamble to the indictment, or with 'intent to endanger the maintenance of law and order within the Republic'. In short, none of those contentions has, in my judgement, been proved beyond reasonable doubt. It follows that, in my opinion, the trial court erred in convicting appellant in respect of paragraph (9) of the indictment.

For the aforegoing reasons, the appeal is allowed; the conviction and sentence are set aside.

BOTHA, JA ⎱ Concur.
TROLLIP, JA ⎰

It is difficult to describe quite what an effect the terms of this acquittal had on liberally thinking people in South Africa. When I was convicted, a wave of fear and caution had run through the Republic. For instance, Professor John Dugard, the Professor of Law at Witwatersrand University was reported as saying, 'The prosecution and conviction of the Dean of Johannesburg has drawn attention once again to the sinister implications of the [Terrorism] Act and the severe restrictions it places upon freedom of speech and freedom of political activity.' Churches and universities would have to take note that certain subjects were virtually taboo and beyond discussion. 'The morality of violence and civil disobedience, for instance, are subjects which will in future be practically impossible to discuss, despite the fact that they are widely debated in most Western countries.'

Many people withdrew from their work with Dependants' Conferences because they understood from my conviction that work with political prisoners' families would render them liable to conviction under the Act, and even if they were prepared to take this risk for themselves, their husbands or wives would not let them.

The appeal court verdict changed all that. Protesting, arguing, defending and aiding *are* still legal. South Africa is not yet totally a police-state (though it is, of course, also legal for a Security

Policeman of the rank of lieutenant-colonel or above to arrest someone *on suspicion* of contravening the Terrorism Act and hold them incommunicado for as long as he likes, and 'no court shall pronounce upon the validity of any action taken under this section or order the release of any detainee'). The extent to which the rule of law is still a reality in South Africa depends on the importance and skin-colour of the person accused and the amount of money and help he can get. If it had not been for those who contributed to the £42,000 which the trial and appeal cost, and for the support and publicity which I had both from within the Republic and from all over the world – above all if I had not been, as the indictment said, 'an European male' (and a British citizen as well) – the outcome would have been very different. It was without doubt the British consul's visit and the wave of international protest which induced the Security Police to start questioning me after only two days, instead of leaving me for weeks to 'cook' in solitary confinement. And I doubt very much whether I would have got bail either before my trial or after my conviction if the same pressures had not been at work. Even with all these advantages, it was only the availability of the money to enable me to go to the appeal court which saved me from five years in prison. I am deeply aware of how privileged I have been, and how far I am from being the 'martyr' which I have sometimes been called. But there are many real martyrs suffering under South African 'justice' and these must not be forgotten.

FROM CONVICTION TO ACQUITTAL

The appeal court verdict was, of course, nearly six months in the future when, after a trial lasting three months, Cillié, JP, gave his judgement. It was All Saints' Day, when we rejoice in the saints of all the ages, known and unknown, and as I believe in the prayers of the saints, that seemed a fortunate omen. But there were other reasons for some optimism; my lawyers were cautiously hopeful, and the public, who to begin with had thought that there was probably no smoke without a good deal of fire, had become very sympathetic towards me; people seemed to agree that the prosecution's case had pretty well fallen to bits. I was advised that if I was acquitted, I ought to leave the country straight away, so I had got a suitcase packed and had invested in a thicker winter suit, suitable for England – just in case. It was therefore with a sense of hope as well as fear, but also of finality, whatever happened, that I drove back to the Old Synagogue for the last time, accompanied by the friends who had been so good to me all through the trial and had done so much to make it easier for me.

The judgement seemed to go on interminably, but on charge after charge I was found innocent and my hopes really began to rise. There was no morning tea-break, and by the time the very short lunch-break arrived I still had not been convicted of anything and I was able to eat with my friends as usual. Then, soon after the lunch, there came the first conviction – and I knew that conviction on only one count was enough to send me to prison for five years. I can't say it was a shock – I had, after all, had long enough to come to terms with the possibility – but it was a tremendous disappointment and I listened to the rest of the judgement in a sort of dazed incredulity. In fact, its quality seemed to deteriorate very much towards the end and Cillié's reading became tired and hurried, as if he was ashamed of what he was doing. But there it was: I had been found guilty of inciting Ken Jordaan, encouraging the Black Sash to break the law, and receiving money from the Defence and Aid Fund – all in furtherance of the 'ANC plan'.

Sentence was not pronounced at once. I was taken by my counsel into a consulting room behind the judge's chair – I suppose it had been a vestry in the old days – and we discussed what should be done next. Suddenly Kentridge made a dash for one of the doors and yanked it open. There was a policeman outside apparently listening to our conversation. Kentridge was furious and complained to the judge, while the policeman protested that he had only been trying to make sure that I did not escape – which, as there was no way out of the room except through the court or via the police quarters, seemed rather improbable. We had, of course, already considered what to do if I should be convicted, and we decided to stick to our previous plan that Kentridge should not make a passionate plea in mitigation, but only a very short speech asking for the minimum sentence and for leave to appeal.

Before the judge gave his sentence there was one curious incident. He asked Liebenberg if it was possible to give me a suspended sentence – implying, presumably, that this was what he wanted to do. Liebenberg was rather floored by this and did not seem to know what the answer was. It was left to Kentridge to tell the judge (what he should surely have known already) that five years' imprisonment was the mandatory minimum sentence under the Terrorism Act.

After this I was told to stand up at the place where I was sitting between my lawyers, and I was then formally found guilty, and sentenced to five years in prison. Again it was not a shock – more of a dull thud and a sense of *fait accompli*, together with a panic that I would not be allowed bail and would be in prison that night. Somehow it was the thought of that night and not the next five years which was so frightening. I also had a considerable sense of injustice. Even if I had been as guilty as the judge said, it seemed excessive to send me to jail for five years for two acts which had had no result at all and for helping people to get the necessities of life. So I felt angry as well as numb and frightened.

Cillié was reluctant to give leave to appeal because, if I remember correctly, he said that his judgement had been based on findings of fact and there was no dispute about the law. Kentridge said, in a very polite way, that other judges might interpret the facts differently, and leave to appeal was given; also, to my enormous relief, an extension of bail was granted, in spite of (presumably routine) prosecution objections.

There was the usual wait of an hour or more while the bail documents were made out and my friends waited outside the court, not knowing what was going on. Then I was allowed to leave and came out of the court into a marvellous crowd, with Africans leading the singing of 'Onward, Christian Soldiers', and cheering, and crying, and sympathy, and congratulations for the lawyers, and, of course, news cameras and reporters. It was all very moving and emotional, and I felt pretty choked. Then I was asked by a reporter what I was going to do and I answered without thinking that I was going to Mass – simply because, it being All Saints' Day, there was an evening Mass at the cathedral and it was my duty to be there. (I had of course said Mass myself that morning as usual and many people had come.) It sounded like a pious remark, but it wasn't meant to be. Because of the traffic-jams, we only got there in the middle of the *Sanctus*, and I stood at the back of the church in the suit in which I might have been travelling to England that night, and said what prayers I could.

The five-and-a-half-months' wait between the trial verdict and the appeal judgement seemed endless. There was absolutely nothing I could do which would affect the issue one way or the other – it was all up to my lawyers. I was partly held together, I think, by the necessity of going through the motions of my job (and, amongst other things, of raising the commercial loan of R2.6 million needed for rebuilding Darragh House, since we had at last got the scheme approved). But the main factors were the care and kindness of my friends, the skill and concern of my doctors, and the friendliness and warmth of so many people. That Christmas I got over four hundred Christmas cards from all over the world, instead of my usual hundred or so, and many of them were from complete strangers. In the street people whom I had never seen before – particularly Africans – would come up to me and shake my hand and say, 'God bless you, Father' and 'Good luck, Father'. One African bus conductor saw me from his bus, rang the bell to stop it, came dashing across the street to shake my hand, and then dashed back to his bus and started it off again – all very much against the rules, but very encouraging. On another occasion a very posh car stopped and a doctor got out (I knew he was a doctor because he had a stethoscope in his pocket). He shook my hand and said, 'We are all thinking of you', and then got back into his car. Who he was I haven't the faintest notion. Sometimes it was a Jewish person, who told me that he was of a different faith as he wished me well.

The trouble was that I did not know *when* I would get an answer. The appeal was heard at the end of February and the beginning of March, and after that we were just told that we would get twenty-four hours' notice of when the judgement would be handed down. It was an awfully short time in which to get ready either to go to prison or to leave the country. In the end, the judgement was given after Easter, for which I was deeply thankful. Not only was I able to celebrate the Resurrection again in the cathedral and amongst the congregation which meant so much to me, but I was also able to finish my seven-year term of office as dean. At least, whatever happened, I did not have to feel that I was walking out without fulfilling my commitment.

In the event, I got much less than twenty-four hours' notice. On Thursday 14 April at about 3.45 p.m. I was told that the appeal verdict would be handed down in Bloemfontein at 11 a.m. the next day. (All the appeal hearings had been in Bloemfontein, but it was entirely a matter for lawyers and I had not been to them.) Ray Tucker arranged for a colleague in Bloemfontein to telephone through the news, and at 11 a.m. a few of us crammed into his office, while others gathered in the passage and a great crowd were in the street outside.

The news came through promptly – one word, '*Mazeltov!*' the Yiddish for 'Good luck!' It was an unforgettable moment and an unforgettable experience. We went out to the crowd and told them – Ian Thompson got us all quieted down and we said the Lord's Prayer. Then off to the cathedral where there was a crowd already waiting. Neville Palmer decided to have a short service and the Africans literally danced up the aisles in their own fashion, singing and clapping their hands. It seemed exactly and entirely right. Then all the practical arrangements – travel documents (the Security Police still had my passport, but the British embassy were very helpful), packing, instructions about money and furniture, and a hundred and one other things, goodbyes to friends whom I loved and to whom there wasn't enough time to say so properly, goodbye to a country which I loved and did not want to leave – but which everyone told me I must. Then the airport, and the hymns, and the choking in my throat – and the ultimate horror of finding that a reporter had oozed his way into a seat next to mine. I could not even be sad and happy in peace, but at least I got him to pay for my whisky on the plane.

CHAPTER ELEVEN

'But what can be done?'

To the end of my life I shall probably be in doubt as to whether or not I was right to leave South Africa. It has been said of me that I deserted my congregation and my people, and that it would have been far better if I had become a martyr, and a good many other things, all of which may well be true. Indeed, I feel in my heart that they are true. But the reasons why I left are perfectly clear to me and they seem intellectually convincing, even if they are not convincing emotionally. My legal team, with whom I discussed the question at considerable length, were certain that I should leave at once if the appeal was successful because the Security Police might re-detain me immediately as they had done with 'The Twenty-two'. My lawyers were also worried about the threats which had frequently been made against my life by right-wing fanatics and which might well be carried into effect if I was acquitted. Still, the fact that there was danger in staying would have been no good reason for leaving if there had seemed to be anything useful that I could still do in South Africa. Of course I could have gone on protesting, but I do not believe much in the effectiveness of protesting by itself. I could not have gone on helping anyone on an individual basis, because anyone I helped would immediately have been victimized by the Security Police. Also my term of office as dean had finished and there was no obvious job for me to do. This in itself seemed to be significant. And so I decided to leave.

The immediate emotional relief of getting on to a plane and getting out of the country was, of course, immeasurable. However, like so many emotional things, that very soon passed and I began to feel very strongly that I should perhaps have stayed and gone on and waited to see what happened. I shall never know whether I was right or wrong to leave, but the fact remains that I went, and now I feel that I must do what I can from outside the country which I love, and which I still feel is my home, to bring about change within it.

As I have said earlier, 'change' is one of the rude words in South Africa. Anything or anybody who sets out to change the 'South African way of life' is an anathema, and this is said, again and again, in official announcements and in parliament. White South Africans have got it good. They look around the world and they see racial unrest. They see Negro riots in America and racial troubles in England's cities, while in the liberated African countries they often see chaos, tribal wars, one-party government, massacre and murder, and (although the murder rate in Soweto is the highest of any city in the world) they proclaim that in South Africa these things do not occur. Everything is fine – for just so long as 'State Security' can keep the lid clamped down on the seething hatred boiling up beneath. For white South Africans know, in their heart of hearts, how precarious their situation is. Always at the back of white consciousness is awareness of the 'Swart-gevaar' – the black danger or black menace – and as the rest of Africa becomes liberated and independent, and black consciousness, black theology and black power increase, white South Africa's awareness of being a beleaguered people grows. Historically it is just not possible for three and three-quarter million white people to maintain seventeen million non-whites in a state of servitude and near-starvation for ever. But as I said in the 'theme' at the beginning of this book, apartheid is essentially a matter of the guts and not of the intellect, and any alternative way of thinking or being is utterly impossible. As was made clear at my own interrogation and trial, the Nationalist Afrikaners believe that anybody who tries to induce change is necessarily out to destroy them and everything that they stand for.

For the Christian, of course, the reverse is true. It is God who does not change. 'He is the same yesterday, today and for ever', but man must change continually. *Metanoia* – repentance, renewal, change – is one of the great Christian words. Christ called us to 'repent, for the kingdom of heaven is at hand'. He came to change death into life and sickness into health, and if the kingdom of God is to 'come on earth, as it is in heaven', it means that not only man's heart must change but also his circumstances and the manner and condition in which he lives. This is one reason why Christianity and apartheid are utterly incompatible. Another reason is that *koinonia* – belonging together – is the essence of the life of the Church. 'By this shall all men know that ye are my disciples, if ye have love one to another', Jesus said, and this is repeated in different ways over and over again in the gospels. The fellowship of the Spirit is *not* 'tea and buns' after church, but a real and costly belonging together at depth, an acceptance of other people which also requires (again as I said in the 'theme') an acceptance of all you dislike most in yourself.

Koinonia is the utter antithesis of apartheid – *separatedness* – which seeks to divide not only the blacks from the whites, but each African tribe into a separate people, and to cut the African off from any sense of being a citizen of the country in which he lives and works. In the 'white' cities he is officially a unit of labour, not a person, and very often he has no real home anywhere, no place in which he can truly feel he belongs. (Since I myself, at present, do not really feel that I 'belong' anywhere, I am acutely aware of how much this matters to a person's sense of identity.) People *must* have some place where they matter and where they are accepted just as being themselves. We belong to each other, we need each other, we are deeply dependent on each other, and we can never grow into human beings except in relationship with each other. I believe that this is an essential part of the Christian gospel (as it is also an essential part of psychiatric theory), and it is, as I have said, the utter antithesis of apartheid.

I am sometimes asked whether, if I believe this, I can accept the Dutch Reformed Church as 'Christian'. The Dutch Reformed Church, of course, supports apartheid, on the basis of various Old Testament texts and particularly on the ground that as God was said to have set the nations apart when he destroyed the tower of Babel, so he means them to live apart from each other for ever. I think that the Dutch Reformed Church in Holland has shown that, theologically, these arguments don't have much of a leg to stand on, but since members of the South African Dutch Reformed Church claim that Jesus is their Saviour, they must still, in some sense, be said to be Christian. It seems to me to be a terribly emasculated form of Christianity because, in essence, they have disregarded the Incarnation.

'The kingdom of heaven is within you' – it is *now* that we are called to be whole. I have always preached, as the appeal judge rightly said, the antithesis of 'pie in the sky when you die'. And apartheid, as I have said so often, leaves both white and black less than whole. Probably Dutch Reformed theologians would reply to this that the white people have been sent into South Africa to care for the black man and to enable him to develop to his full potential, but I think it is manifestly obvious that, even if this paternalism was a right way of looking at things (which certainly both I and the black theologians would bitterly dispute), apartheid policy does not and cannot bring the opportunity of full development to all the peoples of South Africa.

So we come to the question of why there is not a head-on collision between the 'Incarnational' Christian Churches of South Africa and the Nationalist government. There sometimes appears to be. Many individual Christians, from Trevor Huddleston to David Russell, have challenged the government in a direct encounter. But for the most part, the Churches are content to pass resolutions condemning this or that piece of legislation and leave it at that. The government does not mind this very much. It not only shrugs condemnation off, but it uses it in the Afrikaans press to show the Afrikaans people what fools the English are, and how disloyal they are to the whole concept of white South Africa as the Afrikaner sees it.

The trouble is that the Churches consist of people, and their leaders and spokesmen find it very difficult to go further than their congregations will follow. And they will not follow very far. The average churchman is also an average white South African. He may be more liberal than his non-church counterpart (though this is certainly not always so), but he is generally uneasily content to leave things as they are. He knows that dreadful things do happen under the apartheid laws and he does not like them, 'but what', he asks, 'can I do?' He feels that the system seems to work all right, although it is of course abused, and he, like the rest of the white South Africans, suffers from the delusion that there is a clear distinction between religion and politics. He is wrong. Both are concerned with the way in which men live, and you cannot separate them without making a nonsense of them both.

Some Christian bodies which represent the Churches as a whole have publicly recognized this and are trying to do something about it – particularly the Council of Churches and the Christian Institute. Apart from a lot of practical work, they have produced some first-class reports under the heading of 'Spro-Cas' – 'Study Project on Christianity in Apartheid Society' – and these give valuable guidance, not only to the 'converted', but to those who are truly puzzled and want some positive help in understanding the real issues and alternatives. However, the Christian Institute, which publishes the Spro-Cas reports, is itself now under government investigation (along with NUSAS, the University Christian Movement, and the Institute of Race Relations), and it is becoming increasingly evident that the most peaceful and academic discussion of the implications of Incarnational Christianity in apartheid society will become taboo.

Sooner or later, any Christian organization which seeks to practise its faith as well as to proclaim it will be forced to go 'underground', while the conventional Churches go on doing their utmost to avoid a head-on clash with the system and trying to salve their consciences by making protesting noises, which the government completely disregards because they are not backed by any kind of action.

Perhaps the University Christian Movement already gives us some idea of what the underground Church of the future may look like in South Africa, and in other parts of the world as well.

UCM is, I suppose, 'left-wing' in many ways, and it is certainly very experimental liturgically and completely undenominational. Its first general secretary was a Roman Catholic priest but, as far as I remember, you do not have to be a Christian at all, in any formal sense, to belong to it. Many of its officials, like Dr Basil Moore for instance, have been banned, and most of the orthodox Churches are thoroughly frightened of what it is doing. It is to movements like this that really deeply thinking Christians of every denomination, who wish not only to worship together but to work together for a change of society, are being driven. These new 'Churches' will soon be living in the atmosphere of the first centuries AD, when practising Christians were constantly under the threat of persecution and betrayal, and the celebrant said Mass facing the door so that he could watch for strangers coming in.

This, I am sure, is a development of great significance in the whole South African situation, for I am certain that the fight with apartheid is not just a political battle. A power which sets man against man in the name of God is literally satanic. 'We wrestle not against flesh and blood, but against principalities, against powers, against the rulers of the darkness of this world, against spiritual wickedness in high places.' If this evil is not to escalate, the battle must be fought with sacrificial prayer and fasting as well as with political and economic action. I believe that South Africa is in some way the focal point of a global struggle with global significance and that it may well end in apocalyptic violence as forces clash which we cannot fully understand or control.

So I come back to the question which I posed so often when I was Dean of Johannesburg and which the Security Police disliked so much. If the volcanic fury of the African people erupts in the Republic, what is the African Christian supposed to do? As I have tried to show in this book, the South African situation is one which is already extremely violent, not only in such things as police brutality but in the violence which is done to the African's humanity. It kills his children by starvation, it deprives them by deliberately restricted education, and it forbids them to enjoy love and family life. I do not think that it is reasonable or possible to say that it is Christian for a white man to be violent against a black man, but if a black man is violent against a white man, that is sin.

As I have said, it will probably be a very long time before a revolution in South Africa can have any chance of success. But suppose the time comes, as I believe it will, when the black countries to the north of the Republic, aided by forces from the Arab League, or indeed from almost anywhere else on earth, attack the South African régime in what they may well consider to be a just war. What is the African Christian supposed to do then? Is he supposed to fight with the white man to defend the régime which has oppressed him and his forefathers for generations? Or is he to welcome such an invasion as a force which has come to liberate him? And what ought white Christians in the Republic to do if South Africa is invaded? And where would we Christians in England or America stand? Would we side with the apartheid government in South Africa to protect our investments and the Cape route and defend our 'kith and kin' from very real danger, or would we stand with the African?

These questions may not be as far off as we think they are. Perhaps it's time we got down to some real prayer and talk about them. The whole issue was raised as early as 1965 by the Archbishop of Canterbury when he said in a speech, 'If Rhodesia goes over the brink, I believe it is not for us as Christian Churches to give to the government military advice as to what is practicable or possible for it. That is not our function. But if the British government thought it practicable to use force for the protection of the right of the majority of the Rhodesian people, then I think that as Christians we have to say that it would be right for us to use force for that end.'

Rightly or wrongly, the government chose to allow white violence in Rhodesia to pass unchallenged, and so the Churches were able to avoid facing this particular issue, but as violence comes nearer and nearer home in anti-apartheid demonstrations, in Northern Ireland, or at the Olympic games, the question becomes harder and harder to evade. Where do we stand when force can only be met with force? At what point do we feel that we must try to stop the genocide of a people? (Was it really only because we knew ourselves to be in danger that we entered the war against Hitler?) How much do we really care, as long as it is far enough away?

These are uncomfortable questions, but they are questions which Christians all over the world have got to try and answer if our faith is to have any reality in world affairs and is not itself to be a kind of apartheid – a shutting-off from the real issues of the twentieth century in a cosy game of liturgical reform where the crucifixion is forgotten and love involves no cost and no sacrifice.

They are questions which can no longer be openly asked in South Africa itself. I was found guilty of inciting people to violence simply because I warned them that violence was going to come, and any priest or Christian teacher in South Africa who tries to talk with any kind of reality about a Christian's duty when violence breaks out around him will certainly be silenced. Yet, unless the Church in South Africa can preach a gospel which is honest and realistic about the just war and just revolution, the African Christians will be driven to discard the Christian religion as having nothing to say to them in the situation which faces them. And this is another reason why the 'live' Church is being driven underground.

It is sometimes argued that there is no need to take any positive action, whether violent or non-violent, against apartheid, because it carries within itself the seeds of its own destruction. Those who argue in this way point to the shortage of white skilled labour which is very gradually eroding job-reservation; the growing pressure of business leaders, both English and Afrikaans, for relaxation of some of the apartheid laws which make it impossible for industry to run efficiently; the gradual growth of an urban black middle class; and the emergence of a real leadership in the Bantustans which is challenging the government to put its declared policies into effect. There are also a few scattered signs of some change in the political thinking of white Afrikaans-speaking businessmen, academics, and intellectuals, and occasional rumblings within the Nationalist party.

But, as one of the Spro-Cas reports points out, 'white supremacy is no delicate plant which will wilt in a slightly changed political, social, or economic climate', and I myself believe that as economic pressures on apartheid grow stronger, the white population will feel increasingly threatened so that the laws which enforce apartheid will be more rigidly applied. It has always been the least educated and skilled Europeans who have felt most threatened by African advancement, so any weakening of economic apartheid is likely to increase the virulence of social and political apartheid.

Other people argue that the one thing which we must avoid is driving the Afrikaans people further and further into their defensive isolation – that if only they can have enough contact with a multi-racial world, they will realize that their policies are untenable. This may be true for a few individuals, but I am sure that in most cases it just doesn't work. Some of the most virulent Nationalists have had an English university education and it does not seem to have made the slightest dent on their thinking. The average white South African who visits England or the United States does not undergo any real mental change. He is only too glad to get back to his own safe, unchanging society, where everything is thoroughly under control and where black men are kept in their place. He forgets as fast as he can the upside-down world beyond his borders where black men go out with white women, and white men sweep the road and empty the dustbins. 'Dialogue' of this kind is not going to change anything.

In my opinion, therefore, there will be no 'natural' change in South Africa, and war or revolution is eventually inevitable unless we can apply enough non-violent pressure to enforce real change. It is a remote chance, at best, but I am certain that it is our duty to try.

There are three main ways in which this pressure can be brought to bear – by reducing white immigration, by forcing the big industries to accept their social responsibilities, and by cultural boycotts of various kinds.

Immigration is a basic issue. As the South African economy expands, it *must* have more artisans – more motor-mechanics, plumbers, carpenters, electricians, and all the other people who keep an industrialized society going. As long as the government can draw immigrants from Great Britain, Ireland, Spain, Portugal, Germany, Italy, or any other country where the skin colour is 'white', who are qualified in these trades, Africans will never be allowed to do them. These are jobs which could be done by Africans with very little extra training. In the African townships, African mechanics already work on their own cars and apparently manage to keep the most decrepit old wrecks on the road. They are perfectly capable of becoming mechanics in 'European' garages, and they are equally capable of becoming carpenters, bricklayers or plumbers – all of which they do in their own townships.

'Job-reservation' leads to utterly ridiculous situations. For instance, the 'white' bus services in Johannesburg are continually being threatened with cuts because of difficulty in getting Europeans to operate them. There are plenty of African men who drive exactly the same kind of buses (although they are generally much more overcrowded) in exactly the same traffic conditions, but they are paid a fraction of the European rate, and of course they cannot, in any circumstances, be allowed to drive, or collect fares from, European passengers. Another example is bricklaying. Just before I left Johannesburg, rebuilding had started on Darragh House and there were African men bringing the bricks and laying the mortar, but it had to be a white man who put the brick on the mortar. And while European artisans continue to go out there, this sort of nonsense will go on. It is very understandable that they want to immigrate. South Africa is a lovely country, the pay is good, and for the first time in their lives, European artisans are able to employ at least one servant. They can also run a car, and everything is done to provide them with housing and to make them feel that they are really wanted. The fact remains that their good life is bought at the expense of the African and Coloured people.

I have done my best in England and the United States to bring home to trade union leaders how essential it is for African economic advancement that their members should be discouraged from immigrating. But apart from some rather vague exhortation to their members, there has not been much response.

I am told that one of the basic problems is that the trade unions in England have strong ties with the white trade unions in South Africa, and it is of course the white trade unions in South Africa who are most anxious to preserve the status of the white artisan and prevent the rise of any Africans into their ranks by refusing to allow them to learn their trades. When one looks back over the history of the British trade union movement and how it fought from the beginning for the basic human rights of all workers, it seems almost impossible to understand how it can now ally itself in this way with the white unions in South Africa.

But even if one has to accept, sadly, that this is the case, there is still a great deal that the world trade union movement could and should be doing to help African labour to get itself organized. It is still legal for Africans to form trade unions, although they are not allowed to organize strikes, and all sorts of complicated regulations and restrictions are put in their way. (There is, for instance, no machinery by which non-white union dues can be paid directly from the men's salaries, so subscriptions have to be collected outside the factory gates each pay-day.) Skilled support and help from unions in Britain or the United States could make all the difference in getting African trade-unionism off the ground.

I do not feel so strongly about the immigration of professional men and women because there is no possibility for many years that enough Africans will be educated to fill these jobs. (There is, for instance, no engineering faculty in any tribal college.) But I do think that if such people decide to go out to the Republic they ought to realize that they are going to a very privileged life – to a glorious country with a wonderful standard of living, beautiful sunshine, plenty of servants, and good pay. They should be aware at whose expense they are enjoying these things and ask themselves what they are going to give back in return for all that they are getting. I do not suggest that they should immediately launch into political diatribes, which will, in any case, do no one any good. But they should make a real effort to get to know some Africans, and especially their own servants, as people, not as objects. It is equally important that they should make the effort to learn Afrikaans properly and get to know the Afrikaners as real people also. Then they can join organizations like the Black Sash, the Institute of Race Relations, and the Christian Institute, so that they can become informed about what is going on in the country, and, if they pray at all, they can make a real effort to pray deeply about the problems and their own responsibility in the situation. Above all, they should do everything in their power to avoid the insidious creeping acquiescence in the system and the unconscious English arrogance about which I have written and spoken so often.

Then there is, of course, the whole complex question of overseas investment in South Africa. Many people who are far better informed on this issue than I am believe passionately that American and British industry and investment should disengage from the Republic as completely as it can. They argue that even if this is not achieved, pressure on companies to withdraw does at least induce them to put some effort into getting better conditions for African employees, and they quote Polaroid and General Motors as examples of companies making such concessions only because there was a real threat of their shareholders insisting that they withdrew altogether. This may well be true, though I have tended to argue myself that it is utterly impossible in most cases to bring enough pressure to bear really to scare these big companies. The ramifications of their interests and the size of their profits are far too considerable, and I am told that if it came to the point, the South African government would refuse to allow the withdrawal of capital on a really large scale. Indeed, with all the complex system of subsidiaries and cross-investment it is impossible for the most committed anti-apartheid investor to make sure that none of his shares is helping to maintain the South African economy. And even if there were considerable withdrawals from South Africa by English and American companies they would simply be replaced immediately by capital from West Germany, France, Japan, or some other source. Personally I prefer to have British and American investors, with whom I can have some sort of communication, rather than those in foreign countries where it is much more difficult to bring any pressure or public opinion to bear. (An excellent book has recently been published on this whole issue: *The South African Connection* by Ruth First, Jonathan Steele and Christabel Gurney.*)

Whatever the rights or wrongs of total withdrawal may be, the point which I always emphasize is that neither British nor American companies are doing a tenth or a hundredth of what they could do for their African and Coloured employees. Very often, this is because, although the international top management in the parent company is quite 'liberal' and sympathetic, they appoint South Africans to manage their subsidiary companies in the Republic. These men, of course, are like any other South Africans. They are used to the system of apartheid, they find it works and produces good profit, and they salve their consciences by using a personnel department to help in particular cases of hardship. In fact, I have evidence which shows pretty clearly that very often South African subsidiaries do not tell the whole truth about their treatment of their African employees to their head offices overseas.

Even men who have not been born and bred in the country find it becomes extraordinarily easy to accept without question all the rules and regulations of apartheid, and this is true even in matters where they can most easily be challenged. This was most clearly brought home to me by an incident which happened soon after I arrived back in South Africa from Rhodesia. I was invited by the American consul-general in Johannesburg to the celebration of the American Day of Independence on 4 July. The invitation was for about 5.30 p.m., and in South Africa this invariably means some sort of a 'sundowner'. I went to this all dressed up in my Sunday best, and expected to be given, if not good American Bourbon, at least South African brandy – instead of which all I got was Pepsi-Cola. Pepsi-Cola is no doubt an admirable drink,

* Published by Maurice Temple Smith in 1972.

but not one that I am prepared to put up with at that particular time of the day in South Africa.

The reason for this abstemiousness was that the Americans quite rightly had some Africans at their party and there is a law in South Africa which forbids white people to give alcoholic drinks to black men. I don't know how many people ever observe this, but I cannot think of any church party that I have ever been to where we have ever taken any notice of the rule. We share our drinks with our friends, and the government can do what it likes about it. What shocked me was that the Americans were celebrating their own Independence Day, on what was presumably their own territory, with the American flag flying, and yet they refused to be independent enough to do it in their own traditional way, but fell in with exactly what the South African government wanted.

It seems to me that British and American companies which have their bases in countries in which freedom has been hard won and is much treasured should have sufficient guts to try to apply their standards in South Africa, rather than adopt standards that South Africa happens to think are right. Of course people say that large companies are so impersonalized that it is impossible to get them to act according to any principles, other than those of sheer economic profit. But in fact, before God, there is no such thing as a company or a corporation. Each one consists of people, and at the head of each there is a person, or a small group of people, who can change things if they really want to do so. There are also shareholders, big and small, and they too are people. The man in the street who has only a few shares still has the right to ask questions at an annual general meeting or to band together with some of his fellow shareholders.

But it is, of course, the big investors who can bring most pressure to bear. I think myself that there is room for some international body, perhaps under the auspices of the United Nations Organization, which could call together the main investors in South Africa and try to formulate some plan by which they could bring their united pressure to bear upon the South African government. There is no question that the South African government needs these investments, and there is no question that money talks. Companies acting unilaterally against job-reservation, for example, might well be discriminated against by the South African government purchasing departments and in other ways, but if it were possible to bring together a great number of the industries concerned and get them to combine on some of the basic issues, the South African government would be very hard put indeed to deal with them.

Much of what these industries could do is, of course, in the realm of pay increases, in-service training, trade union organization, and so on. But companies could and should show much greater concern for their employees' living conditions, opportunities for further education, chance of a proper family life, and other matters which do, of course, greatly affect their efficiency as workers.

There is one area in particular where I believe that a few big industries could take action at comparatively little cost in a way that would have a really vital effect on the whole apartheid system. This is over the enforcement of the 'pass laws'.

It is a well-known fact that the daily prison population in South Africa is approximately double that of Britain although its total population is something like a third of Britain's. Most of the people in prison are what can loosely be called 'pass-law offenders', that is to say people who have the wrong reference-book for the place in which they are, or an incomplete one, or simply have not got it with them. It has recently been stated that the average time it takes to sentence a pass-law offender in a Bantu commissioners' court in Johannesburg is three seconds. This may seem impossible but it can be done because they are tried (if that is the right word) in batches, and so a whole lot of them are sentenced at one time. The courts can do this *because there are no lawyers there to defend the people concerned.*

If every big English or American company used a member of their legal department to provide legal defence for any company employee or employee's relative who was caught up in the pass laws, the situation would change almost immediately. Alternatively, a group of firms could get together to finance a legal service in the big cities to which any African or Coloured person who was in this kind of trouble could come to ask for help in his defence. The immediate result would be that it would become impossible to convict and sentence prisoners automatically. Of course, this would mean that men would be kept even longer in prison awaiting trial than they are now (and the present six weeks' average is long enough). But it is possible for arrested men to be allowed bail for these offences *if* their employers can discover where they are being held. I myself have spent days trying to discover the whereabouts of cathedral employees who were in trouble so that I could bail them out. If the big companies made enough fuss, they could get the system of notification improved and be able to arrange bail – which would mean that they also got their employees back at work.

If a fair proportion of the pass-law offenders were defended in court, the police would be a lot more careful whom they arrested and on what grounds – because they themselves would have to go to court to give evidence. More important, the Africans concerned would not feel quite so utterly helpless and caught in 'the system' as they do now. They would know that they had some status in belonging to a particular firm and that their employers cared what happened to them. The firms would benefit too, because I believe that better labour relations and better work would result.

The danger is that responsibility for carrying out ideas like this might get left to the personnel departments of the big firms and, quite frankly, I have found them almost completely useless. The personnel manager is never really one of the top brass in an industry, and, if it is to be of any use, a project such as I have suggested has got to come as an order from a director who is prepared to make sure that it is carried out properly. For example, the lawyers who are retained must be men of a calibre who will not let themselves be browbeaten or bullied by the commissioner or the magistrate concerned. But if the top management of a number of firms really took a scheme of this kind seriously, I believe that it could be of inestimable importance in cracking open the whole cumbersome machinery which keeps apartheid going.

Another, and quite different, area in which I believe pressure could be brought to bear much more effectively than it is, is in the great Afrikaans universities. We hear a great deal about student protest in South Africa and we tend to forget that the students who protest are mostly NUSAS members from the English-speaking universities, Witwatersrand, Natal, Rhodes, and Cape Town. But there are of course also Afrikaans-speaking universities which are dedicated to keeping alive the old teachings of the Dutch Reformed Church amongst the youth of the country. It is noticeable that when members of NUSAS protest about some issue, it is the Afrikaner students, as well as the police, who are in the forefront of any attempt to break the protest up, and there is serious and bitter hatred between the two groups.

The whole emphasis at these Afrikaans-speaking universities is that South Africans must preserve the whole policy of apartheid. It must be prosecuted with the utmost vigour because South Africa is the last bastion of white civilization throughout the whole wide world and unless the students dedicate themselves to preserving the South African way of life, the Republic will disintegrate into corruption and racial strife, as the rest of the world has already disintegrated. The newest of these universities, the Rand Afrikaans University, is specifically dedicated to eradicating 'socialism, communism, and liberalism'. (There is a much more liberal attitude at Stellenbosch, which I suppose stands about half-way between the English-speaking and Afrikaans-speaking universities, and, as a result, has been the subject of a great deal of pressure from the authorities.)

I cannot help feeling that there would be good grounds for universities throughout the world refusing to accept the qualifications, especially in Arts subjects, of students who have been educated within the system of these Afrikaner universities. What can they possibly know of the whole great stream of Western thinking if their education is intended to eradicate 'socialism, communism, and liberalism'? When I have raised this point with academics in England, it has been pointed out to me that it is extremely dangerous to take any political setting as a criterion on which to decide whether or not a university's academic standards are acceptable, and I take the point. Nevertheless, I am sure that more could be done to bring academic pressure to bear on institutions which seem to me to be devoted to controlling thought rather than liberating it.

Then there is, of course, the vexed question of sports and cultural boycotts. The effect of this kind of thing is, admittedly, superficial. It is not going to alter the deep emotional and economic roots of apartheid, one way or another. Nevertheless, I do think that these boycotts are worth staging. They do hit where it hurts. The South Africans love their rugby more than almost anything else in the world and they really do care about being excluded from international matches. Any move in this direction is immediately given full coverage in the Afrikaans press and it does bring home to them what the rest of the world thinks about the South African system.

Apart from this, I think there is a moral issue involved. It is arguable that economic and political pressures force us to have a business relationship with the Republic – to trade with it and to invest in it. But nothing forces an individual to play games with a person whose behaviour he detests, and the same goes for a country. A person plays games with his friends, and I think we should say to white South Africans, 'While you go on treating human beings in this way, you are not our friends.' It is as simple as that.

As I said earlier, it is arguable whether any of the changes which can be brought about by economic and social pressures of this kind can be really radical. I have no doubt that the exponents of Black Power would say that they are the typical woolly palliatives of a typical woolly English liberal, and that they would only obscure the real issues of black/white confrontation. I think that this is very probably true, and although I am sad about it, I can understand why they feel like this, and I believe that a black/white confrontation may well be a necessary phase in the development of mankind.

For centuries we white people, and perhaps particularly we missionaries, have taught black people all over the world that the way they can be most acceptable to us is to imitate the way in which we behave, as exactly as possible. We made them wear our clothes, speak our language and adopt our table manners and our customs, and the closer they approximated to us, the more 'civilized' and acceptable we felt them to be. The implication of this is that a black man is at his best when he is an imitation white man. Of course he can never be a white man, so even his best is bound to be second-rate. It is against this attitude that I think the black man is now rightly rebelling. It is true that the European nations have had a great deal to give to Africa and Asia, but the giving has not been disinterested – there has been a lot of exploitation in it – and now the time has come for us to accept as well as to impose, to enter, with the other races, into the common heritage of the whole of mankind.

The best way in which I myself can understand this is to think about St Paul's remark that 'there is neither Jew nor Greek, there is neither bond nor free, there is neither male nor female: for ye are all one in Christ Jesus'. Theologically, of course, that is an admirable and unexceptionable statement, but taken at its face value it is extraordinarily stupid. Whether St Paul liked it or not, men and women do not lose their sexual natures by becoming Christians. They remain male and female, but they need each other, and they complement each other. It seems to me that exactly the same is true of the different races. We complement each other, and we cannot be whole people unless we can accept our need for each other. Even at a conscious level, for example, Africans have a great deal to teach us about the proper responsibilities of kinship. (When an African talks of his 'brother' he very often means his second cousin twice removed, but he does think of him, literally, as his brother, and he often makes far greater sacrifices for him than most of us would for 'real' brothers.) Africans have a great deal to teach us, too, about spiritual awareness and the whole reality of psychic levels of being, and about patience and lack of anxiety, and many other things.

As I say, we have not begun to explore the depths of this relationship, and it seems to me that we shall never find out how much we need each other and how much we mean to each other until black people can stand and look us in the face as black men and women, not as imitation white ones. This will mean radical changes on both sides. For Africans it means abandoning bitter anger and resentment, but for us Europeans it will mean reinterpreting many of the archetypes which are buried deep in our consciousness.

As long as whiteness and goodness are somehow synonymous, it is going to be very hard for us to recognize our need for blackness, and to stop seeing our skin-colour as being somehow a sign of natural superiority. The Bible, in particular, is full of metaphors which encourage this kind of thinking. Washing, whiteness, cleanliness, holiness – they all go together. Even the detergent advertisements carry the same message. But 'wholeness' is a much better image than 'whiteness', and as I said at the beginning of this book, I believe that wholeness depends on our being able to recognize and accept the whole of our own nature, with all its lust and envy and arrogance and fear, so that it can be opened to change and redemption. If we can do this, there will then be no need to convince ourselves that we are 'good' by projecting all our 'badness' on to people of a different colour or creed or social class.

'Theme' repeated

It will be obvious to anyone who has read this far that there is a great deal in myself for which I need forgiveness, and I can only hope that God can use my weakness to help others to accept themselves as they are. I know that this does sometimes happen. A man came up to me in the United States, when I was doing a tour there recently, and said that he had listened to other religious speakers – men like Trevor Huddleston who look so obviously ascetic and absorbed in God – and had felt remote from them. Then he had listened to me, and said to himself, 'This is a perfectly ordinary bod, if he can go through this and get on top of it, perhaps I can too.'

Certainly, I am most deeply aware of what a vulnerable person I am, not only because of my occasional 'breakdowns', and my liking for alcohol and appreciation of feminine beauty, but also because of my need to 'be needed' and to be a success in what I undertake. I remember vividly, as a boy in New Zealand, how I pretended to have a weak ankle in order to avoid playing rugger because I was afraid that another boy was a better player than I was and would be picked for the team in my place as scrum-half.

I am certain that if I had not been called to be a Christian and a priest, either I would have ended like my father, dying of alcoholism with a string of broken marriages behind me, or I would have become extremely arrogant in order to disguise my insecurity and my obsessive fears, and so would have used what talents I have solely to boost my own ego and destroy other people. Certainly fear, and the need to defend myself against fear, would have played a great part in my life. Even now, I am not a 'nice' person, but I am absolutely certain that my vocation to the priesthood was a right and true one, and that I could not have been, with any integrity, anything other than a priest.

Salvation, I believe, is knowing that by myself I am hopeless and helpless and yet that, if I want to be accepted, God accepts me. One of my favourite quotations is St Teresa's saying, 'Oh God, I do not love thee. Oh my God, I do not even want to love thee. But, oh my dear God, I do *want* to want to love thee.' This has been the basis of my own faith and my preaching.

Many people say that I am much too easy-going on sin, and I am sure it is true that I am much too easy-going on myself, but I do not believe that I ought to be hard on other people. For instance, I knew that in my various congregations there were a good many practising homosexuals. I never felt that it was my business to stop them, and I did not enquire about their relationship to each other. It was not my business that some of them were living together. If they wanted to come to church and worship God and serve him, as many of them did, most devoutly, I certainly felt myself to be in no position to refuse them. (I do, however, have what is perhaps a puritanical feeling that I could never celebrate a homosexual marriage, and I am not sure why this is so. Certainly a homosexual relationship can have the deep commitment and expression of love which is part of marriage, but it somehow seems incomplete, perhaps because it is bound to be physically sterile.) In any case, I do know from experience that the Church can give great joy and fulfilment to such men and can also receive a great deal from them.

Sometimes a priest who is (as I have said before that he ought to be) 'unshockable and unflappable' can give a love and acceptance to men and women which they may not be able to seek from psychiatrists or social workers or any other source. There is an old story of a man who came in very great trepidation to a Roman priest in the confessional and said, 'Father, I have committed murder', and was patiently asked, 'How many times?' And this I think is the right attitude. If a priest can accept a person, he can go on to show how much more God will accept him, and from *that* point *metanoia*, changing, rebirth, can begin. As the Samaritan handbook says, it is useless to talk to people about the love of God unless you can demonstrate the love of man.

There is, of course, the complementary problem of Christian discipline. My first rector, Tom Savage, was absolutely rigid about this. He would not, for example, accept the children of nominal Christians for baptism. I am sure that in essence this is right, and that it is no good being wishy-washy about presenting the demands which the Church makes on its members, but I am also sure, as I look back over my ministry, that I have often been too harsh in the way in which I have expressed this. Some people have been attracted by 'toughness', but others have been turned away who, with more gentleness, and more concern to show them that they really were wanted and cared about, could perhaps have been brought in without any of the essential disciplines being lost.

Sometimes, of course, there simply is no answer, and this is particularly true of the tragic problems which arise when a person is divorced and has remarried. I think that a great deal more thought and prayer needs to be put into this whole issue. It is simply not good enough to wash our hands of it. Personally, I am inclined to think that we should be much stricter about investigating a couple's real commitment and sense of responsibility before we allow a marriage to take place in church and 'before God', with all that this implies, and should accept that registry-office marriages may not be made with a full Christian intention. Then, if a marriage goes wrong, you have a basis of faith to work on, with a 'Christian' couple, and a means of allowing 'secular' divorcees to start again with a clean sheet and, if they really desire a full commitment, with a church wedding. But this is an issue on which I think the moral theologians of the Church ought to give much more help to the clergy.

Priesthood is, of course, a terrible responsibility, and I am almost sick sometimes with the realization that I have given people wrong advice, or failed to give them the kind of help that they needed.

Sometimes I do not realize it for years afterwards and sometimes I know immediately, but in either case it is no good wringing your hands and moaning about it. A priest is supposed to be trained to give proper moral advice, and if people come to ask for it you can only do your best, put your mistakes right if you can, and pray like blazes for guidance. This I think is the crux. Unless you are really praying, day by day, and trying to become sensitive and obedient to the will of God through prayer, you cannot expect to know what to say when people come for help – and, indeed, they probably will not come unless they sense that you are a person who prays. What can a priest, as a limited human being, say to a man or woman who is lonely, troubled or suicidal, or who has got an impossible marriage or a mongol child, or whatever their tragedy may be? From your own resources you can do precisely nothing.

For this reason, it has never been my habit to go out directly after Mass to shake hands with my parishioners. For me, one of the most effective times for prayer is after I have received the Holy Communion, and if, as I believe, I have received our Lord himself, it is right that I should be quiet and attentive to him afterwards for as long as I reasonably can. If I am to teach other people to do this, they ought to be able to see me doing it myself. (I am aware, of course, of all that was said in the New Testament about the Pharisees praying 'that they may be seen of men', but I really do not think that that is our danger today.) The Mass is the heart of the Church, which is the body of Christ, and it has so many aspects – sacrifice, communion, worship, the glory of holiness, universality – that I could go on for pages about it. If a priest, or any other Christian, really tries to grow in true awareness of its meaning, his faith will live and he will be able to communicate it to others.

According to the rubrics of the Anglican Church, another part of a priest's work, which he is bound to do day by day, is the saying of the offices of morning and evening prayer. I know that some of the younger clergy find this obligation absolutely 'dead' and cannot bring themselves to do it. But I have done it, day by day, throughout my life, ever since I was ordained, with practically no break at all, and I am very deeply thankful that I have had it to hang on to. This regularity may well arise from the fact that I am an obsessional neurotic, and I have sometimes gone to perhaps absurd lengths to preserve it – including getting out of bed in the middle of the night to go down to the church after suddenly waking up and realizing that I have forgotten to say evensong.

I am certainly not saying that everyone should imitate me by carrying things to these lengths. But it still is good to have some basic habit or practice of prayer which does not require any emotional response, or even a peaceful setting, and which you can do no matter where you are or how you are feeling. The office can be said on holiday, in aircraft or trains, or in a car (provided someone else is driving); it can be said without any kind of spiritual exaltation or desire, and no matter how depressed or sinful or faithless you are feeling, and at such times 'going through the motions' is, I know from experience, of enormous value.

However, it is a priest's real personal experience of his own humanity and its redemption in God's love and forgiveness which gives him the authority to mediate that love to others, and I am sure it is a great mistake to try and make spurious efforts at being different and behaving differently from your own true nature and social background. Even an honest effort at temporary identification with another way of life is bound to be false just because it is temporary. For instance, when I did a course at the Urban Training Centre in Chicago a few years ago we were asked to start with what they called a 'plunge' – that is to go off into the depths of Chicago for about four days and see what it was like trying to survive with practically no money in hostels and shelters, doing casual labouring and so forth. Obviously this is a useful educational experience for people from rich middle-class families who have never seen this side of life, but doing it for four days, knowing very well that it will finish soon, and that if you get into real trouble you can always pick up a telephone and ask for help, is a very, very different matter to being really poor.

The real trouble with poverty is not the day by day grind, though that is bad enough, it is the hopelessness, the blackness and emptiness, and the fact that there is no way out. No amount of 'plunging' can enable people with a secure professional background to experience this hopelessness. The danger is that they may not realize this, and so will believe that being short of food and sleeping rough for a few days enables them to be truly identified with the destitute. The same is true, in my opinion, of clergy who try to identify themselves with hippies or drug addicts or 'youth', and who dress oddly or get up to other antics in order to try and show how 'with it' and unconventional they are.

Unless behaviour comes from the living experience of the person himself, it is bound to come over as phoney, and in the long run I believe it defeats its own ends. You should have the courage and integrity to be yourself, wherever you are (and, as I learned so painfully in New Zealand, if you have pyjamas when working with a sheep-shearing gang, then you should wear them). This generally works with people of any age. For example, it is no good my pretending that I am interested in pop music, because I am not, and if it is being played by young people with whom I am talking, I ask them to switch it off because I cannot listen to that ghastly row and talk to them at the same time – and this is accepted. A priest *must* find his own identity, and the closer he is to Christ, the more likely it is to be a true identity, but trying to pretend to be either holier or more unholy than you really are is a mistake – we should do our best to be our real selves.

All of this is, of course, equally true of laymen, and I have rather begged the question as to how, if at all, the vocation of a priest differs from that of any other Christian. The trouble is that I am not at all sure that it does. In the past, of course, the difference was that the clergy were paid, full-time servants of the Church, and they were ordained and licensed to administer the sacraments and preach. As a young man, I used to have very exalted 'Catholic' notions about all this, but as I have got older, and more and more adept at using the gifts of my parishioners to make up for my own deficiencies in time or talent, I have realized more deeply the meaning of the 'high-priesthood' of Jesus Christ and, in him, the priesthood of all believers. Spiritual direction can be given just as well by competent laymen and laywomen as it can be by an ordained minister, and there have been magnificent examples of this in both the Roman Catholic and the Anglican Churches. Equally, we could have far more people who are doing ordinary jobs but who are ordained to administer the sacraments in homes and offices without a church building (and a move in this direction has of course already started).

Personally, I believe that these are straws in the wind, and that the Church will move far faster and more radically than we expect into quite a new mode of 'being', leaving perhaps remnants of the institutionalized Churches stranded in our great ecclesiastical buildings.

This is already happening in all sorts of Christian group movements which cross the denominational boundaries, and it is for this reason that I have taken on the Wardenship of the Servants of Christ the King, which is a group movement combining corporate silent prayer and commitment to action. Other organizations, like the Samaritans and Shelter, have by-passed theology in order to find a practical expression of the meaning of sacrificial love. As I have said, I believe that it is also happening in South Africa, where there are signs of an 'underground' Church being born.

For myself, this does not mean that I have to discard any of my beliefs, but that my horizons have widened and that I have learnt (particularly through my brief experience in prison) to be much less obsessive about many things which I previously thought were more important than I now believe them to be. I have become freer in my own prayer and more aware that God's power and love uphold me, however paralysed I may be by fear, or consciousness of sin. But I have also learnt that words are not enough, and that faith must explode into action when I am called to it, not just into gestures of protest. (It is one of my lasting regrets that I was too afraid of jeopardizing the work I was doing for prisoners to become personally involved with the people whom I was helping, and that I deliberately avoided meeting and talking to Winnie Mandela and her friends. I believe now that I should have been more courageous in using my right as a priest to go into the African townships and should have become much more deeply involved with the African people than I was.)

But since I have been living in England, I have come to realize that, in some ways, we in South Africa were fortunate. At least we had an obvious glaring evil to fight and we could not disguise from ourselves what we were, or were not, doing about it. In England it is all so complex and so 'soft' that it is only too easy to evade the challenge of our faith to 'change' and to 'belong together'. There are many ways of practising apartheid which have nothing to do with colour or race (though, goodness knows, colour and race are live issues in Great Britain as well as in southern Africa). If we are to fulfil our vocation as Christians and be catalysts in our society, the leaven in the lump, we should be doing far more than we are to confront the real problems of twentieth-century man and to work for a society where there will be no 'discarded people', and where belonging and caring are more than pious platitudes, a society where greed and fear can be challenged and men can be made whole.

What the future holds for myself and my fellow Christians, I do not know. But I am utterly certain, from my own experience of the Church's life, that it is true that the 'gates of hell will not prevail against it'. I know this from the power of the prayer of so many people which upheld me so strongly when I was in prison. I know it from the great crowd of every denomination who flooded me with their love and support, because they found that in a crisis we belonged together. I know it from the courage and sacrifice of men who say that they have no faith and yet are willing to risk everything to fight for justice on earth. For this living body of Christ, as for so much else, I give thanks.

Prison diary

The diary which follows was written in prison in the days after the British consul's visit, when I was allowed to have a pencil and paper. I knew, of course, that the Security Police would read it, so I had to be careful what I said, and when I left prison it was taken away from me. Subsequently I was allowed to have a typed copy, but the original is still in the hands of the Security Police, and I have, of course, no means of knowing whether what is reproduced here represents the original exactly. Clearly in some places the typist misread my handwriting and, although I have corrected this where I can, in some cases I cannot now remember what it was that I wrote and have had to leave gaps in the text. Apart from these changes and some alteration of the typist's punctuation and spelling, the printed version reproduces the typed version with all its peculiarities.

FRIDAY 22nd
(4.00 p.m.)
It's awfully difficult to believe that I've only been here for 42 hours if my arithmetic is right – I finally got to my cell (No. 211) about 10 p.m. on Wednesday night. (At this point I was called and asked if I would give a voluntary statement which I agreed to do and have been doing since about 4.00 p.m. and have just returned at 9.40 – I was allowed to finish as soon as I was tired) – and I'm going to say evensong and go to bed. But I feel much better because I had my first wash and shave since I've been here this afternoon and was allowed to smoke!

I do want to write about the goodness of God – but when I

shall get around to it I don't know because I gather the giving of
the statement, in the form of answering questions, is going to be
a pretty full-time job. But I am full of gratitude for the goodness
of God directly: and also in a lesser way for the visit of the U.K.
consul this afternoon, the news that he brought me that people
all over the world were praying for me: and for the amelioration
of my conditions that were given me as a result of his (the
consul's) intervention. (In light vein, the Psalms for the 22nd
evening of the month which this is, could hardly be bettered for
a first day of interrogation!)

SATURDAY 23rd
(8.30 a.m.)
I have just had my cigarette which the policeman on duty brought
me with my Rautrax.* It's amazing what a difference a cigarette
makes, although I was astonished at how well I got through the
first 40-odd hours without a cigarette. I thought that I would be
in a terrible state: but it is part of the goodness of God that I
wasn't too bad: except for this beastly business of weeping. I've
always been inclined to this in emotional stress situations and
particularly when people are kind to me. I've cried three times in
the last couple of days: once on my own, which I think was just
self-pity when I thought that nobody knew where I was or what
was happening to me: once when the two doctors first came in
on hearing from Bill Miller (bless him) and were kind and
reasonable: and once, most of all, when I saw the U.K. Consul
and that was in front of Col. Botha, Col. Coetzee and some of the
Security men who were at the interview. I wish that I didn't
do this because it is, and looks, so weak – but then that's what I
am – and very frightened – in spite of all the comfort that God
has given me. This I find hard to describe. It all starts, I suppose,
with the new light that I got on the Faith through this Eastern
conception of religion which I've been thinking of for the past
few months and have had time now really to experience in these
last few days. I try to think out beyond the immeasurable

* A heart medicine.

distances of all the stars and universes, and then down through the millions of years of history, long before history itself began and try to make real surprisingly easily that God (went for shave, wash and then questioning and returned at about 12.30 for lunch and the afternoon 'off' by agreement – so I've rather lost the thread of what I was writing) is – before, behind and without all that and whatever other universes and histories there are: and yet so wholly, utterly personal within each bit of those universes and histories and especially in a weak man: and of course, wholly and completely in Jesus His Son – and the glory is that I share not only in God's presence in man the beloved creature: but in Jesus the God man. This is where the wonder of Redemption lies –in that I blot out, discard the God within me by sin, and by neglect, but Jesus restores it – he won't be pushed out. All this talk too of the 'Goodness of God' – our love being so far below the true Being and Nature of God – they are words which we have to use: just as we have to use 'He' and 'Him': but the unalterable glory is wholly beyond words, concept, vision – everything. And all this is completely impossible to put into words or even into concepts. It is something which is 'given' to man – I have no illusions at all that I receive the Beatific vision or anything like that: I have no vision or visions: but I have a completely satisfying (or almost completely satisfying) knowledge that God is.

I think my writing is even more illegible than usual. I have no table but write on one of the two concrete benches in my cell – which I have checked *is* no. 211 – it's written on the board downstairs. I don't quite know what to make of the interrogation. In some ways it's a great relief to get out my cell and walk over to the room where I am being questioned: but it's not a pleasant experience although I have been subjected to no kind of physical violence whatever. But from time to time one of the questioners will branch out in polemics about the country and its policies and it's not pleasant to be shouted at and called a communist, a hypocrite, told that I'm not a Christian, etc. It's an unnerving experience because part of the time they seem perfectly ordinary decent chaps and then suddenly they turn on me and let me know how much they hate me. I think that there is a good deal of misunderstanding on both sides of this whole business and it's a great pity Christians on both sides of the apartheid fence can't get together: we should be able to iron out something: but we can never do so by shouting at each other – and perhaps we are already too far apart.

Since the Consul's visit my conditions have very much improved but, as the Security men have said, I can't expect the President Hotel and I certainly haven't got it. But I am getting some cigarettes a day (I have of course to ask for them individually because they and the matches are, inevitably, kept downstairs) and my meals are sent over from 'the mess', what I suppose is the police mess but I don't know. I've gotten an electric battery razor today from Laura and I must try to arrange a time for a shave and a change of clothes: it's difficult, presumably because of my own nature. As the Security men have pointed out to me, all these things in here now are privileges and not rights so I don't particularly want to abuse them – and I don't know at all what is the most suitable time for such things – if only I could get together with one of them and talk about it so that we could fit in the most suitable time it would be easier all round: but they aren't frightfully inviting of discussion.

I get up just before 6.00 each morning and join in with Cathedral staff at matins at 6.00 and then say what I suppose we would call a 'dry' Mass at 6.30. It is surprising how real this is – I've only got the BCP* rite but I interpolate a good deal into the Prayer for the Church and put the Prayer of Oblation after the 'Consecration', the Humble Access, etc., in its right place: and somehow the 'consecration' seems very real – and so does the Spiritual Communion. It obviously is not the same but I find it satisfying and I ought to think and write more about this. I've never understood this business of being 'conscious' that other people are praying for one – but I am very constantly conscious of it here – not so much at periods of stress, e.g. in questioning when my mind just goes blank (mostly I think with fear – I don't

* The Book of Common Prayer.

know why or what of – although I get these irrational fears of
being killed) but when I'm alone and particularly at night and
I suppose at 'Mass'.

This business of writing at any angle is frightfully uncomfortable and gives me a crick in the back – so I'll say my
midday intercession (it's now 1.15) because the coffee and
cigarette haven't come yet: investigate my new razor set and
towel – and can read the BCP – I started on 'the 39 articles'
yesterday – ugh! But now I've got pencil and paper I may even
try to work out some of these Golden number things!

(2.30 p.m.) My cell as a matter of fact isn't at all bad. The door
as I first approached and didn't know what lay behind presented
a most terrifying aspect – small and yellow and with a peephole
in it. However the cell is quite big and airy and light and quite a
good size. It is about 8 of my good paces square – I imagine
about 20′ × 20′ and it takes about 22 of my paces round it –
although the actual measurement by putting toe to heel – it's $17\frac{1}{2}$
of my feet (E to W) and $16\frac{3}{4}$ (N to S) ... of course, I cannot walk
right round its circumference. Inside the door is a big steel grille
with an inner door forming a kind of cage – I imagine to protect a
warder coming in from a violent criminal. On the right as you
come in is a wall and a window on to the corridor, through which
the light shines all night on to the bed in the opposite corner of
the room from the door and gate – but it's not all that bright and
with a handkerchief over my eyes I can sleep pretty well when the
cell light gets turned off – which is either too early – e.g. about
7.00, or too late – e.g. about midnight: but as I request them to
leave it on I suppose I can't complain if it isn't put out until too
late. Anyway, in the corner on the same side as the entrance is
a WC – for which I am very profoundly grateful. It isn't luxurious
– it is 'open' with two patches of wood on each side: but it works!
And there is a low dividing wall projecting about 3′ between the
WC and the bed, which latter is surprisingly comfortable. It is a
low iron 'truckle' bed with a rubber mattress on a spring frame –
an 'under blanket', two cover blankets and a bigger thick blanket
rolled up to form a pillow. The blankets are quite soft which,

since I can't have pyjamas and sleep in my pants and vest, is just as well! Then on the wall facing the entrance there are 3 windows – all of course heavily barred and wired and at least I can open and shut the narrow windows – very important when it's as cold as it was the other night when there was a cold East wind – these windows face, as far as I can make out, due East. Apart from these windows the wall is blank and then along the North wall of the cell are two concrete blocks each about 3′ 6″ long and knee high and separate from each other by a gap of about 2′ 6″ – which makes a very convenient gap in which to kneel and say my prayers and offices which I do facing west (very wrong liturgically), i.e. facing the grille and the door – although for saying 'Mass' I stand facing East – (not that I thought of that) but there is a kind of cross of wrought iron between two of the windows which makes it very suitable.

The possessions which I am allowed to have here are my Office Book (for which I can never be grateful enough to the Bishop for sending in to me: my first morning's attempt to say a kind of Office and a kind of 'Mass' from memory was absolutely shambolic!). This pencil and paper, my new battery electric razor (which the Security men got Laura to buy for me – and for which I must pay some day), my towel and soap and my Celestoderm ointment. Also on my 'eating' block (the most westerly!) are as usual dirty mugs and plates which will be exchanged at the next meal. I am as glad of the spoon that comes with my meal as anything – my attempt to eat with my fingers was neither pleasant nor successful and I'm grateful for the spoon – of course I cannot have knife or fork but I can manage. I keep my Office Book, paper and pencil on the most easterly block which I call my sitting room rather than my dining room which is the other block near the gate.

(4 p.m.) Somehow the great words like Love and Peace take on an unduly different dimension. It's not that I feel Love or Peace in any way really: but it's as 'attributes' of God they seem much more real – more intrinsic to Him: but here again using the words 'attribute' and 'Him' bring it all back into dimensions.

I do feel very much loved by some – at this moment a lot – of people – (just as I am hated by the men who question me) but that isn't the point: it's catching glimpses of the love that is an aspect of God – that mean be . . . (as tho' I cared) because God is love: but he is so much more. It isn't much good rambling on about this: I must remember Archbishop Geoffrey's remark about 'not knowing what you mean until you can say what you mean'. So I must go on seeking and looking until it comes, if it ever does – to a point where I can say what I mean. It's probably all very simple really and I've got it complicated.

4.40. These Golden number tables in the BCP are about impossible for me: it isn't just the mathematics but the English which fogs me completely. But talking of privileges there are faint markings on the walls which I find rather depressing: presumably the dates on which other prisoners have been imprisoned here – one Col is written May 28th after the last day of the month through . . . to January 31 (no years given) and then a sum which I cannot work out which seems to conclude with 37 weeks 6 days (these on the N. wall) and on the S. wall one which runs through from May 20 – Febr. 16 and another one from June 30 to Jan. 31. And someone with a very educated hand writing a more cheery thing, 'Whoever you are, Whatever you've done, My sympathies, God be with you': and in the same handwriting is a rather scathing account of a couple of days' menus – with one reference to '2 boiled eggs – (not bad) (just lousy) and the pap ("ugh")' – at least some folk seem to be able to preserve their sense of humour. Another chap has drawn a picture of a man in shorts (an African!) with his two arms raised, each arm bearing a part and a broken manacle obviously indicating 'Freedom' and entitled '*Xmas Die Droom*! *Droom*!!! – dreaming that he would be free by Christmas.

(8.00 p.m.) I've just had my supper – having sat in the dark a bit which isn't unpleasant – they put the lights on when my supper came and the policeman has gone to get the coffee and a cigarette – I must remember to save my matches for tooth-picks because I get meat stuck in my teeth all the time and I'm bereft of the magnificent tooth-picks which Janet used to leave in my flat for me – but matchsticks aren't bad.

I can't of course read the Bible right through because I've only got my office book but I'm starting at Septuagesima with Genesis and see how I go. It's good the way John echoes the 'In the beginning . . .', it always has been good but now it's magnifical, to use one of Abp Geoffrey's words. (I've just noticed with the electric light on that there is a light patch around the sketch of the little 'freedom' man on the wall – it looks just like an aura all round him: but I think in fact it's just where they've tried to wash his sketch off the wall and left a light patch – but it's quite striking.)

9.20 and still no coffee and cigarette – I still have hopes of the latter: but I've been drinking water and notice how curiously delightful water tastes out of a metal cup compared with a glass – I wonder why – could be some very mild electrolytic action or something?

SUNDAY 24th

I have just 'finished' my Matins and 'mass' – very unorthodox and interrupted – but in a way I think that my own religion is much more real (God's religion) than it has been since the days of my first 'conversion' – although I've never been conscious that it has ever been unreal and in spite of my sins and unfaithfulness in a number of ways – particularly three, and spiritual communion is very real: although again it's only reassurance of the inner presence of Jesus at all times day and night. Which makes me think again – it re-emphasizes what in fact the Catholic Church has always taught, that the Sacrificial aspect of the Mass is the first one and *not* communion, which follows from it – at least that's what I have always taught and I should say that the BCP Catechism certainly says so. But the Communion aspect obviously is wholly important and what I visualize here is how much it is communion with fellow Christians who are doing this 'at the same time' everywhere. Perhaps I am wrong but I had the feeling this morning that there were (are) thousands of Christians throughout the world with me – a most extraordinary, glorious, truly comforting and strengthening feeling – although I know I must not be dependent upon feelings. But the whole thing was very disorderly – I shall have learned a lot about the 'fussiness' of the 'orthodoxy' ways which I have been too long insistent by the time I've finished this lot – 'sweet are the uses of adversity'.

Part of the trouble is that you never quite know, sometimes within an hour or two, when things are going to happen here. I got up at 6.00 and shaved (with my new electric razor, thank God! and Laura), said matins which I finished exactly at 7.00. It's pretty slow but good to read the Psalms, canticles and prayers 'antiphonally' although I don't do that with the lessons. So I was just starting 'Mass' at 7.00 with the collect – when in comes breakfast. Since it was already pretty cold I had it and then started off again. Just before the 'Consecration' the warder arrived with my a.m. cigarette and since I can only light it while he is here with the matches, I had that (and very welcome it was – but shades of my ideas about fasting and non-smoking communion! – presumably if I was a real saint I'd have cold breakfast and done without the cigarette – but what the hell! – it seems to work this way!) – I then went on to 'consecration' and communion. I think in some ways the 'consecration' is more meaningful even than communion under these circumstances – perhaps it's something to do with this Sacrifice business. This will need more thinking about. But it's all been lovely – and what the day holds I don't know – I'm supposed to have a shower shortly and get some clean clothes – but will wait and see: and whether there's to be further interrogation today I don't know – I'm not sure how strong their sabbatarianism is!

(8.45) Back after a really good hot shower and change of shirt, socks and underwear – much better. I was thinking during my shower how agonizing this sort of thing must be for a married man – to have someone outside in perpetual agony for the man inside – knowing nothing and fearing everything. I've thought over and over again in these past few days that it must be pretty agonizing for these few that love me – but not quite the same I expect as man and wife – and somehow I feel particularly sorry for Bar who has done so much for me recently and is a particularly sensitive person – not that there aren't dozens of others who have done a very great deal for me in different ways – but she's pretty sensitive and needs help – I do hope (and expect) that they will be supporting each other.

(9.20) Apparently they are not sabbatarians. The warder has just been up to say that 'they' are coming to fetch me for 'investigation' – and it gives me a beastly feeling in the pit of my stomach – whether this 'contradicts' my religion I don't know but I don't feel that it does – to feel fear presumably is natural: Jesus seems to have felt it. But then I'm not Him! and I don't quite know where or what I am.

At about 9.45 they came to fetch me – it's now 1.05 p.m. and I've just returned. I've had an awful hammering but of course only verbal. But it's very frightening indeed – because they will shout at me, e.g., that I don't preach Christianity but that I preach 'shit' and most fantastically that I am a well-trained Communist spy (and Alison is also). It sounds fantastic – they can't really believe this: but the really frightening thing is that perhaps they do – and that SCK* is a Communist organization. These statements are so out of reality that they ought to be laughable, but when they're made in that atmosphere, with shouting and only enemies present, they take on a horrifying aspect. Again I had an emotional weeping fit – but not for very long and again only over a not very relevant point – my supposed hatred of the Afrikaner as such which isn't true anyway. Presumably I'll feel better when I've walked about in my cell and done some 'formal' religion. It's 'funny' to think that all this was going on this morning while the High Mass was going on in the Cathedral – and perhaps other services throughout the world. They are very skilled and competent questioners and know just how to unsettle you psychologically and raise all your anxieties – they must be very well trained and yet one of them was complaining about the lack

* The Servants of Christ the King.

of Afrikaans advertisements in the streets. I just don't understand it but it frightens seven bells out of me.

(2.45) I've been trying to do my intercessions . . . It's taken me about an hour because of the impossibility of concentration, which is not a good sign, it's all so fantastic – the suggestion that Julia (Logan) should be a Communist spy (what on earth Fairacres would think of this I just can't think – die of shock or something) and even John Lascelles – who is probably the archest of all Conservatives – although I suppose that Janet would probably be Labour – she's 'anti' most conventional things. But the whole thing wheels around in my mind as though it was all a phantasy. I was surprised to know just how much they knew about Alison's visit last year – they must have followed her all over – she apparently never noticed it – even down to the Transkei.

(5.30 p.m.) I seem to have developed a stinking headache and a runny tummy – I suppose it's not really surprising, it's my normal sort reaction to strain – oh hell. Anyway the warder has just been in and given me a light for a cigarette which is a comfort. There seem to be some young Chinese prisoners of some sort on this floor lower down who come in with him and bring the food around – but as to who or what they are doing here I've no idea. I've passed quite a few youngsters of one sort or another – I wonder if they're using this as some sort of remand place for youngsters before going off to a Reformatory? If they are and are keeping them separate from the criminals in the Fort then good for them – but I don't know. I'm going to get on with some more (very amateur) 'work' on Genesis.

(5.45) Supper arrived – 3 eggs and chips – these doctors are curious – cut my cigarettes right down and fill me up with cholesterol – I suppose that there are subtle ways of killing people with high blood pressure – but I've done my best to leave most of the yolks. So on with Genesis until it gets too dark.

(5.30) (Not having a church calendar, I must try to work out when Septuagesima is if I'm to read the right lessons. I think Ash Wednesday is Feb. 18th – today is Sunday 24th, next Sunday 31st – the next 7th, then 14th – then Ash Wed.: must be

17th, ∴14th is Quinquagesima, 7th is Sexagesima – so next Sunday 31st must be Septuagesima and I must change over the lessons then.)

(8.05 p.m.) Evensong is now on in the Cathedral and I suppose that poor dear Dick is preaching – unless of course they've arranged something special because of me and put the Bishop on soon something? I've been wondering why on earth they took John Austin Baker's *The Foolishness of God* away from the flat – I saw it in the office here the other day – what on earth could be the reason for that? – except that I marked a lot of passages – I wish they'd let me have that to read – it needs real re-studying and I was going to take it to retreat – tomorrow!

I asked the chap who very kindly brought me my last cigarette to put the light out because I wanted an early night – I think he misunderstood me completely (his English is nearly as bad as my Afrikaans!), said 'Oh' happily and went off. I think he thought that I asked for it to be left on – so now I'm stuck with it for the next 3–4 hours presumably and even though I cover my face with my jersey the light shines directly into my eyes and I cannot sleep.

I've been asking S. Stephen to pray for me, for obvious reasons, and feel a little 'comforted'. – It is now midnight – and still the light is on – no sleep. I am a fool to think this is accidental, it must be deliberate. But it's no good panicking about it.

MONDAY 25th
(7.30 a.m.) I quite forgot that last night was the 1st Evensong of S. Paul and said the wrong office but '*maak nie saak nie*' – I've said the right office of S. Paul this morning and they're comforting – even spiritual communion seems to flow right into the bones and sinews and renews the whole of me.

My compulsive obsession about 'order', etc., should disappear at this rate – breakfast arrived at 5.50 – and I wasn't even up owing to the beastly night. It was brought up by a white steward in a steward's white jacket – I think it was an attempt – bless somebody's heart, to bring it to me warm – but of course it failed. It consisted of some good toast, eggs (cholesterol), cold tomato, and haddock. I ate one piece of toast, keeping the other for 'tea' (there isn't any!), the whites of the eggs and a bit of haddock – ugh!

(8.00 a.m.) Glory Halleluja – I've been allowed to walk up and down the corridor (23 paces) for about ten minutes (my first official exercise outside the cell) for exercise – glorious – and the PC told me to swing my arms higher to exercise shoulder muscles (I don't think I've got any) but it certainly helped.

Anyway, to go back, I therefore had to say matins and 'Mass' after breakfast – but that again was good. But now I await with the usual dread the day's interrogation and try to remember (but always forget) the presence of Jesus – but I've got Paul and Stephen to remember too. But the less I think about the day to come the better – the now is as good as it can be under the circumstances because God is so good.

(3.30 p.m.) I've just returned from interrogation and it's been an awful day . . .* I'm more defeated and discouraged than I can say. . . . I suppose one must pay for one's sins: and I'm too fed up with myself to write more – I'll try to say some prayers. I am glad . . . that I can have cigarettes now in my cell but no matches – and should be able to get a light off a warder when he comes in – but that doesn't lighten the load . . . and I suppose that's only the calm before another hell tomorrow – my birthday. I should just be arriving at S. Benedict's for the Retreat at this time. I don't feel like doing Genesis – or anything tonight, but I'd better try. The forgiveness of God, if not of men, is the one thing to hang on to. . . .

26.1.71, MY BIRTHDAY – TUESDAY

(7.30 a.m.) I was mistaken about the light last night – it eventually went off, thank God, at about 8.30 and so I got some sleep – of a sort – and very considerably interrupted by the young man on duty who I think must have been drunk or something – he came in I should think more than once every hour, put the light on –

---

* The gaps in this section refer to a personal matter which involves other people.

twice offered me a smoke (at about 2–3 a.m. I ask you!) and indulged in some strange door banging on my own door and down the corridor – what it was all about I don't know. I got up at 5.45 in view of yesterday's experience in the a.m. and I managed to get Matins said by 6.30 when breakfast arrived – no toast, but I had a piece left over from yesterday morning – one egg, cold tomato, haddock and the coffee not so cold as usual. Then I said 'Mass' and some prayers and although I received much comfort – and I have Polycarp today as well as Stephen and Paul amongst human beings – I am still very sick at heart over this . . . business – I have never realized before what the expression 'sick at heart' means – I do now, with a vengeance.

(4.05 p.m.) Just back from interrogation. Surprising how good it can be to be back on my own again – I suppose 'good' is a comparative term in this respect! It was a fairly 'easy' day – no shouting methods which I simply can't stand. I think they tried to make it easy because of my birthday – they had cakes for tea – but I suppose I ought to discount this, but it all sounded pretty genuine. I almost feel like saying 'Bless them' – but I expect it will all change tomorrow – however the Bible is pretty clear about 'not being anxious for the morrow': which is easier said than done. Most of today's questioning I simply didn't understand – all about where I was during the 3 days of the Archdeacons' Conference – and who had access to my flat in that time. It sounds as though something must have happened during these days?

I had 3 bouts of weeping today – blast it. Once in talking to the two doctors who came to see me – they tell me my blood pressure is down which surprises me but is good – once talking about this damned . . . – and once when a birthday card arrived signed by the Bishop and 19 others all around the Parish and Diocesan offices. I've been allowed to keep it and it's a very great blessing indeed – I've gotten it stuck up behind the bars of the window on the West side of the cell where I can see it whenever I sit down on my 'sitting room' block – for reading, office, writing, etc.

I had my fingerprints taken today, a rather frightening business

– but very effectively done – palm-prints, fingerprints the lot – so now I feel like a fully fledged criminal. I've been told that it's for some documents. I suppose it's these damned leaflets – but the only one of them that I handled was one the police showed at me, saying 'Look at it', or something like that – I'm a complete fool – if I'd been more sophisticated I'd have refused to touch it: but I was too shocked to think.

I've said my intercession and I'm going to look out of the window for a little and say Evensong – I had quite a good spell of exercise (about 10 minutes) in the corridor this morning. One of my main thoughts from this morning is of our Lord Himself saying the Mass – not me or anyone else – e.g. at the Last Supper week, with God, even Judas present and Thomas – Peter . . . so that however bad I may be I do stay and I don't, like Judas, have to go out 'and it was dark' unless I have to, thanks be to God. Jesus saying the Last Supper is very vivid – although when conventionally visualized – I can't get away from the orthodox 'Last Supper' pictures.

(7.00 p.m.) I've just had my supper and have been watching the Indian children playing – they didn't seem very resourceful or organized and much quieter than any group of European children.

WEDNESDAY 27th

(7.30) A week today I came in: it seems like several months – and I wonder how much longer it's going to be – they told me yesterday that it could be 'another 100 days', why quoting that figure I don't know. I've had no cigarette yet this morning – although I have had breakfast – in the midst of doing my religion at about 6.30, just as I finished . . . I graduated to a knife and fork this morning – it must be an oversight – it's much easier to cut eggs (on toast) and sausages with a knife and fork than with a spoon. The warder knows I want a cigarette because I asked him for a light at breakfast time – he promised to bring one but still hasn't arrived. Anyway 'Why should I bother'!! is probably his attitude – it's a pretty frequent one in and out of here.

I had never realized what a total destruction, giving, immolation, oblation of Himself is implied by the words of consecration – 'This is my body which is given for you, this is my blood which is shed for you, DISSOLVED FOR YOU – with love of you.' It's magnificent. Even his soul was torn apart – separated from God in the giving of Himself – His whole self – all for us/me.

The indictment

IN THE SUPREME COURT OF SOUTH AFRICA (TRANSVAAL PROVINCIAL DIVISION)

The Attorney-General of the Transvaal, who prosecutes in the name of and on behalf of the State, informs the Court that:

GONVILLE AUBIE FFRENCH-BEYTAGH

an European male (hereinafter called the accused) is guilty of the offence of PARTICIPATION IN TERRORISTIC ACTIVITIES in contravention of section 2(1) of Act No. 83 of 1967 and read with sections 1, 2(2), 4, 5, and 9 of the said Act.

WHEREAS:

(a) During 1961 the African National Congress, South African Communist Party, South African Indian Congress, South African Coloured People's Organization and persons to the prosecutor unknown, formed a plan to prepare for, and to commit, acts of violence in order to bring about the overthrow of the State;

(b) This plan was put into effect in 1961 and is still in force at the present date;

(c) The plan to commit acts of violence comprised the following stages, to wit, the commission of sabotage on private and public property, the training of fighters and participation in guerrilla warfare;

(d) The plan to train fighters and thereafter take part in

armed attacks on Rhodesian and South African Forces was put into effect in 1967;

(e) The overseas branches of the organizations mentioned printed, published and distributed pamphlets in which non-whites in the Republic were incited to take part in an armed uprising against the State and to give active support to the trained guerrilla fighters;

(f) The accused accepted the said plan and worked actively towards its implementation;

NOW THEREFORE:

During the period between 26 April, 1965 and 21st January, 1971 within the Republic and elsewhere, the said accused did, wrongfully, unlawfully and with intent to endanger the mainten-ance of law and order, within the Republic, participate in terroristic activities, to wit, did commit or attempt to commit one or more of the acts set out below, and/or did conspire with one another, the persons and organizations mentioned in annexure A, to commit or aid or procure the commission of one or more of the said acts:—

(1) During the period between 28th August, 1967 and 21st January, 1971 the accused possessed for distribution and/or personally or through the agency of IAN THOMPSON or per-sons to the prosecutor unknown, distributed to WINNIE MANDELA and others to the prosecutor unknown, pamphlets, detailed below, published by the overseas branches of the organizations mentioned, in which readers were incited to support, prepare for or take part in, a violent uprising against the State, to wit,

(a) 'We bring you a message – The ANC calls you to action' (Issued by the African National Congress)

(b) 'Sons and daughters of Africa' (Issued by the African National Congress)

(c) 'These men are our brothers, our sons' (Issued by the African National Congress)

(d) 'The ANC says to Vorster and his gang' (Issued by the African National Congress)

(e) 'We are at War' (Issued by the African National Congress)

(f) 'Freedom' (Issued by the S.A. Communist Party)

(2) At a gathering held at 43 St Davids Road, Houghton, Johannesburg, on 12.1.1968 he incited or encouraged the persons present to support a violent revolution with the object of effecting social, political and economic changes in the Republic;

(3) During the period between January, 1968 to January, 1971 in Johannesburg the accused prepared written notes for purposes of propagating the need for a violent revolution within the Republic in order to overthrow the present State;

(4) At a conference of the S.A. Council of Churches held between 5 and 6.2.1969 at Auden House, de Korte Street, Johannesburg, to discuss the subject, entitled 'Generation Gap', the accused incited or encouraged the persons there present to support a violent revolution in order to effect the overthrow of the State;

(5) On or about the 15th day of May, 1970 in England, the accused participated in a decision taken by the overseas branches of the said organizations to grant financial aid to the FRELIMO guerrilla fighters in order to expedite the overthrow of the Portuguese rule in Mozambique and Angola as a necessary step preparatory to the overthrow of the South African State;

(6) During May or June, 1970 in England, he advocated the need for sabotage and a violent revolution in South Africa to bring about social, political and economic changes and reaffirmed his intention to continue to assist in the achievement of the said aims by administering in the Republic the monies received from one CANON COLLINS and/or the Defence and Aid Organization, London;

(7) At a meeting of the Black Sash Movement, held at 4A – 2nd Avenue, Parktown North, Johannesburg, on 2.12.1970, he incited or encouraged the persons present to contravene

the laws of the Republic and to support and prepare for a violent revolution with the object of bringing about social, political and economic changes in the Republic;

(8) During the period between 18.8.1969 and 17.10.1970 in Johannesburg, he incited or encouraged one LOUIS HENRY (KEN) JORDAAN to support the commission of acts of violence and to take part in preparations for a violent uprising against the State, inter alia, by making the following statements on the dates mentioned below:—

(a) *On 18.8.1969*: that he had large sums of money available to finance activities directed against the safety of the State; that boycotts could be effective as a means of undermining the authority or safety of the State; that one Major Swanepoel of the Security Police was a sadist and should be killed;

(b) *On 25.8.1969*: that there should be an organization in existence to control and direct the commission of acts of violence, in the event of it being resorted to; that WINNIE MANDELA was recruiting youths in furtherance of the aims of the African National Congress;

(c) *On 21.1.1970*: that he could arrange training in methods of sabotage for the said Jordaan in England; that he distributed monies in South Africa in order to further the achievement by the African National Congress of its aims to overthrow the State by means of a violent revolution;

(d) *On 5.10.1970 & 17.10.1970*: that it was decided by the overseas organizations that their major financial support should be given to the FRELIMO guerrilla fighters as the downfall of the Portuguese Government in Mozambique and Angola would facilitate the destruction of the South African State; and that the said Jordaan could receive instructions in England in the use of explosives and electronics in the commission of acts of sabotage;

(9) (a) During the period between 18th March, 1966 and 21st January, 1971 in Johannesburg, the accused, in furtherance of the said plan, received from the Defence and Aid Organization, London, through the agency of one ALISON NORMAN

or other persons to the prosecutor unknown, monies amounting to R51,400 or thereabouts, which monies he paid out in the Republic, as set out in Annexure B hereto, to:—

i) members of the aforesaid organizations and of the PAN AFRICANIST CONGRESS, who were charged with, and/or convicted of, offences against the safety of the State, and/or restricted by ministerial order issued in terms of legislation dealing with the safety of the State and/or detained in terms of the aforesaid legislation and/or who left the Republic in order to participate elsewhere in activities against the safety of the State;

ii) the dependants of such members and

iii) other persons or bodies who were engaged in activities regarded by the accused as furthering the aforesaid aims;

(b) ALISON NORMAN, in collaboration with the accused, opened a banking account at Barclays Bank, Johannesburg, to which account she transmitted monies from the overseas Defence and Aid Organization, London, and authorized the accused to operate the said account;

(c) ALISON NORMAN visited the Republic during the period November, 1969 and January, 1970. She received reports from the accused and/or other persons to the prosecutor unknown on the affairs of the aforesaid organizations which she conveyed to the Branches in London;

(d) ALISON NORMAN procured one NICOLAAS JOHANNES ZWART, in January, 1970 during her journey to the Transkei to co-operate with and act as an agent of the Defence and Aid Organization in the event of the need therefor arising in the future;

(e) During January – February, 1968, the accused arranged with ALISON NORMAN, SYLVIA MCKEE and HOWARD TRUMBULL that a banking account be opened in Durban in the name of SYLVIA MCKEE so that the Defence and Aid Organization, London, could transmit money through such channel for use by the said HOWARD TRUMBULL;

(f) During the period between 18th March, 1966 and 21st

January, 1971 the accused conducted correspondence with members or agents of the aforesaid organizations, submitted reports to them personally or through the agency of ALISON NORMAN, about activities and financial needs of the persons concerned with the implementation of the aforesaid plan, and received instructions from the said organizations which he carried out thereafter.

(10) During the period 4.8.1967 to 21.1.1971 in Johannesburg the accused discussed or was party to a plan to commit acts of sabotage at buildings or installations to the prosecutor unknown·

IN case of conviction the said Attorney-General prays for judgement against the accused according to law.

K. D. M. MOODIE
Attorney-General
(*Transvaal Province*)

ANNEXURE 'A'

LIST OF CO-CONSPIRATORS

1 AFRICAN NATIONAL CONGRESS
2 S.A. COMMUNIST PARTY
3 DEFENCE AND AID, LONDON
4 AMERICAN BOARD MISSION
5 CANON COLLINS
6 DIANA KING
7 ALISON NORMAN
8 SYLVIA MCKEE
9 JOHN TURNBULL
10 HOWARD TRUMBULL
11 LOUIS HENRY KEN JORDAAN*
12 PERSONS MENTIONED IN ANNEXURE 'B'†
13 PERSONS TO PROSECUTOR UNKNOWN

* Louis Jordaan's name was deleted from the list of co-conspirators when the case came to court.

† This is a list of political prisoners and their relatives whom I had helped.